IMAGES
of America

BUILDING NEVADA'S HIGHWAYS

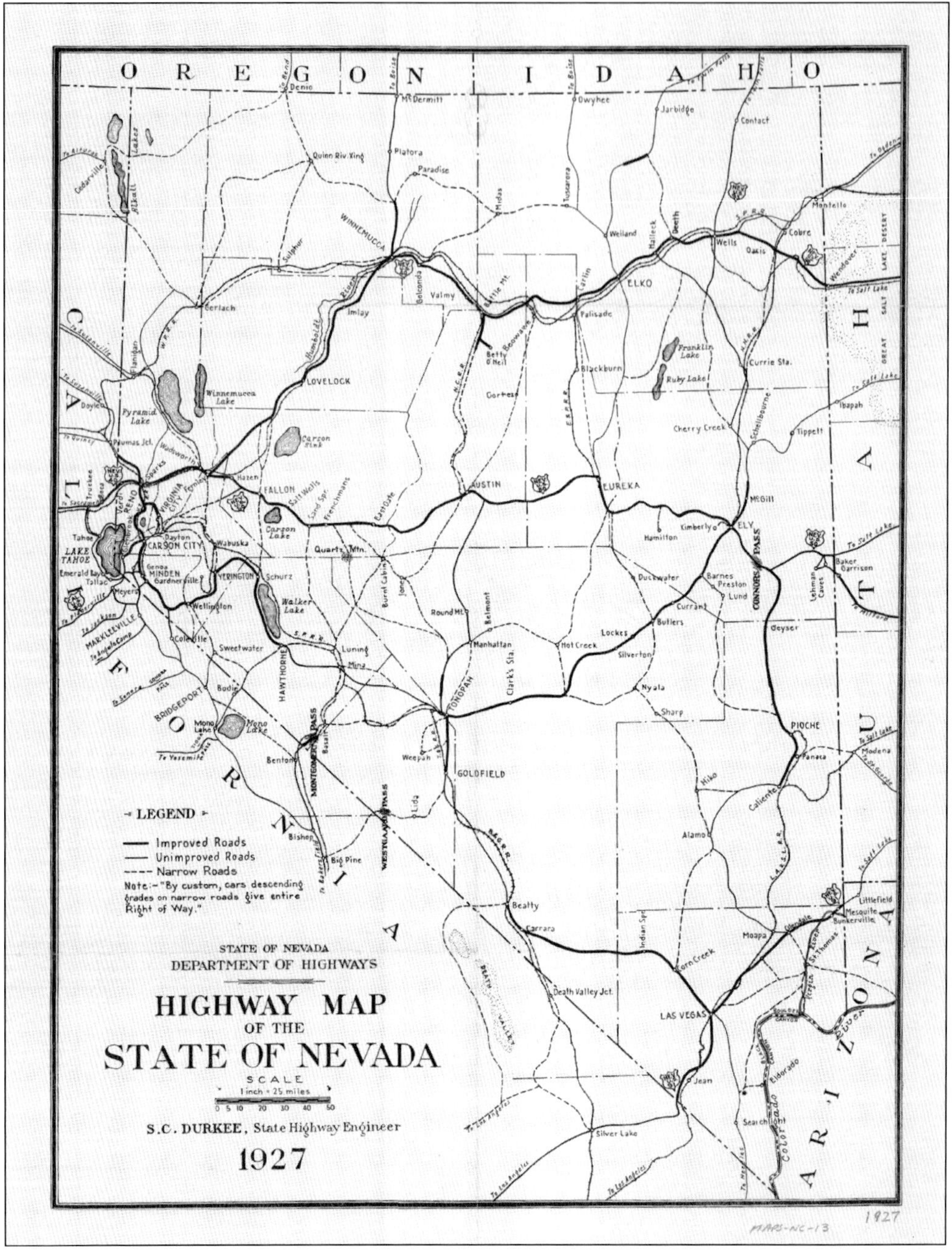

This is the official 1927 Nevada highway map as produced and issued by the state highway department. Improved roads are shown in a thick black line, unimproved roads in a finer line, and narrow roads in a dashed line. (Courtesy of the Nevada Department of Transportation.)

ON THE COVER: Featured here is a c. 1938 photograph of an early automobile enthusiast cruising along the newly constructed and scenic Geiger Grade, the road connecting Reno and Virginia City. (Courtesy of the Nevada Department of Transportation.)

IMAGES
of America

BUILDING NEVADA'S HIGHWAYS

Jennifer E. Riddle and Elizabeth Dickey

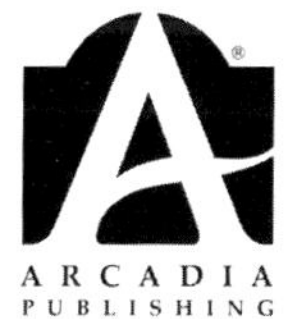

ISBN 978-1-4671-3406-4

Published by Arcadia Publishing
Charleston, South Carolina

Printed in the United States of America

Library of Congress Control Number: 2015948001

For all general information, please contact Arcadia Publishing:
Telephone 843-853-2070
Fax 843-853-0044
E-mail sales@arcadiapublishing.com
For customer service and orders:
Toll-Free 1-888-313-2665

Visit us on the Internet at www.arcadiapublishing.com

This book is dedicated to those who, in the words of the Nevada Highway Department in 1946, "have so loyally served . . . [Nevada] that we may have and enjoy a fine highway system."

Contents

ACKNOWLEDGMENTS

Without the help of Nevada Department of Transportation (NDOT) photographer Sholeh Moll and NDOT multimedia man Barron Lauderbaugh, you would have to find another book to read because this one would not exist. Thank you Sholeh and Barron for going the extra mile for us. We very much appreciate the support of Meg Ragonese, who thought this was a good idea from the start; Roger Miles, for all his wonderful help; and Julie Duewel, who set the organization of NDOT's ponderous photograph collection into motion. Thank you to the unknown NDOT intern who spent an entire summer cataloging thousands of photographs in a windowless basement room. We owe several libations to Michelle Austin, Jim MacDonald, and company in exchange for hogging their scanner. Thank you to the nearly 100 years of amazing NDOT photographers—we hope this book does your photographic work justice. And thank you to NDOT for allowing us to use this fantastic collection. Unless otherwise noted, all images in this book appear courtesy of the Nevada Department of Transportation.

Thank you to Esther Ciammachilli for your awesome eye and your S-curve cover pick. Thank you to Tom and Mary Riddle for existing and for being delightful. And thank you to A.J. Thompson for answering randomly texted caption questions and also for being delightful.

Thank you to Jim and Sophia Dickey for some spelling advice that was soundly ignored. Thank you to James and Gretchen Fagin, who know a factoid when they read one. And, finally, thank you to Steven Van Patten, who loved Nevada's history and a good road trip.

INTRODUCTION

Nothing behind me, everything ahead of me, as is ever so on the road.

—Jack Kerouac, *On the Road*

What is a road? The humble road, that ancient piece of technology so embedded in our human culture that it almost blends seamlessly into the background of our daily lives and yet so full of promise—the promise of adventure, the promise of connecting with friends and family, and the promise of connecting with the most basic staples of life.

Roads are the nervous system of a society upon which goods, services, people, and parts are transported. They often develop organically, starting out as a simple footpath along the most logical route between two places. In the past, very often the logical footpath became a horse path, which became a wagon road, which became an automobile road.

In 1916, the face of American transportation profoundly and irrevocably changed after the US government passed the first Federal Aid Road Act. The act was groundbreaking because, for the first time, it allowed the federal government to give states money with which to build roads. Prior to the act states were on their own, which in Nevada, given its huge tracts of land and relatively small population, was an untenable burden. When passing the Federal Aid Road Act, legislators had two primary goals in mind: to create a network of roads for the benefit of the US Postal Service, and to ensure that roads built with federal aid money were designed and constructed by qualified engineers under the direct supervision of the state. To achieve their goals, the federal government created a list of terms each state had to agree to before qualifying for federal aid money. Among other things, states had to pass legislation formally agreeing to the Federal Aid Road Act and all its provisions, and states had to create a highway department. On March 23, 1917, Nevada responded to the federal government by passing an act to provide a general highway law for the state of Nevada, and thus, the Nevada Department of Highways was born.

A component of Nevada's highway act was to create a network of roads to serve the Silver State. As originally defined, there were four routes in the network: Route 1, which eventually became Interstate 80; Route 2, which became US 50; Route 3, which became US 95 north of Lida Junction; and Route 4, which became US 6. The 1917 legislation completely excluded Clark County from the federal aid program; however, the oversight was corrected in 1919 when Nevada's highway act was amended to include Route 5 (now US 95 south of Lida Junction) and Route 6 (now Interstate 15).

Passage of the 1916 Federal Aid Road Act and the subsequent creation of state highway departments was a first step in bringing the nation's roadways up to a quantifiable and defined standard. Prior to the federal government's attempt to exert control over national highways, thoroughfares were typically created and maintained by groups of automobile enthusiasts. Also known as trail clubs, the groups became public relations machines for their routes. They installed highway markers, held conventions, and generally tried to help the economies of the towns through which their routes went.

Trail clubs gave their routes catchy names, such as Lincoln Highway, Victory Highway, and Arrowhead Highway, among many others. However, with the number of automobiles—and, consequently, roads—skyrocketing, the lack of road-building oversight became a genuine detriment to the public. There was no continuity in how road information was conveyed, be it road hazards, directions, or even road names. Many routes overlapped to the point of confusion, and some trail clubs only routed roads through towns willing to pay them, even if building through a specific area meant adding needless miles to a route. With the lack of standard road specifications, the rampant and confusing road-naming conventions, and the self-serving nature of many road builders and communities, America's burgeoning roadway system was rapidly becoming a quagmire of individual pathways rather than an engineered and cohesive network of highways designed in the best interest of the motorist. Therefore, the last step in reigning in the chaos came in 1925 when a federal and state joint task force called the Joint Board on Interstate Highways designed a comprehensive 75,800-mile numbered highway system.

In general, the system was designed as a grid in which, beginning at the Canadian border and working south, important east-west roads were numbered in intervals of 10, except for the northernmost east-west road, which was designated as US 2 rather than the awkward US 0. Less important east-west roads were then assigned even numbers based on their location relative to the main highways. Beginning on the East Coast and working west, north-south highways were assigned odd numbers ending in either a 1, for the most important routes, or a 5, for secondary routes. The numbering system was not absolute and applied to the early highway system—the interstate system followed a different round of discussions—but, in general, the early highway numbering convention has held.

Not surprisingly, not everyone was happy with the new system. Many trail clubs were upset over losing control of their routes, and many cities and states were upset over which number was assigned to routes in their territory because there was an idea that certain numbers held more prestige. Nonetheless, it was against the aforementioned national backdrop that Nevada's highway department was formed and began its work—work that has continued for nearly 100 years.

The last century has brought numerous changes in technology and engineering, but the one constant throughout the years is that roads are the ties that bind us all together, from the most basic footpaths to the most complex interstates. Without roads, we would all have to be completely self-sufficient, creating our own food, clothes, and housing. And so it is to roads and the people who built them that this book is dedicated, specifically Nevada's roads and how they transformed the Silver State from a place that immigrants, such as the forty-niners, were desperate to escape to a proud member of the Union that people are eager to explore.

One

By Horse or By Rail
Early Transportation and the Birth of the Highway Department

Many of Nevada's major roads follow paths first blazed by Native Americans and later expanded or modified by Nevada's earliest Euro-American explorers, such as Jedediah Smith, Capt. John C. Fremont, and Capt. James Simpson. After the Comstock discovery, Euro-Americans began settling in the Silver State in droves. Driven by a need to move large and heavy ore, equipment, and goods, enterprising folks started building wagon toll roads, and lots of them. Toll franchises were handed out by the legislature, and the practice became so ubiquitous that Nevada darling Mark Twain himself wrote about it in his novel *Roughing It*, in which he stated, "The legislature sat sixty days, and passed private toll-road franchises all the time. When they adjourned it was estimated that every citizen owned about three franchises, and it was believed that unless Congress gave the Territory another degree of longitude there would not be room enough to accommodate the toll-roads. The ends of them were hanging over the boundary line everywhere like a fringe."

The wagon toll roads, like the automobile roads that followed, varied hugely in terms of engineering and maintenance. When cars became more popular and booster clubs more active, Nevada's road system became even more of a hodgepodge, and it was into this largely well-intentioned yet slightly chaotic web of roads that the Nevada Highway Department was born.

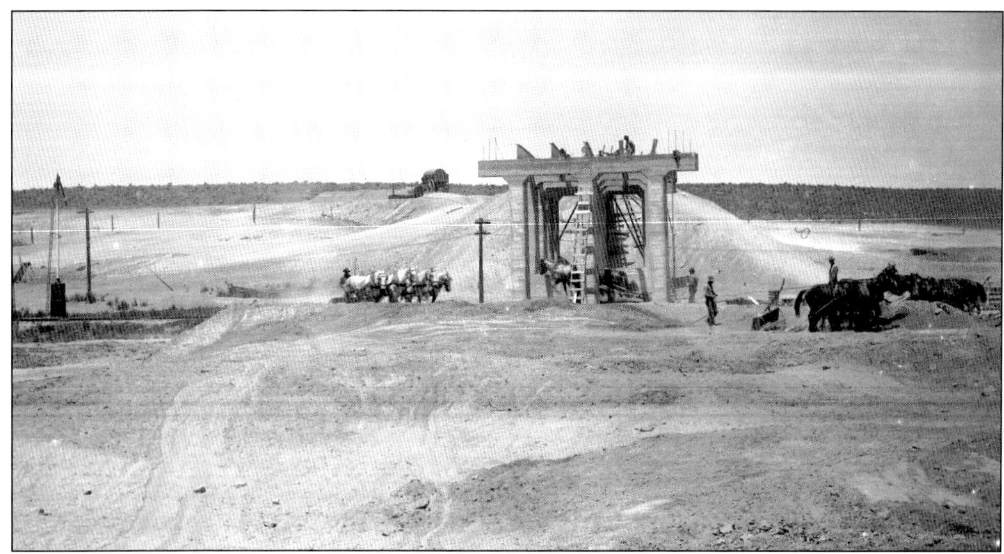

Building the original automobile roads was a monumental undertaking. Imagine constructing a fully engineered route designed for the latest transportation technology—the car—where only railroads or wagon roads existed. As seen in the 1920s bridge construction near Deeth pictured here, many of the early routes were built using horse-drawn equipment.

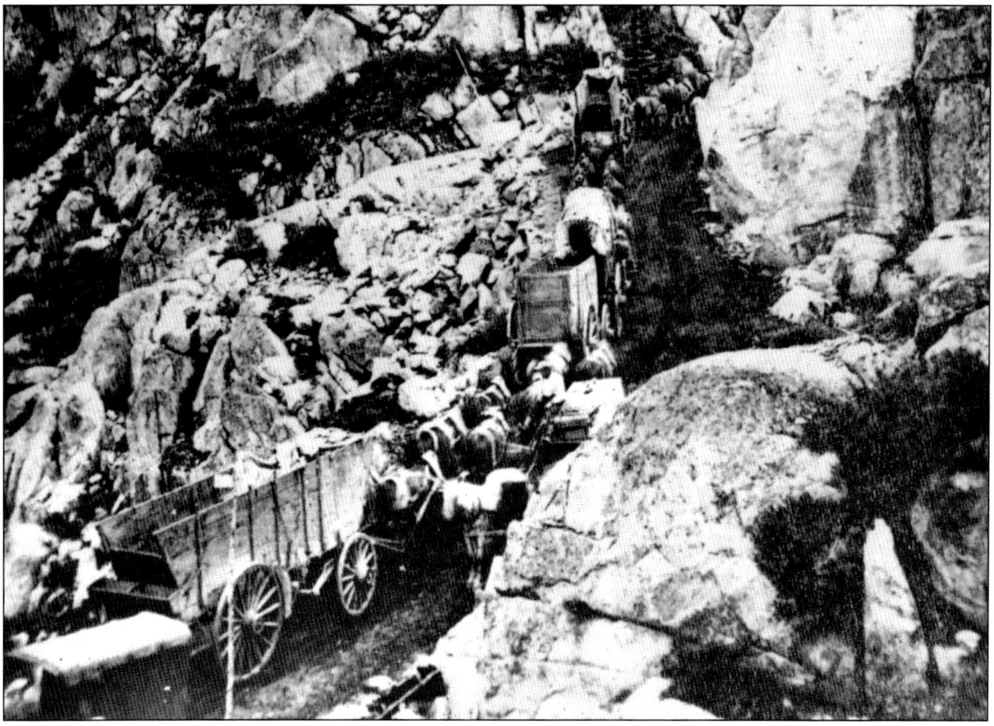

The California Trail was one of the earliest routes through Nevada, coming in from the east and following the Humboldt River to the west. In the early 1840s, the Stevenson-Townsend-Murphy party blazed the Truckee River Route branch of the California Trail, and in so doing became the first group to get wagons into California by way of the trail. Nonetheless, as shown here, the journey through the Sierra Nevada was harrowing.

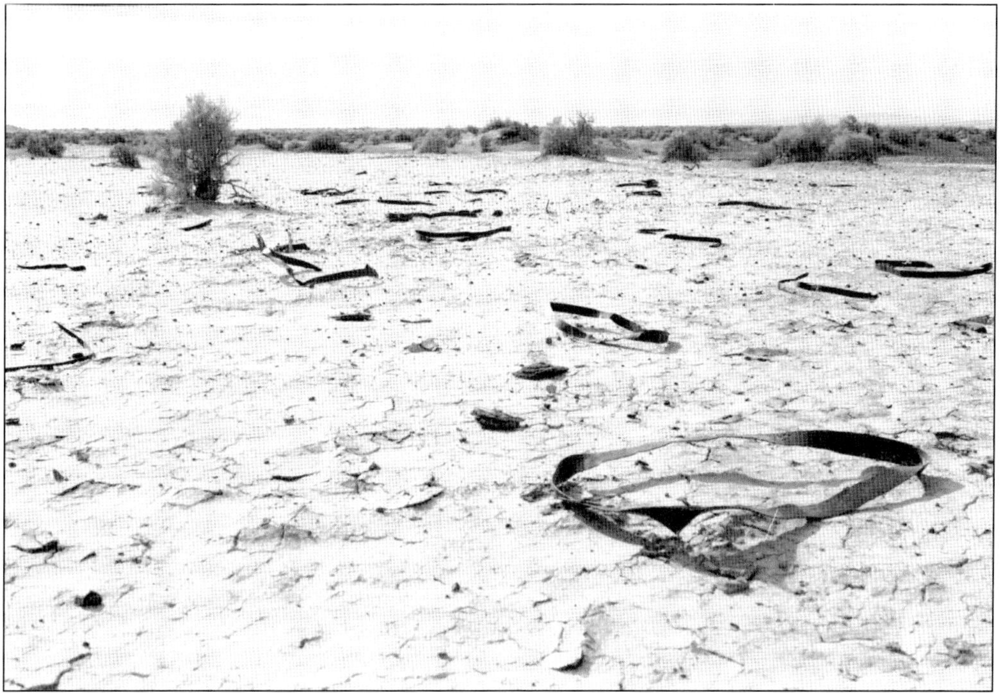

The Truckee River Route began near the Humboldt Sink, then went southwest through the treacherous Forty Mile Desert. Shown strewn alongside the trail are water barrel straps, abandoned by people struggling to stay alive. As one survivor of the trek wrote, "Even the very wagons seem to know that we are off today for the great adventure—in sand, volcanic ash, alkali, furnace heat, and the stench of putrid flesh."

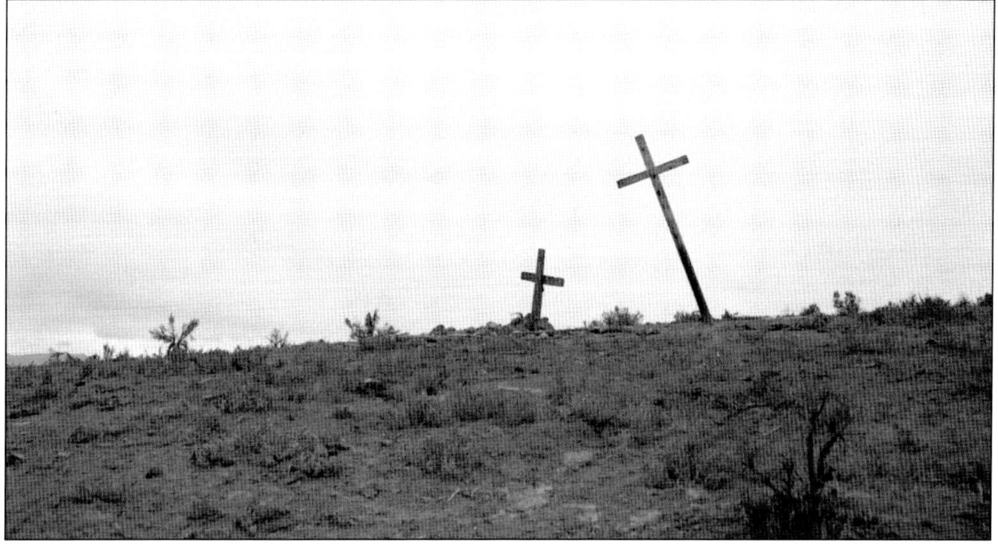

As this photograph indicates, many emigrants died during the harsh journey across the unforgiving desert. The survivor quoted in the previous caption further wrote, "We crossed along the edge of an immense baked plain with the fetid stinking slough for a guide, although the wreckage along the way almost paved our route . . . It must have been here that one emigrant said he counted a dead animal every 106 feet."

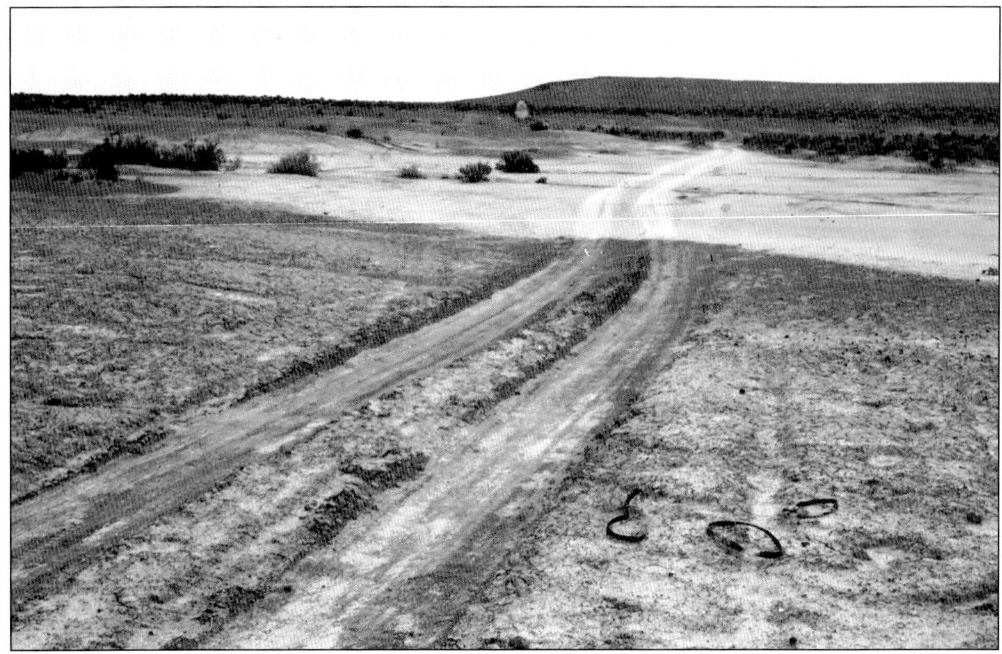

By 1848, a new path to California known as the Carson Route had been blazed. The Carson Route still went through the Forty Mile Desert but became the more popular trail because, overall, it was easier to traverse and because the Donner Party tragedy of 1846–1847 cast a pall on the Truckee River Route. Nonetheless, as this photograph illustrates, the landscape was still uninviting.

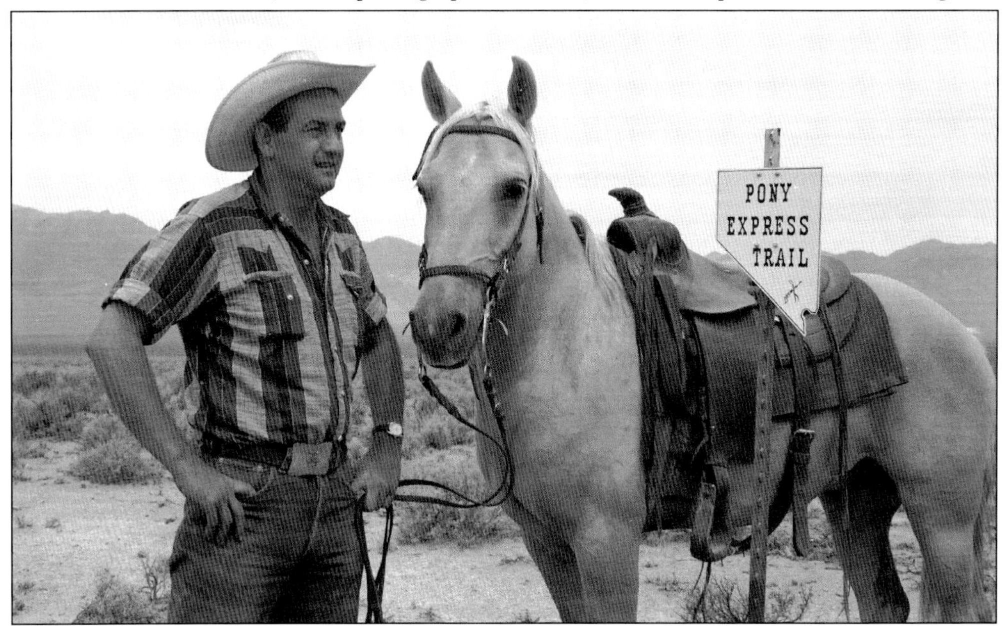

By 1859, Capt. James Simpson established the Overland Trail. The trail, which also crossed the Forty Mile Desert to then overlap part of the Carson Route, was designed for wagon trains and dramatically shortened the distance between the Great Salt Lake and San Francisco. Among those who used Simpson's route were the legendary Pony Express riders, whose lore was celebrated on the company's centennial, as shown here.

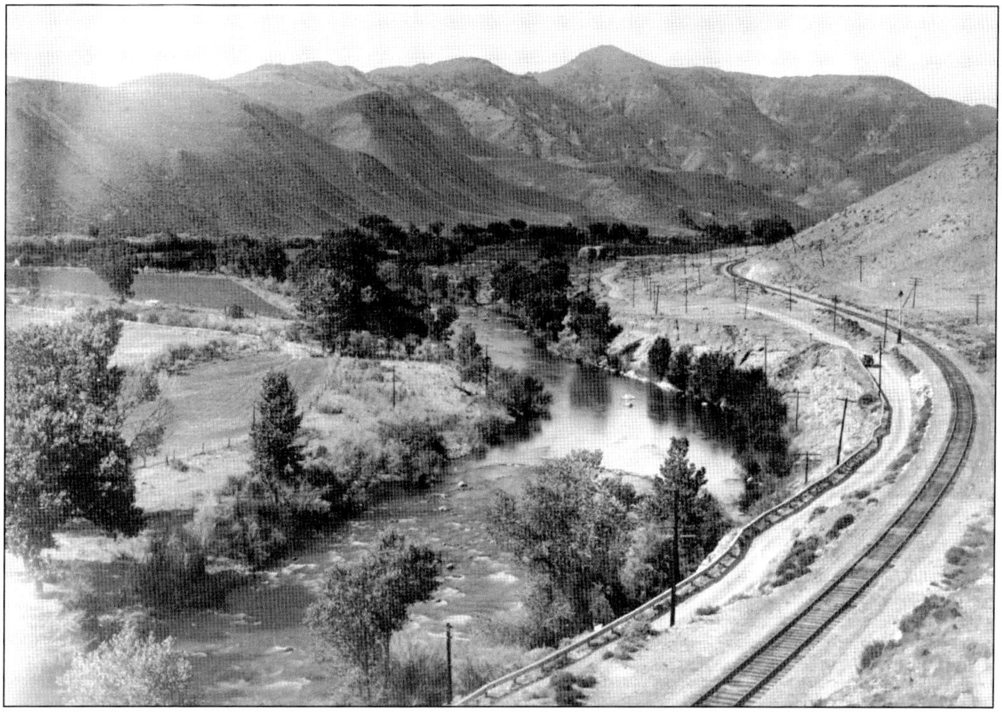

The Forty Mile Desert was finally tamed, and the Truckee River Route corridor became the general path of the Central Pacific Railroad. The railroad corridor then became the path of the Victory Highway, one of the first transcontinental routes and a rival of the Lincoln Highway. The Victory was subsumed into Nevada's Route 1, and in the 1920s was re-branded as US 40, which then became Interstate 80.

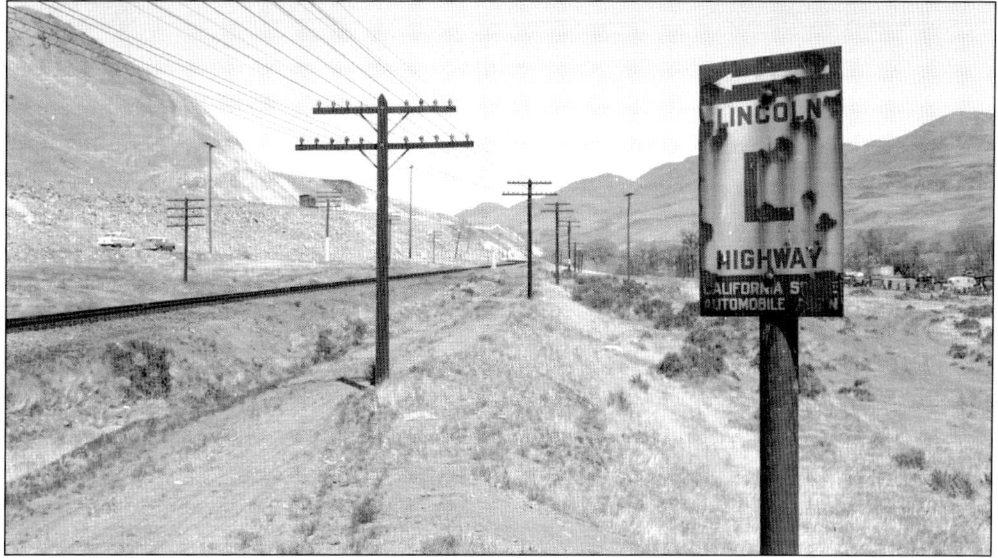

The Carson and Overland routes ended up being the foundation of the Lincoln Highway, also one of the nation's first transcontinental highways. The Lincoln was subsumed into Nevada's Route 2 and today's US 50. As with its Pony Express forbearer, America's "loneliest highway" has found a place in the American psyche evoking images of the Old West.

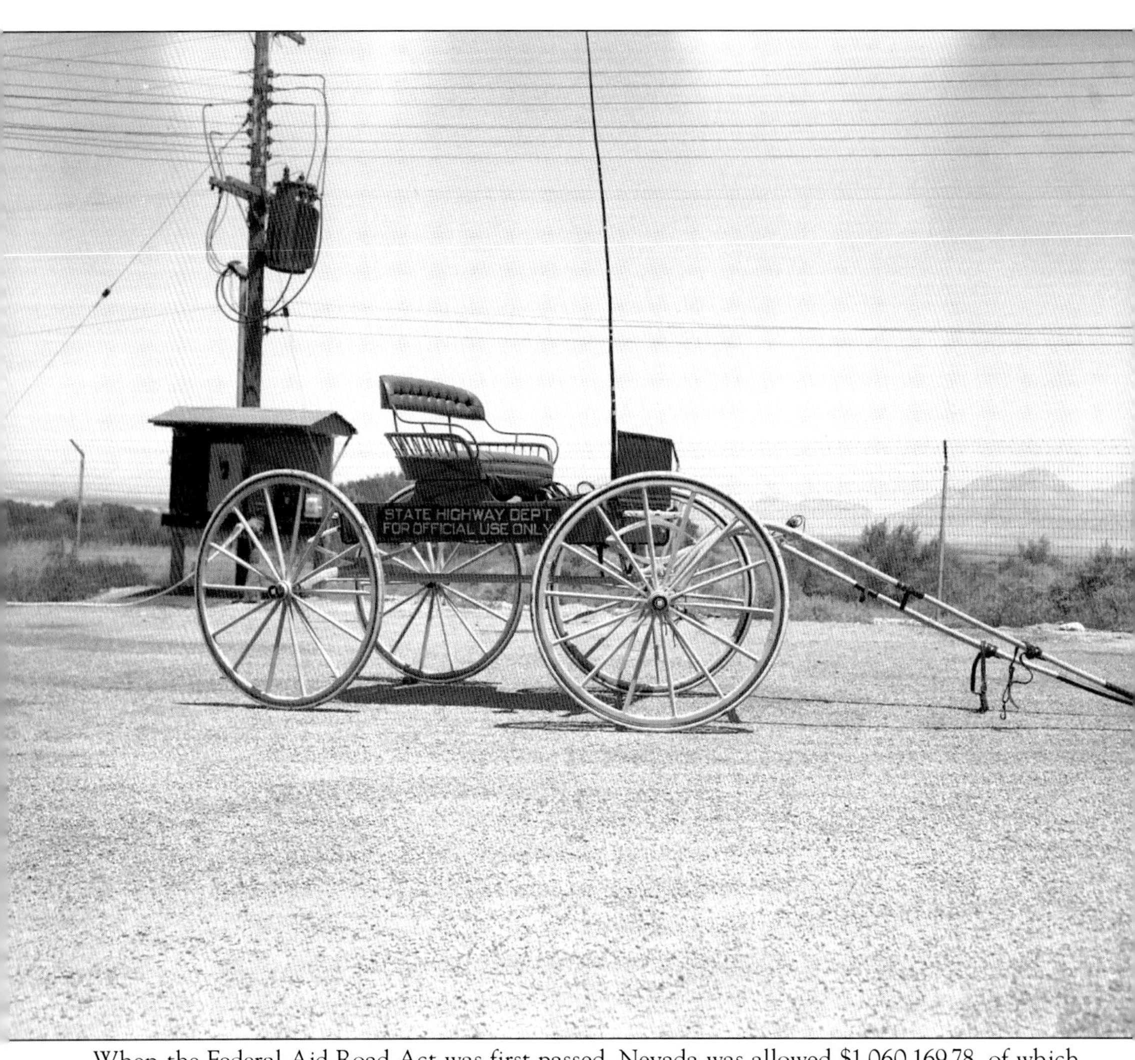

When the Federal Aid Road Act was first passed, Nevada was allowed $1,060,169.78, of which $95,000 had to be spent on routes going through national forests. The remaining $965,169.78 had to be spent on routes used by, or potentially used by, the US Postal Service. Meeting the national forest route requirement was relatively easy. The postal route requirement, however, was problematic. The highway system that Nevada designed through 1917 legislation consisted of 1,450 miles of would-be road. Unfortunately, less than 250 of those miles could be considered "post roads." To make matters even worse, the US Postal Service used less than 20 miles of what would become the transcontinental Victory Highway/Route 1 (now Interstate 80). To spend the money on routes beyond the 250 miles of postal roads, the highway department had to prepare arguments, supplemented by evidence, to the Department of Agriculture proving that a given route might one day carry mail.

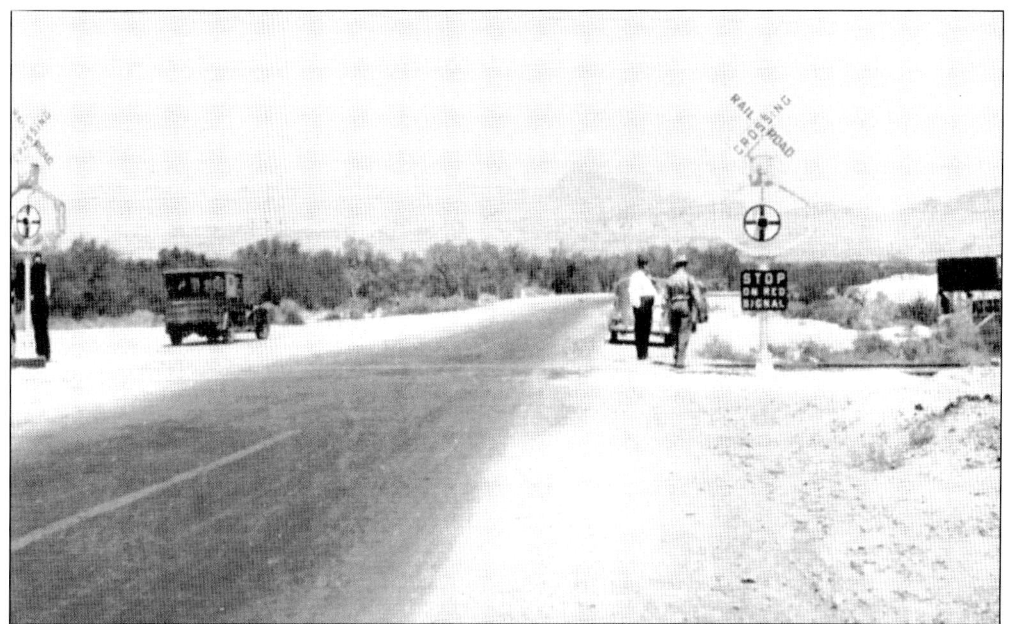

Collectively, Jedediah Smith, Antonio Armijo, Capt. John Fremont, and early Mormon explorers, among others, blazed the Old Spanish Trail and the Old Mormon Trail. The Arrowhead Trail, Nevada's original Route 6, very generally followed the corridor and offshoots of the Old Spanish and Old Mormon Trails. Route 6, shown here, became US 91, which was then upgraded to today's Interstate 15.

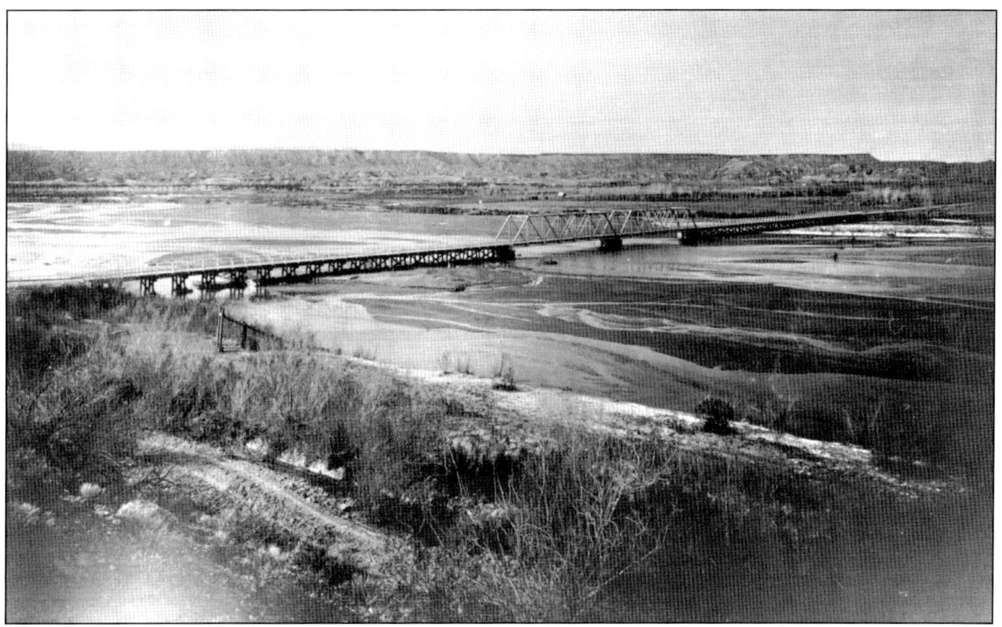

The Virgin River Bridge in Clark County carried the Arrowhead Trail over one of its major obstacles. Before the highway department constructed the first bridge at St. Thomas, travelers were obliged to pay $2 to have their car hitched to a team of horses and towed across the river. On February 9, 1932, a catastrophic flood destroyed the 1920 wood trestle and metal truss bridge pictured here.

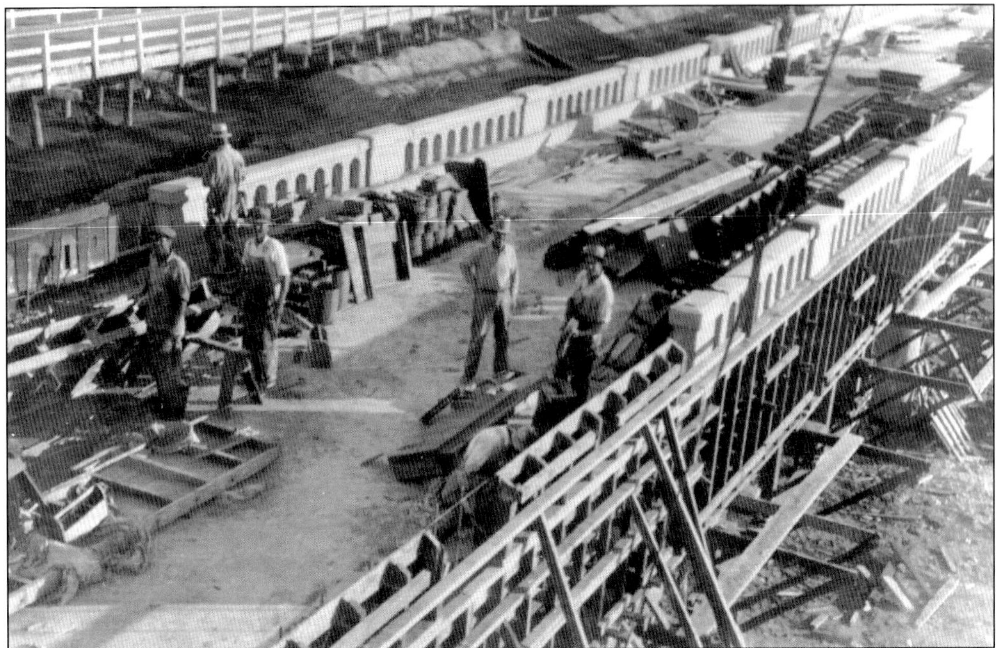

When the 1932 flood demolished the steel and wood truss bridges across the Virgin River at Riverside, the highway department endeavored to build a flood-proof bridge. Here, workers prepare the wood forms for the new cast-in-place reinforced concrete bridge. A temporary wood bridge can be seen in the background. Floodwaters would destroy the temporary bridge two times before the department finished the new bridge in 1933.

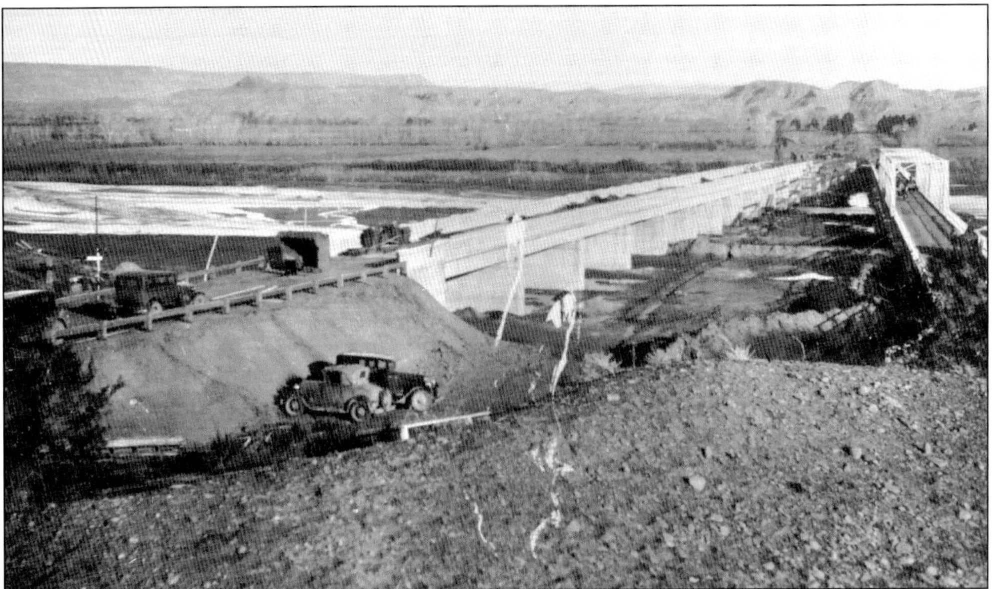

The highway department built the new Lower Virgin River Bridge next to the old bridge. To link the road to the new bridge required a slight realignment of the Arrowhead Trail, which connected Salt Lake City with Los Angeles via Las Vegas. These expensive infrastructure improvements to the Arrowhead Trail were justified by the growing traffic through southern Nevada as people came to work on Boulder Dam.

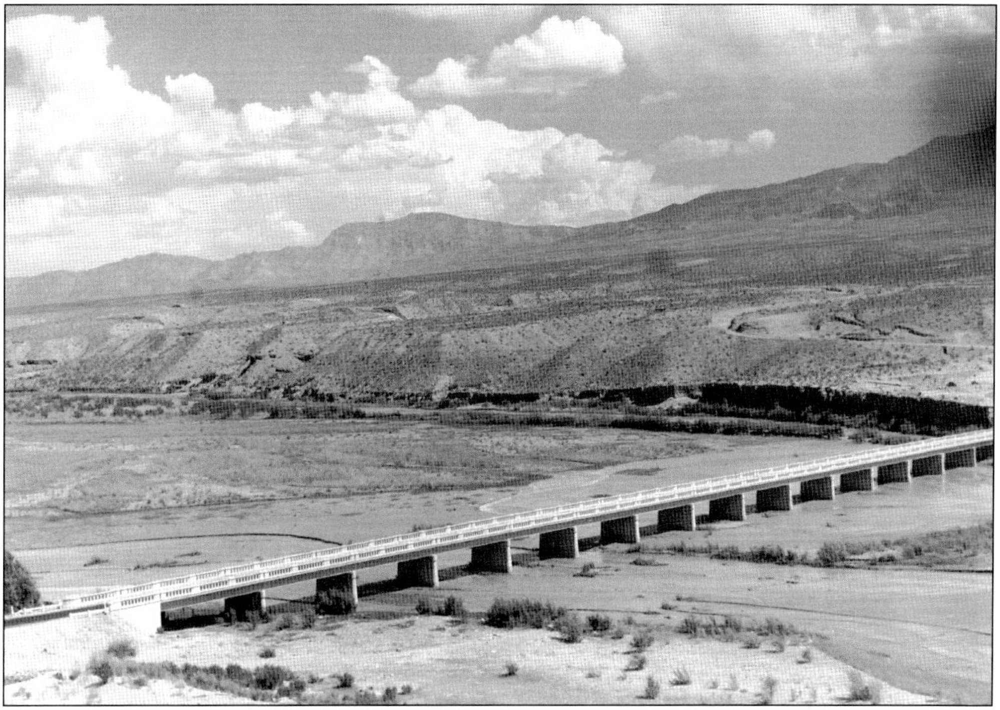

The highway department designed the new Lower Virgin Bridge in the Beaux-Arts style, with an elegant barrier rail of arched windows. At 845 feet long, this was the second-longest bridge in Nevada at the time. The only longer bridge was the Mesquite-Bunkerville Bridge, which measured 945 feet long. Completed in 1933, the Mesquite-Bunkerville Bridge also crossed the Virgin River.

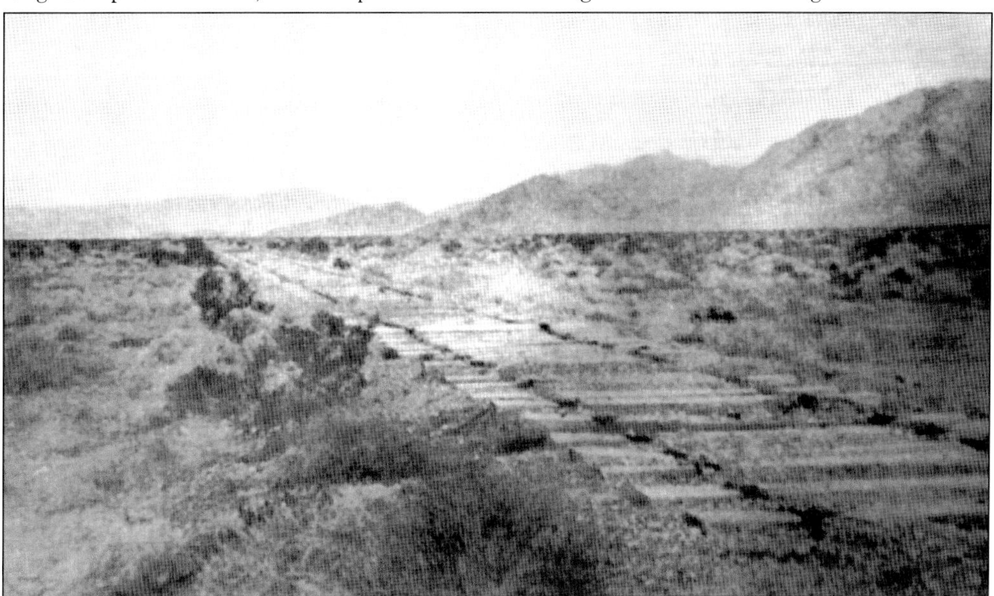

Many of Nevada's major roadways were built on old railroad grades. Nevada's Route 5 (now US 95) was built on the abandoned Las Vegas & Tonopah (LV&T) Railroad berm. The highway department took possession of the right-of-way in 1919 as the legislature scrambled to amend the highway act to include Clark County. Pictured here is the berm as it existed when the state took possession.

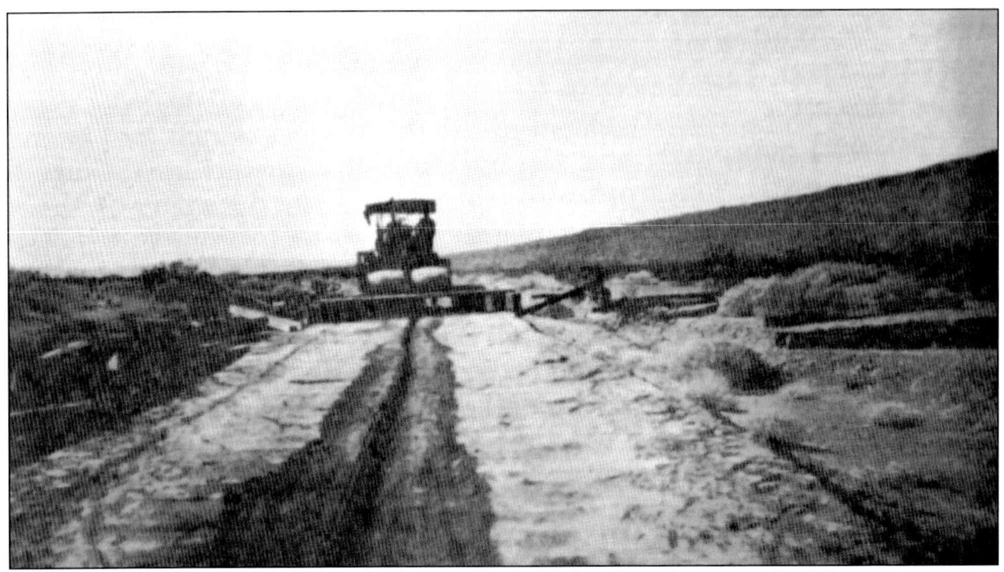

The highway department tossed aside the ties, then ran a heavy drag the length of the railroad bed to remove imprints left by the ties. Next, the department reduced the height of the berm by 8–12 inches and widened the driving surface to 16 feet. The driving surface was primarily dirt except for areas prone to washouts, which were graveled.

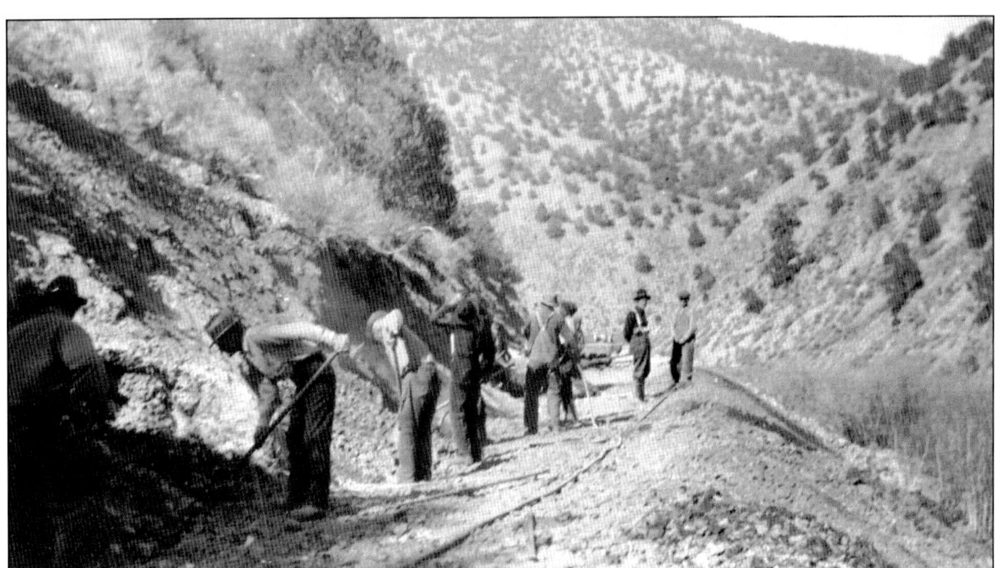

Gravel roads required sustained maintenance over several seasons before becoming satisfactory for highway traffic. Maintenance included dragging, sculpting, adding new material, and removing debris. Consistently watering the surface was also important, which the highway department found economical so long as a water source was within one mile of the section of road to be maintained. This c. 1923 photograph shows a crew constructing the Lincoln Highway over Carroll Summit.

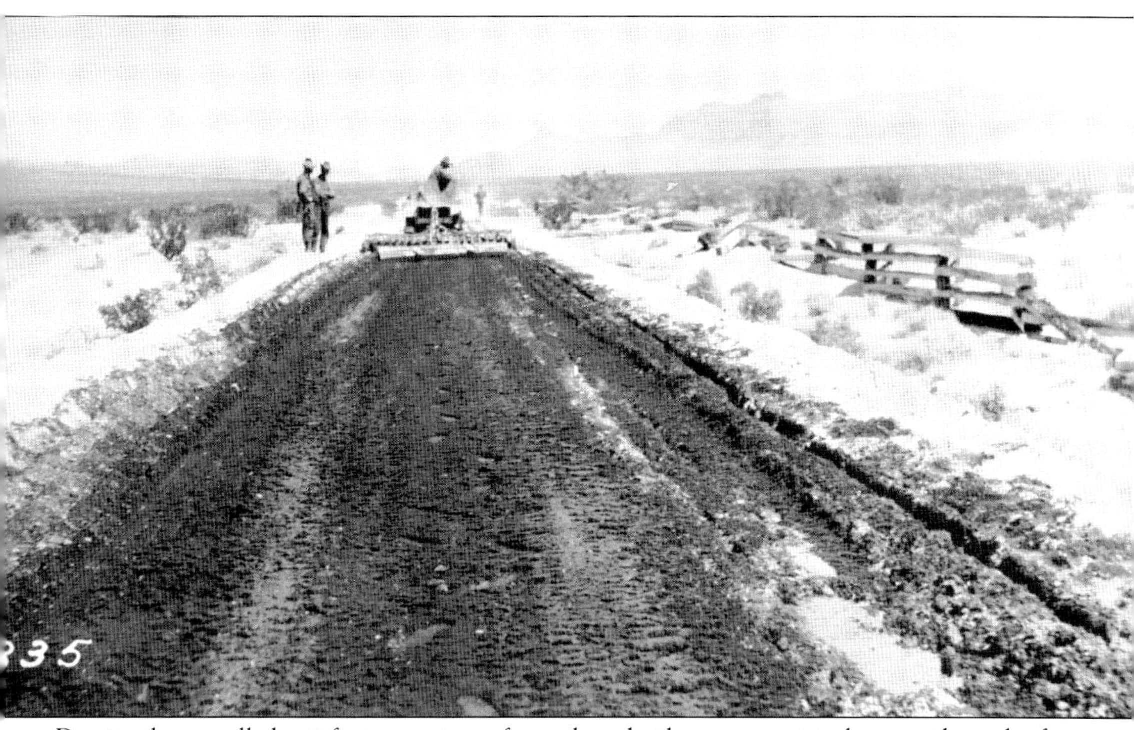

Despite the so-called satisfactory nature of gravel roads, they were not truly up to the task of handling large volumes of traffic. However, gravel roads were relatively cheap, particularly when compared with concrete roads. Concrete roads had the advantage of being very durable, but they came with a high price tag, and just like today, figuring out how to pay for roadways was a contentious task. In fact, many of the funding sources proposed in the 1920s, such as a gasoline tax, a vehicle tax, and a license tax, sound very familiar today. In an effort to balance road construction costs with perpetual maintenance costs, the highway department began experimenting with different types of road surfaces. In 1921 and 1922, experiments in mixing various thicknesses of asphalt with gravel were undertaken just north of Minden. The following year, the department experimented with sand-and-oil combinations. As seen here, the department mixed oil with sand until there was a surface a few inches thick. The surface was then compacted by dragging and rolling the mixture.

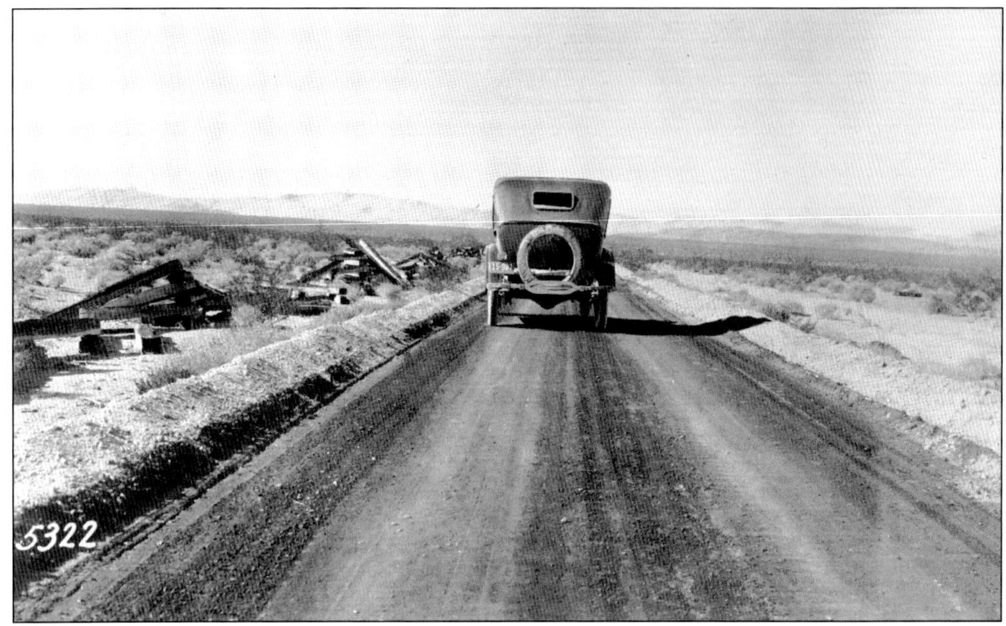

The initial sand-and-oil experiments took place just north of Beatty and were a success. Pictured here is a car being driven on the completed sand-and-oil surface. This cost-effective and durable road proved to be the solution to what had been a prevalent and vexing problem of building an efficient roadway through highly sandy areas.

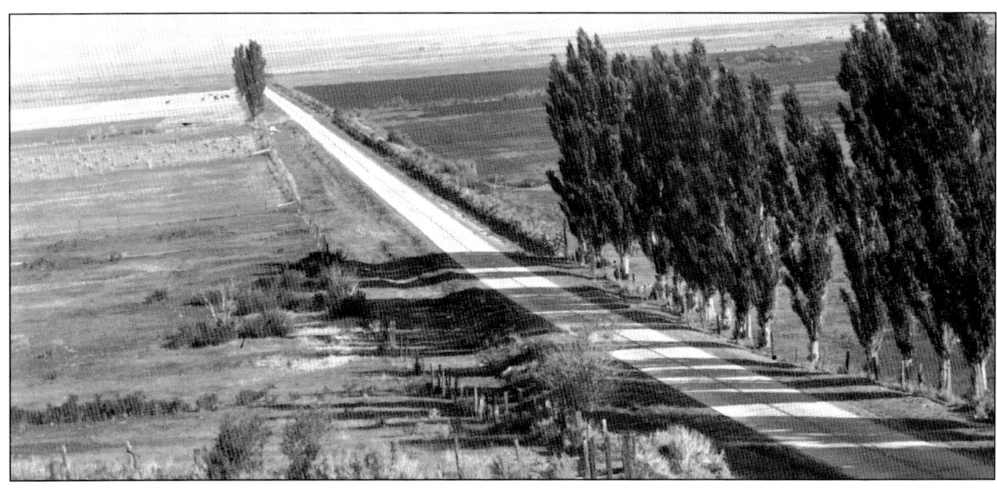

Pictured here is a concrete road through Washoe Valley connecting Reno and Carson City. In 1922, the highway department began a safety campaign in which workers painted a four-inch-wide black stripe down the center of concrete roads, black being more visible than white. The black centerline stripe helped prevent accidents caused by motorists drifting into oncoming traffic.

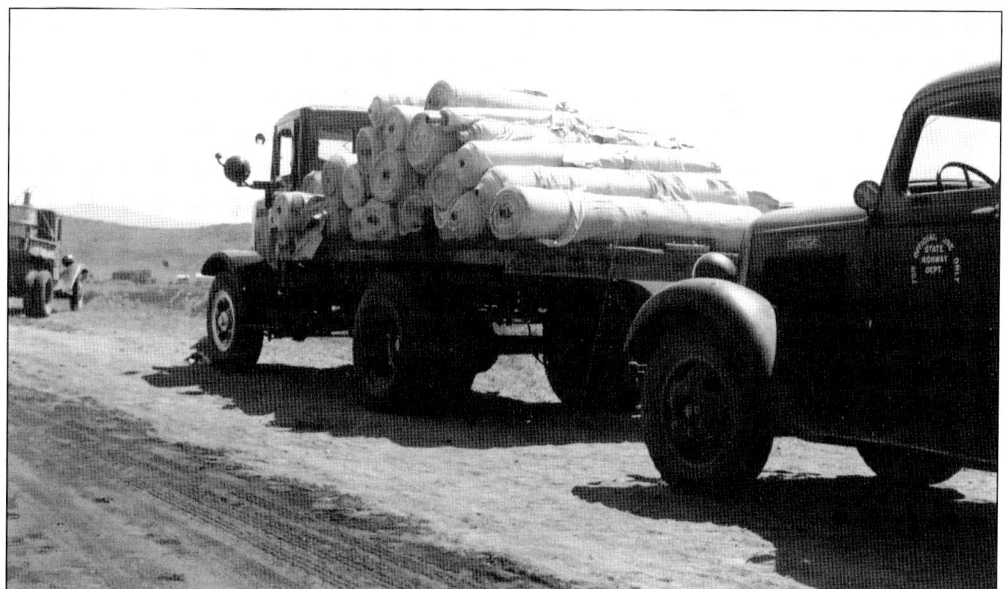

By the mid-1930s, the highway department had begun experimenting with cotton roads. Nationally, the cotton road movement began in the early 1920s in response to the more annoying aspects of bituminous surfaces, mainly edge crumbling and potholes. Nevada experimented with a four-mile stretch of road on the Pyramid Lake Highway. Pictured here is a truck delivering cotton rolls.

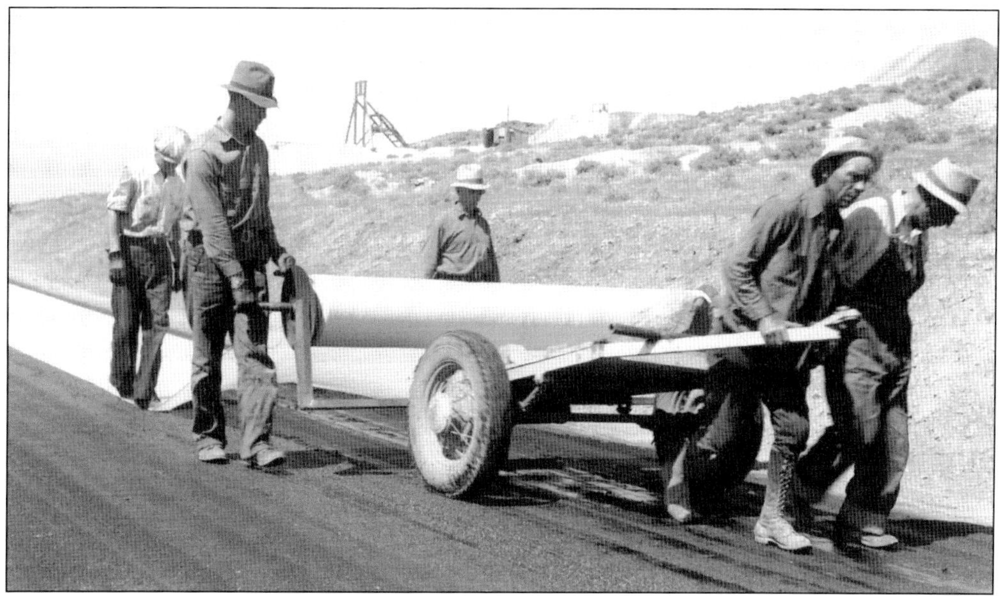

Inspired by tire construction that also used cotton, engineers postulated that fabric would act as a binder for the bitumen and create a stronger driving surface. Although appetite for the experiment faded quickly in the 1920s, it was rekindled in the 1930s due to an increase in roads with enough traffic to quickly wear out the standard bituminous surface, but not enough traffic to justify the expense of a concrete road.

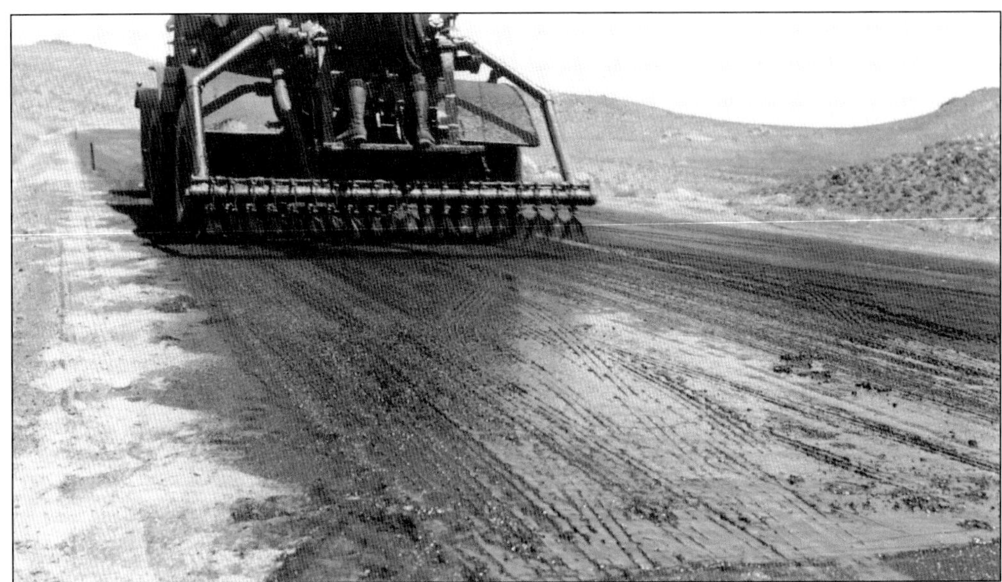

Both the Great Depression and America's loss of traction in the cotton market further fueled cotton road experiments. In an effort to rebuild the South's cotton industry, the Department of Agriculture offered all the highway departments a share of a $1.3 million pot to begin the road experiments. Shown here is the application of bitumen.

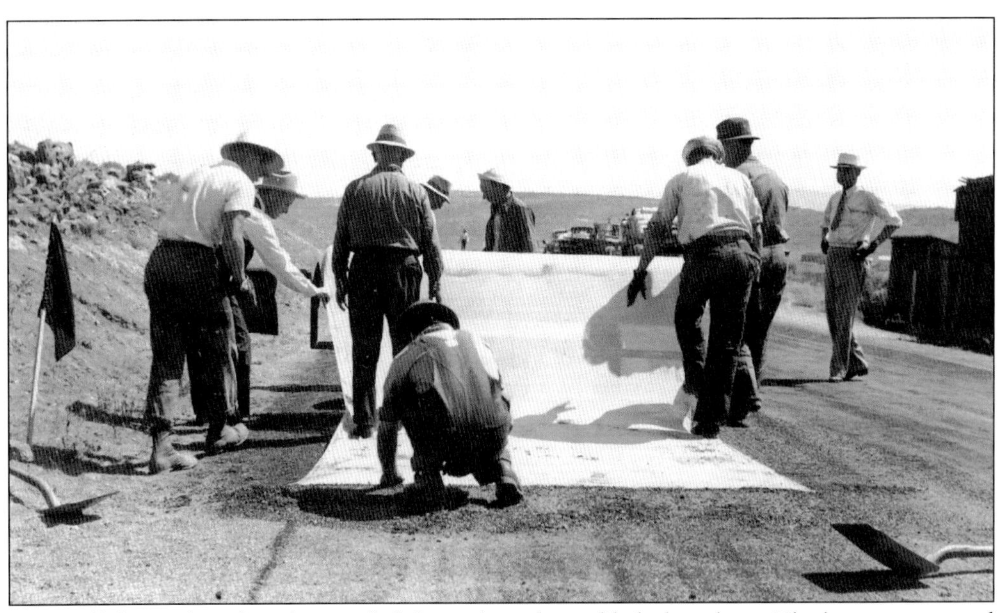

To install the road, workers first graded the surface, then added a base layer. The base was covered with a layer of bitumen, and while the bitumen was still sticky, a layer of cotton was added. When all the layers were completely dried, a layer of hot bitumen was placed on top of the cotton, then rolled by a large machine.

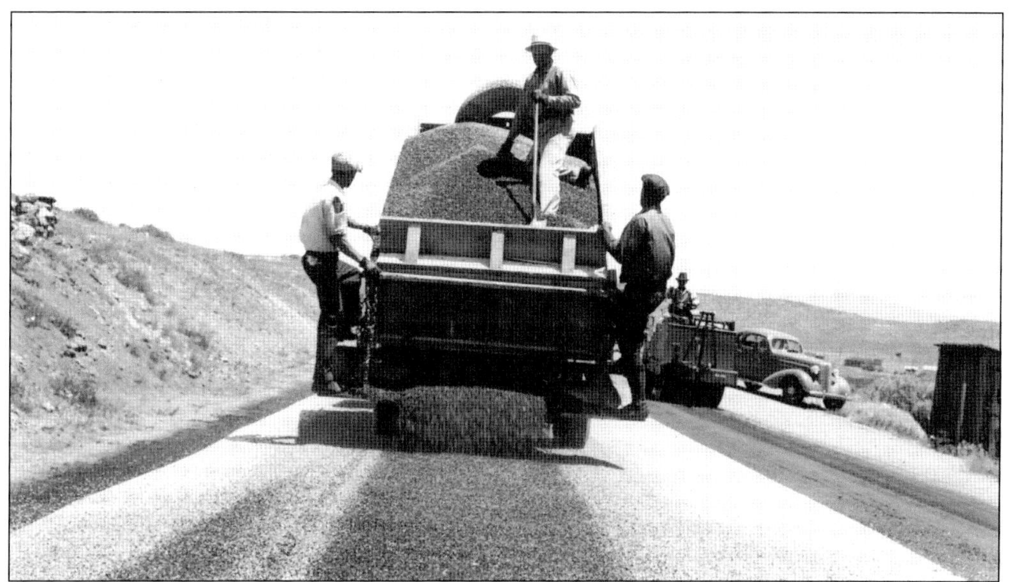

Pyramid Lake Highway was used in the cotton road experiment because of traffic density and prevailing weather patterns. The test zone was sectioned into four parts, each of which was one mile long. The first section was built using a fine cotton mesh, the second with a medium-gauge cotton, and the third with a heavy-gauge cotton. The fourth section was a control where no cotton was added.

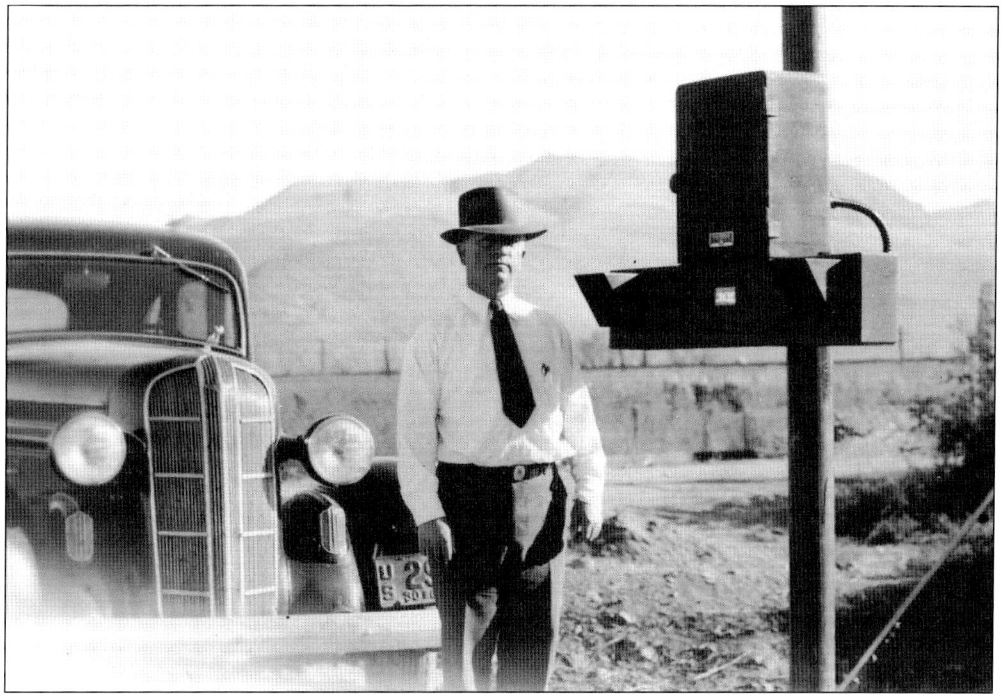

From its inception, the highway department employed a variety of techniques for deciding which roads needed attention in order to prioritize the most needed improvements. Traffic counts were an important tool in making improvement decisions. This photograph, taken in the 1930s, shows the traffic recorder mounted on a pole a few feet off the road.

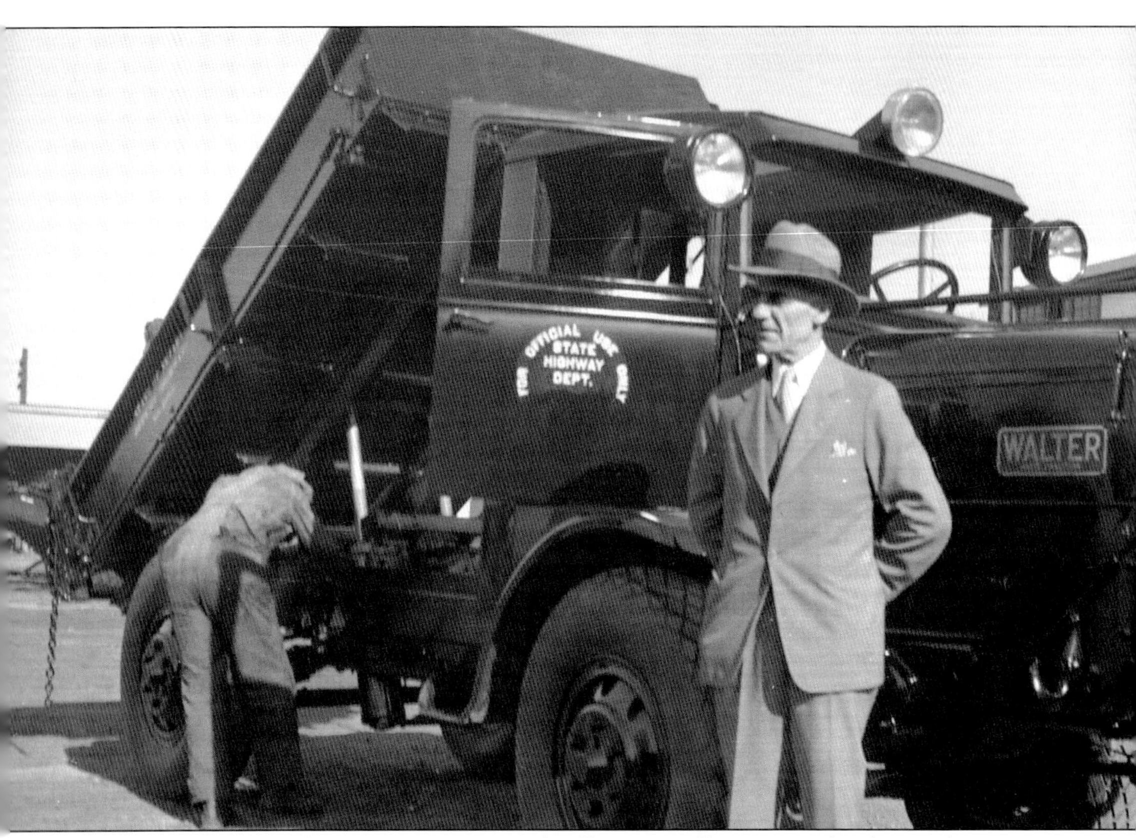

On the ground, road construction was, and still is, typically overseen by the resident engineer assigned to the project. As part of an ongoing effort to standardize and thereby streamline the road-building process, the highway department published a handbook titled the *Engineers' Manual of Instruction*. The handbook, produced between 1929 and 1930, outlined the duties of the resident engineer (RE) and made it clear that the RE had to keep a daily diary, including details on what time events occurred, "salient developments," and "important understandings with the contractor." In addition to dates and costs, the RE was also obliged to record "important conversations relative to the work," as well as any data not provided in other documentation that "might have a bearing in the future, should details come into dispute." Finally, the RE was required to keep a daily log of "all information relative to equipment, labor, materials used on extra work" and to provide "explanations for additional and extra work."

A safely engineered and constructed system also needed a set of rules with which every driver was familiar, yet when cars were new, so too were the regulations surrounding driving. Part of reigning in the chaos was creating and installing uniform signage throughout the Silver State. The highway department kept fabrication in-house by creating the Sign Production Unit in the late 1930s.

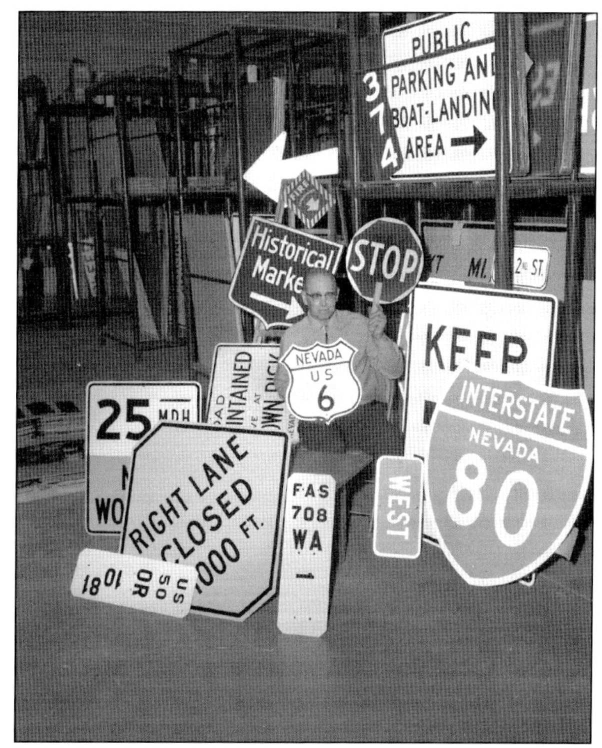

The highway department used this massive electric baking oven located at the Reno sign shop to make enameled metal signs. The oven was made by the Minnesota-based Despatch Oven Company. By the 1940s, durable metal signs had replaced wooden signs. Like their wood predecessors, they featured bold black letters and symbols on a white background.

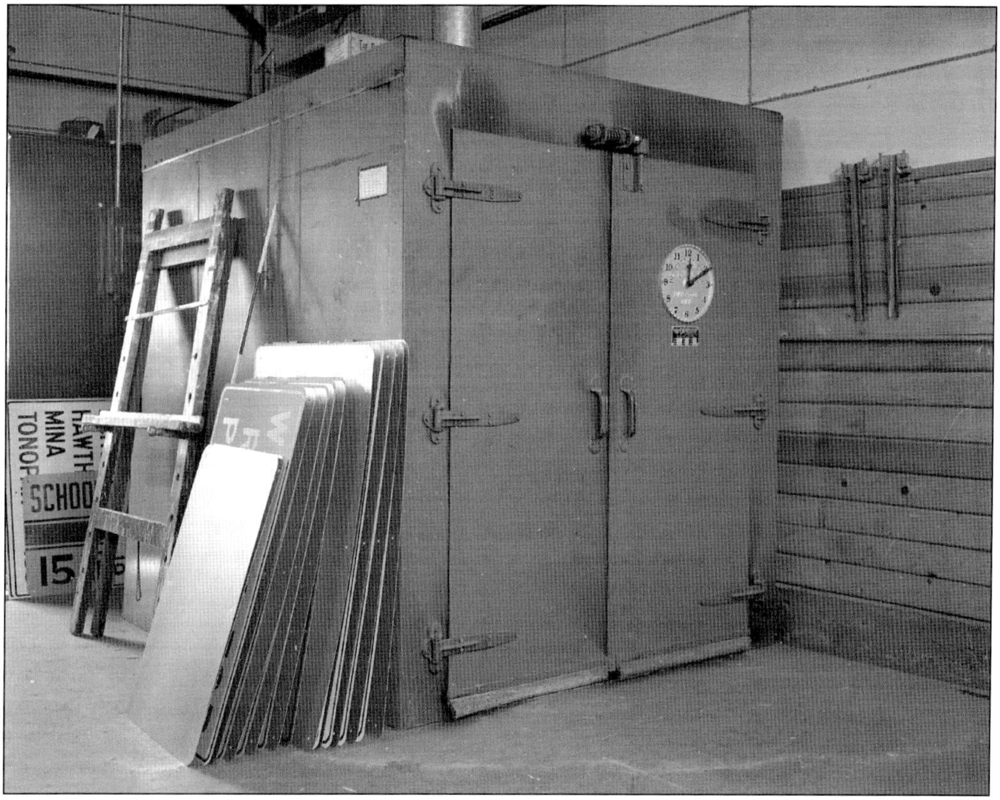

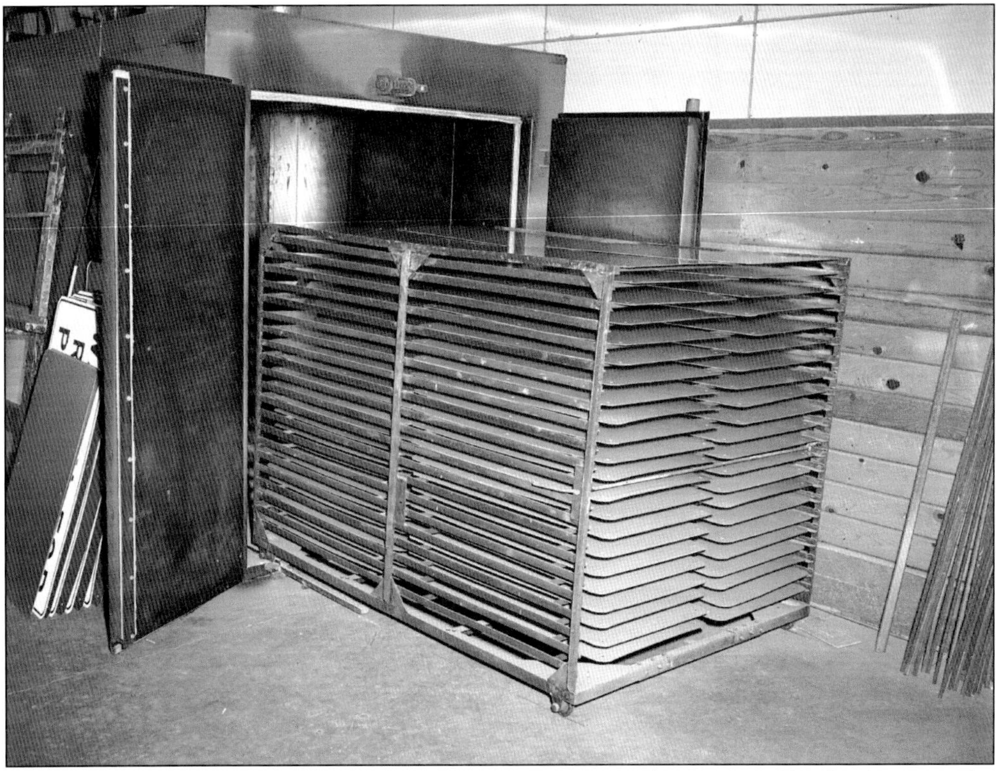

The oven could bake the enamel finish on up to 84 signs at one time. Similar to a pottery glaze, porcelain enamel was made from powdered glass in a suspension that could be painted onto a sign. Each color had to be fired before the next color could be added and the baking process repeated.

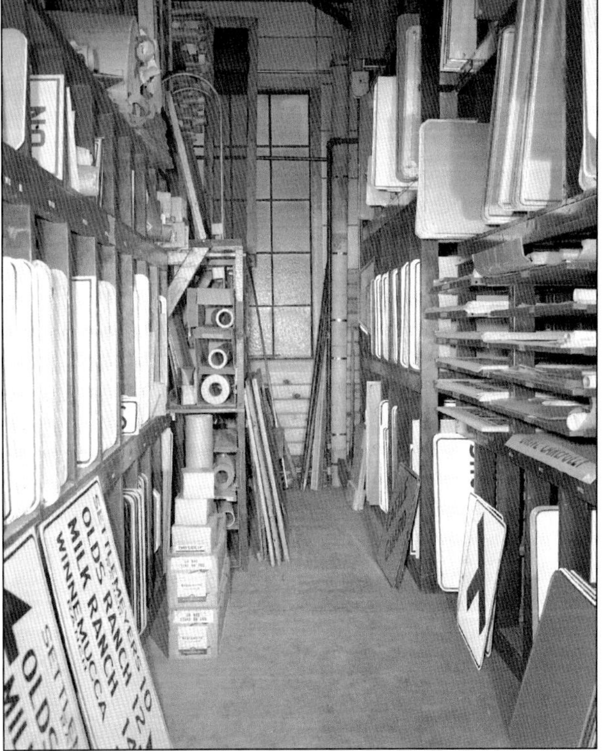

The finished signs were stored at the Reno sign shop until needed. When signs were damaged, they were either replaced or retouched and repaired in place. Typically, signs were damaged because motorists would shoot them or break or steal the reflector buttons embedded in each sign.

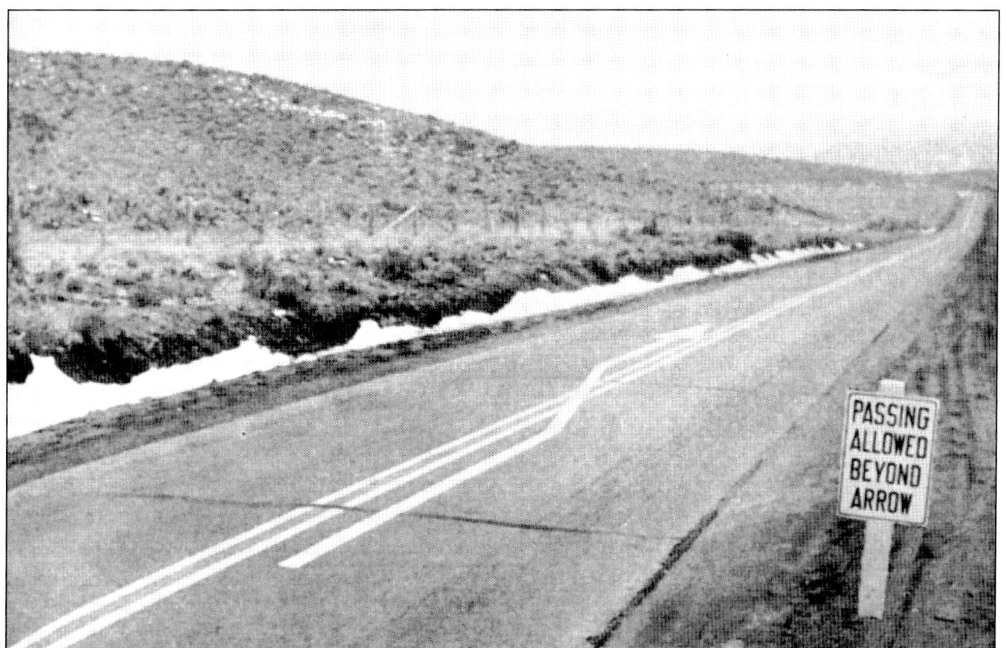

In addition to signage, symbols painted on the driving surface became a way to convey conditions and rules. As seen in this c. 1938 photograph, symbols to indicate passing lanes have changed over the years. At the time, according to *Nevada Highways and Parks* magazine, "The cross-over arrow permits crossing of the double line on the down side of a hill where visibility is good."

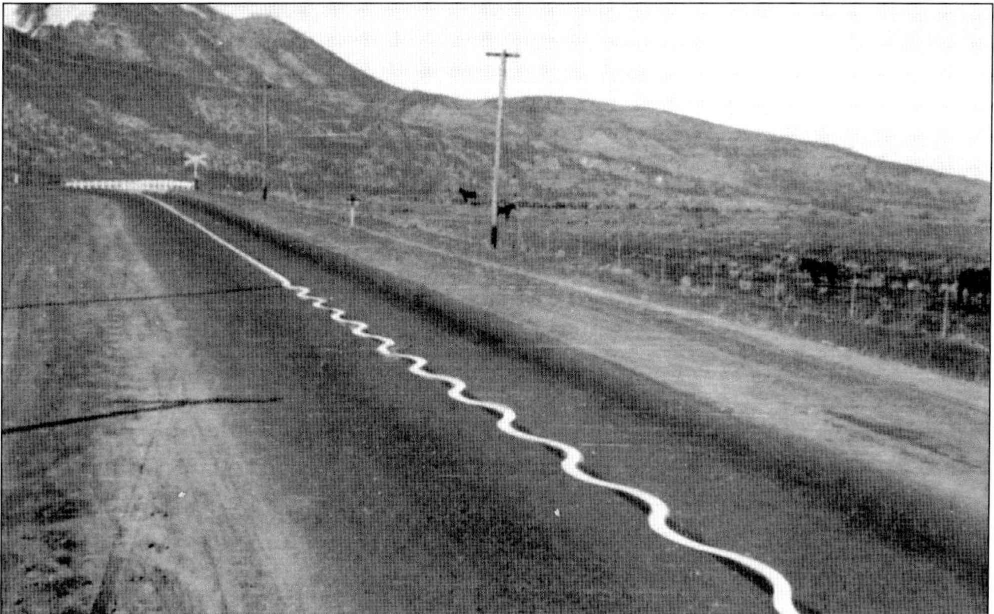

This photograph, taken along the Reno-Carson Highway in the late 1930s, shows the "wavy white line," an innovative technique used to indicate a railroad crossing at the end of a curve in the road. According to statistics from 1938, accidents were reduced by 85 percent after the wavy white line was installed. Another effort to regulate the roadways required each driver to obtain a license.

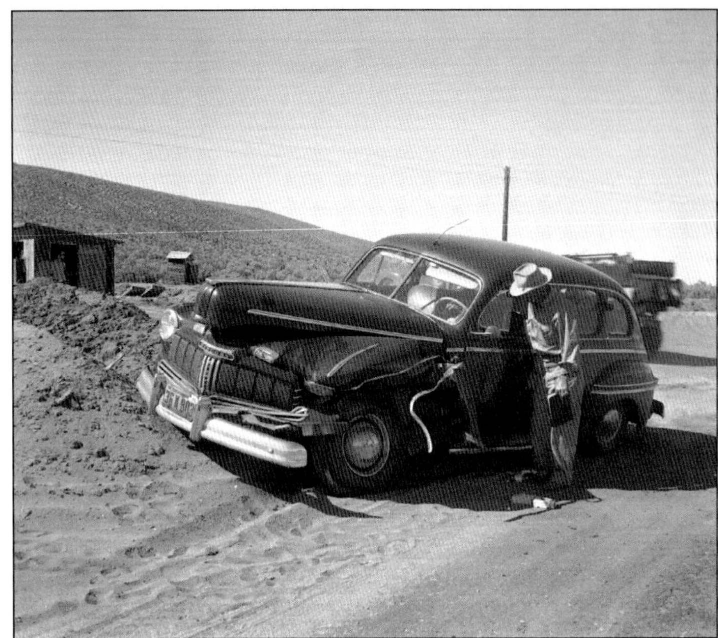

Prior to 1941, driver's licenses were issued by the county assessor. The main licensing requirements were completing an application and paying a fee, so not surprisingly, the competency of the driving public was spotty at best. The highway department bemoaned the lax requirements, stating, "We have designed and built our road system primarily from the safety viewpoint, yet the roads can be driven by people with all degrees of mentality."

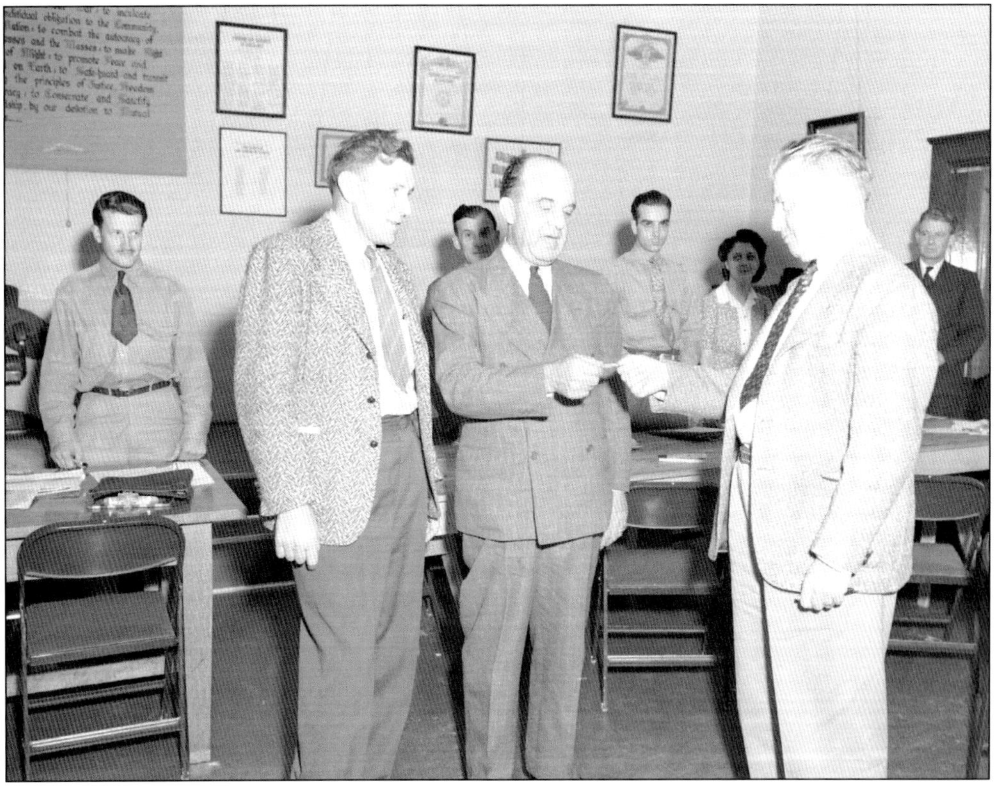

At the direction of the state legislature, the highway department took over the responsibility of issuing driver's licenses in 1941. All previous licenses were declared void, and every driver had to reapply for a license, this time passing a test on road safety if he or she had less than a year of driving experience or a record of unsafe driving. The public was not pleased with the new restrictions.

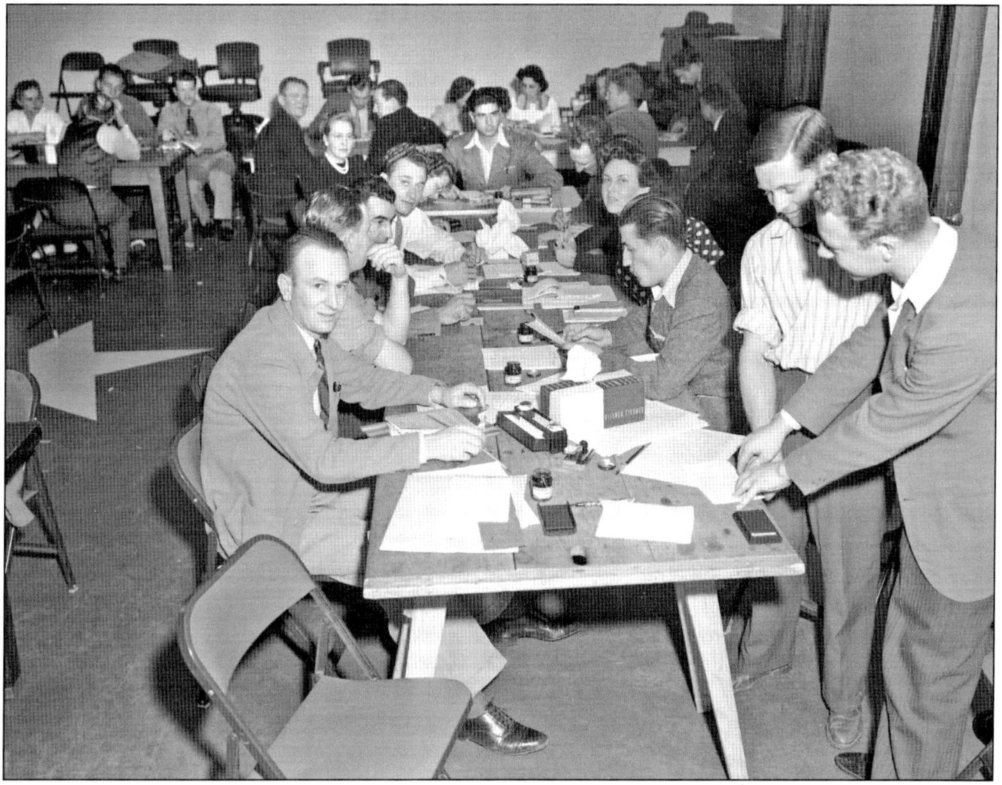

The 1941 Uniform Motor Vehicle Driver's License Act also required that licenses be issued in the county seat, meaning some rural residents had to travel long distances with an invalid driver's license. Shown here is the Las Vegas Driver's License Department in 1942. For the convenience of Nevada's rural residents, the highway department sent crews to small towns to sign up drivers for new licenses.

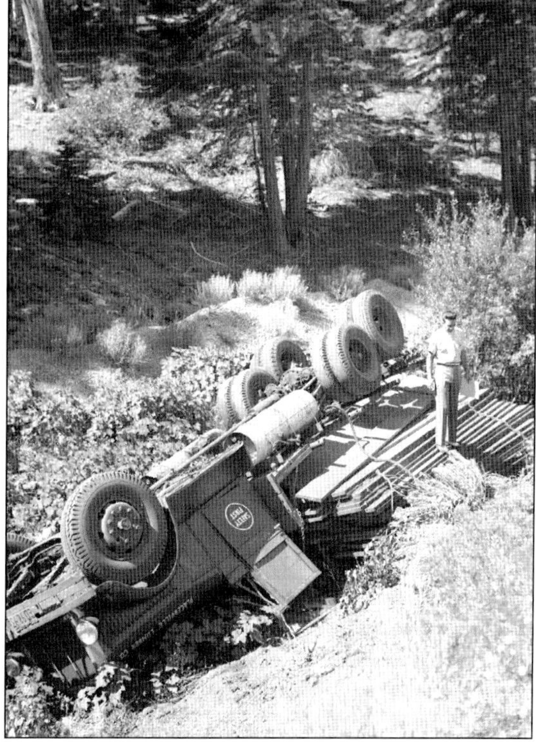

In the mid-1920s, the highway department lobbied the legislature to remove the speed limit of 45 miles per hour, which officials felt was too high in many circumstances, and replace it with a limit of "sane and safe driving." The idea was that drivers would make sensible decisions about their speed and hopefully avoid the same fate of this lumber truck in 1949.

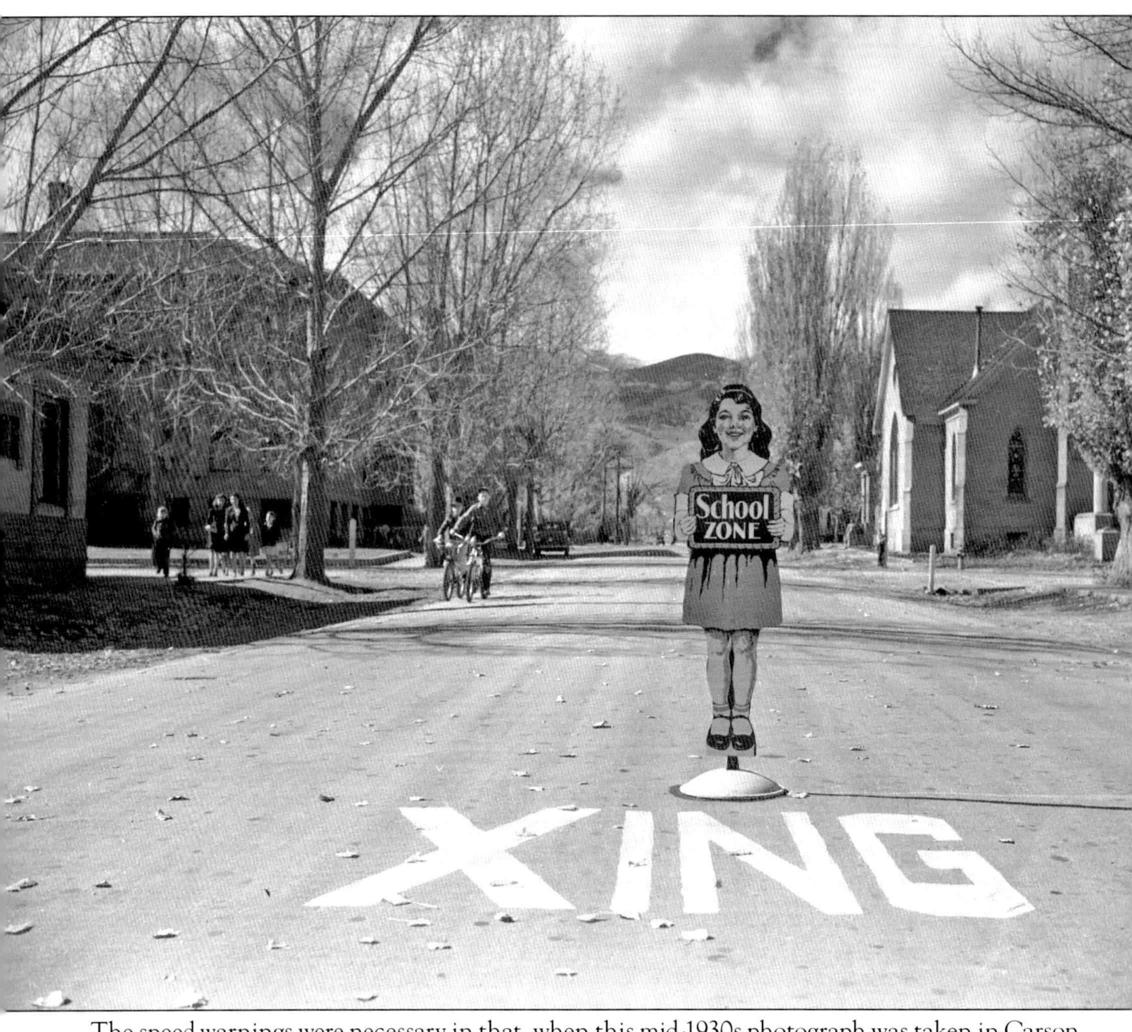

The speed warnings were necessary in that, when this mid-1930s photograph was taken in Carson City, there was no speed limit in Nevada's open country. Speed limits were not imposed until drivers approached cities, school zones, and intersections. At the time, the Victory Highway (US 40) was particularly accident prone, so many anti-speeding efforts were focused on that road.

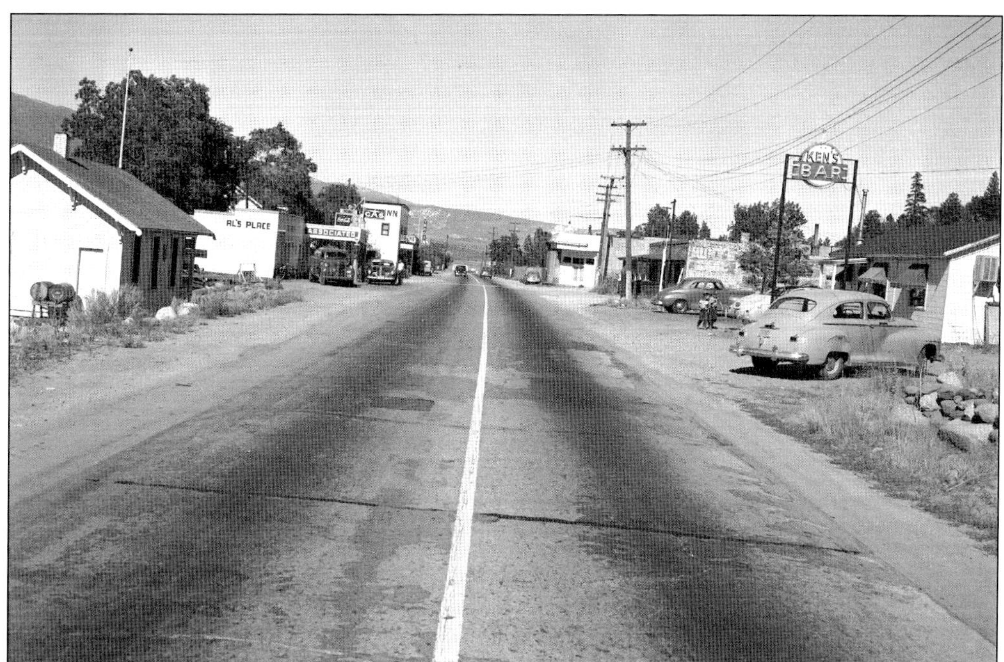

The centerline, shown in this 1940s photograph of a stretch of highway through Verdi, was considered one of the most important roadway safety features in use. The line was instrumental in keeping drivers in their own lane, especially during periods of poor visibility. Prior to World War II rationing efforts, the white center stripe was a solid line.

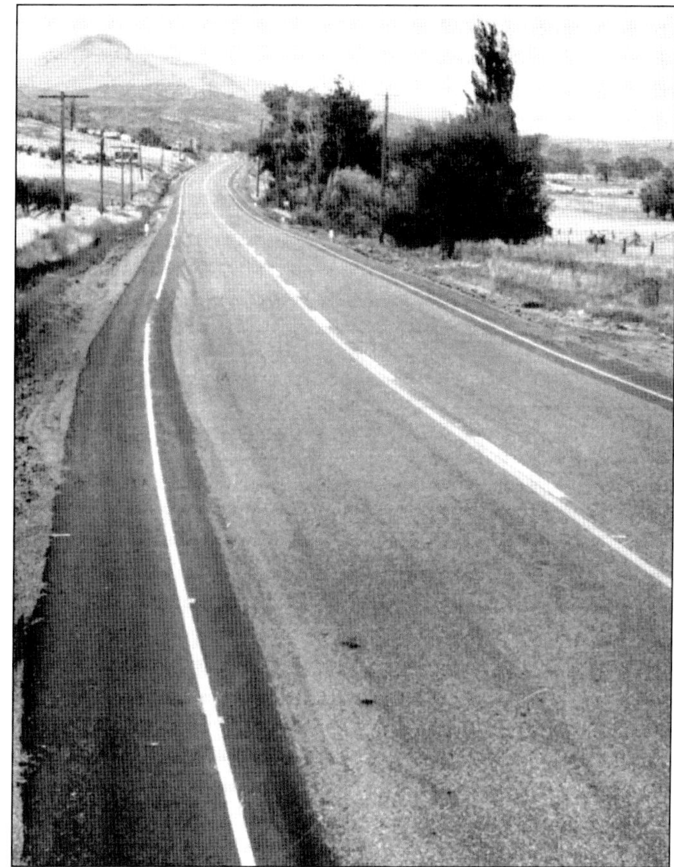

In 1956, the highway department began experimenting with marking shoulders along roadways as well. The first experiment, pictured here in Washoe Valley, proved successful because the line discouraged drivers from using the shoulder as a passing lane and because it gave drivers a clearer view of where the edge of the road was at night or during bad weather.

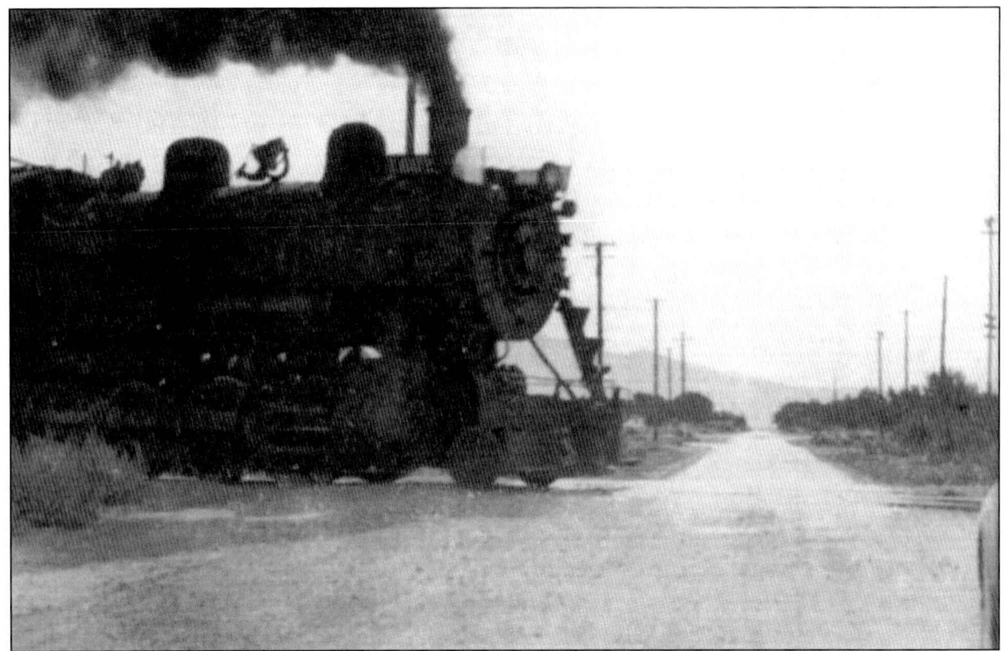

Grade crossing, or the intersection of the railroad grade and the highway grade, was a major road hazard and one that the highway department has worked to eliminate through grade separations since beginning its work on the highways. Photographed in the late 1940s, this image shows the grade crossing along the now extremely busy Charleston Boulevard in Las Vegas.

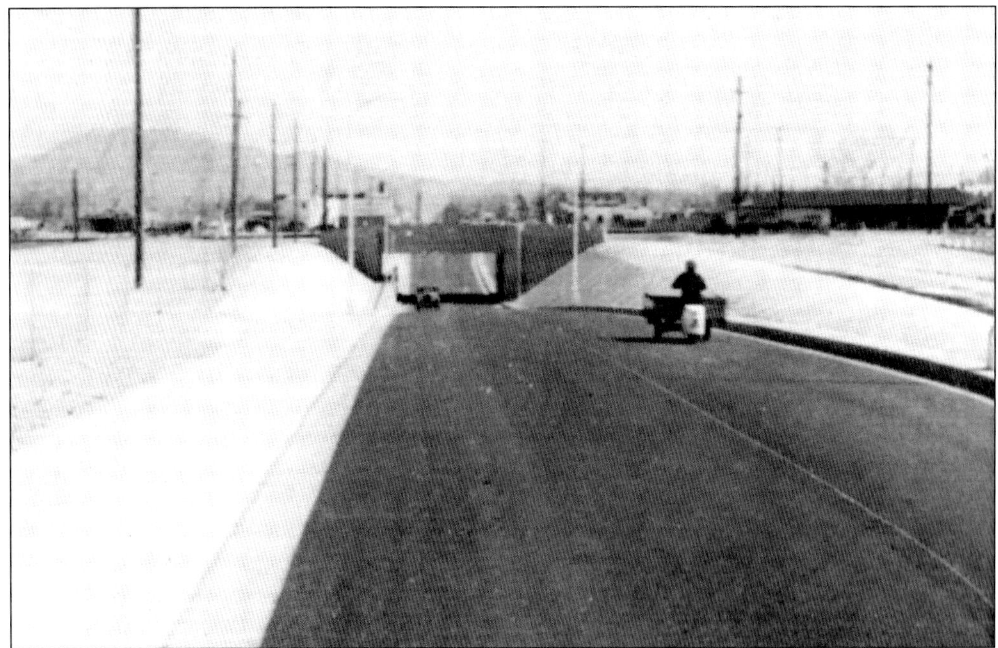

Pictured here is the "after" version of the image above. In 1949–1950, the highway department separated the grades and created a much safer driving experience. In the department's words, "The Charleston Underpass in Las Vegas, not only made highway travel safer, but also aided in the beautifying of the adjacent area."

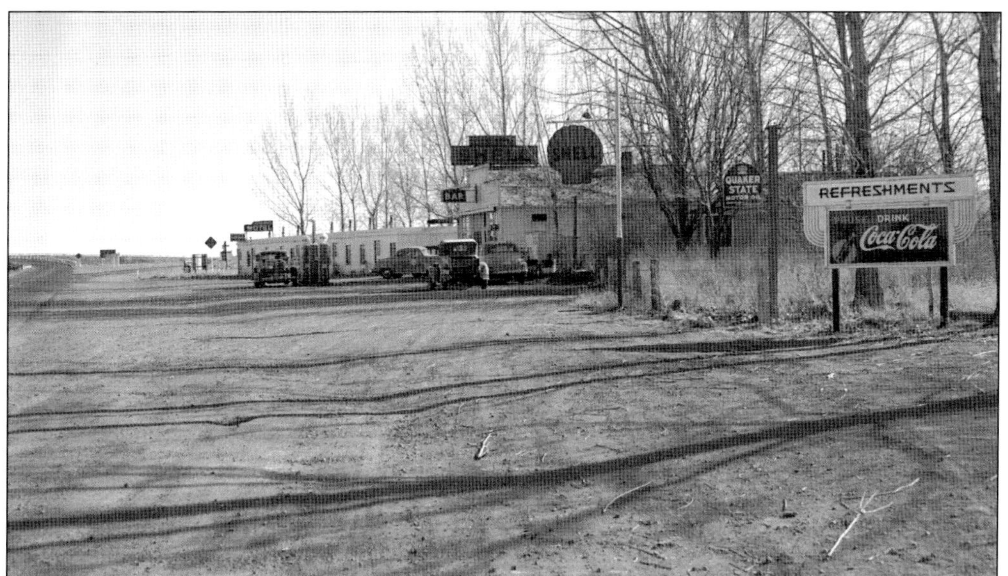

Safe roads have been the highway department's common theme for nearly 100 years. In 1936, the department partnered with the Red Cross and began the process of installing first-aid kits in every highway maintenance station and highway patrol station, as well as in established stores and gas stations along the roadways. Together, they also provided first-aid training on how to assist injured or ill motorists.

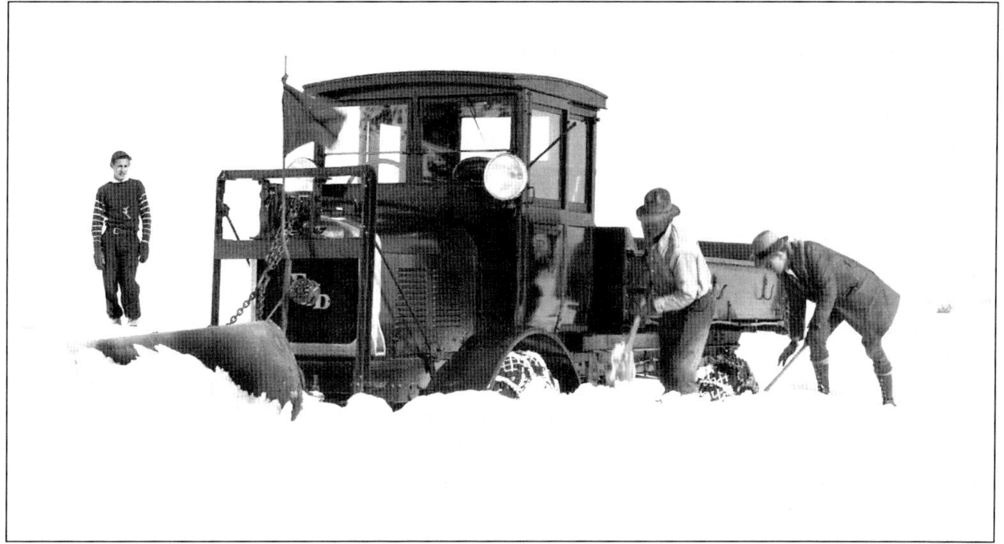

An early challenge facing the highway department was keeping roads drivable during periods of heavy snow. It was not long after the department was formed that a large and sustained snowstorm blew through Washoe Valley and covered the highway connecting Reno and Carson City. The storm came in waves starting on December 19, 1921, and the department had to clear the road nearly every day until February 23, 1922. During the first weeks of the storm, the department used a V-plow towed by a pair of four-wheel-drive trucks to keep the road clear. However, with nine-foot drifts and an intensifying storm, the department had to switch tactics and attach snowplows to tractors. Despite the conditions and makeshift equipment, the road was open every day, with the exception of three days when the equipment had to be repaired.

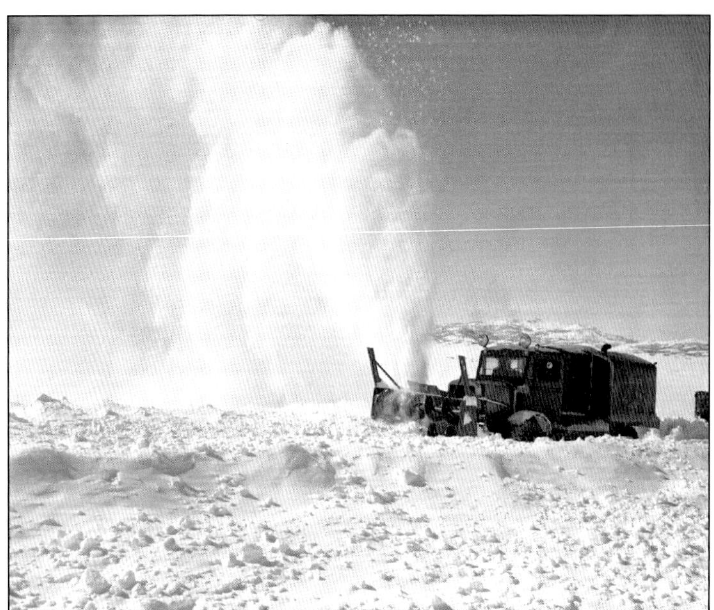

After the 1921–1922 snowstorm, the highway department purchased proper snowplows and installed portable snow fences. By the 1930s, the department had acquired numerous plows and blowers, which were then stored in strategic locations so that the equipment was in place before bad weather hit. Crews to operate the machinery were also on call 24 hours a day.

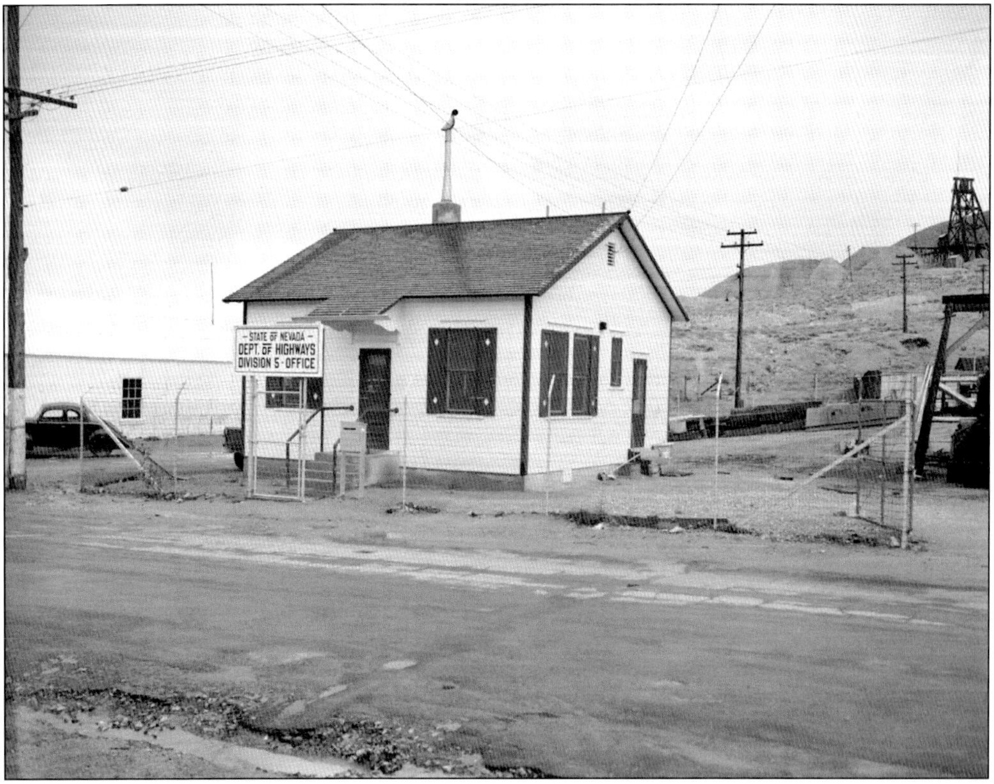

As the highway network grew, so too did the infrastructure required to maintain the system. Consequently, the highway department itself had to grow considerably, and given the vast size of Nevada, had to do so efficiently. As a result, the department split into regionally based divisions, each with its own set of engineers, maintenance workers, and support staff to respond quickly to issues within its territory.

Two

The Team
Surveyors, Engineers, Construction, and Support

Prior to departmental efforts, there were no paved highways in Nevada, only a series of dirt and gravel roads upon which most of the major highways were built or a blank canvas upon which new routes were created. By 1932, however, the highway department had paved 800 miles of road and had taken over responsibility for 2,100 miles of unpaved roads. By 1958, that number had grown to over 4,200 miles of paved road, and as the road system grew, so too did the department. Building more roads created a greater need for personnel to maintain those roads, and changes in technology and design complexity created a need for new and innovative divisions within the department.

By the 1950s, the highway department had expanded from a dedicated handful of engineers and surveyors to a sophisticated machine comprised of specialists in planning, mapping, traffic patterns, road life, safety, design, bridge construction, photogrammetry, materials testing and research, law, finance, maintenance, communications, and computers, among others. In the nearly 100 years since the department was formed, the collective team of highway specialists has created a statewide network of 1,000 bridges and 5,400 miles of roadway. If those 5,400 miles were a linear road that could cross an ocean, it would stretch from the Paris casino in Las Vegas to the city of Paris in France.

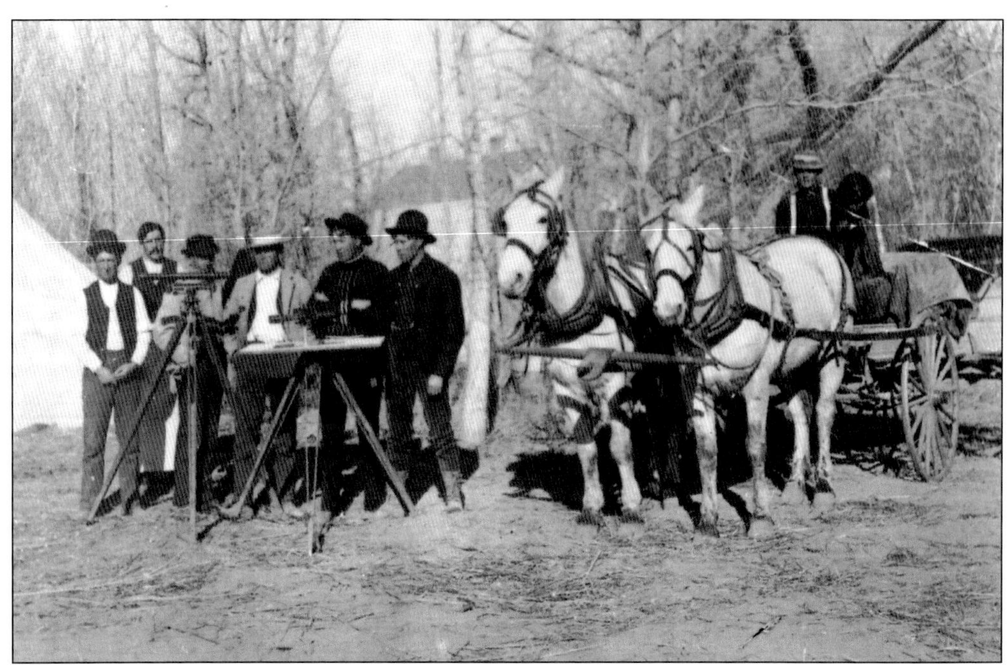

Pictured here is an early survey crew. When the highway department was formed, the nation was in the throes of World War I, and as a result, highway construction was on hold. However, surveys and planning continued, and in 1919, the department proclaimed, "The era of state highway construction in Nevada is about to be entered with the utmost confidence in the preparations made by our organization."

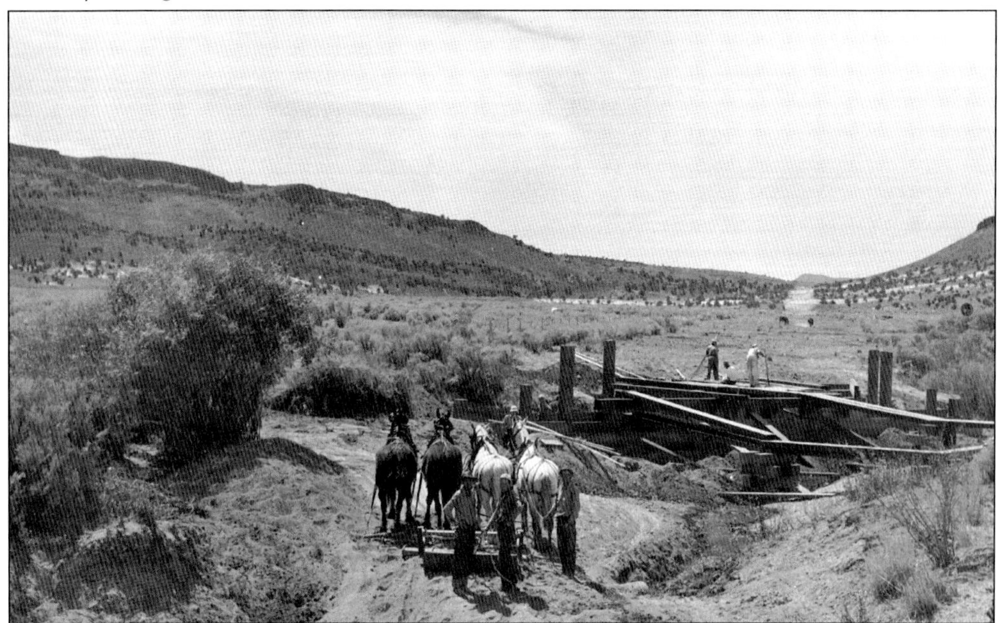

Shown here is a construction scene from the 1920s. In outlying areas, where there were no real roads to work with, horses were often the means by which equipment was powered. Construction was not the only challenge, however. Planning a road where none previously existed required plotting a route with relatively gentle curves and grades, but also not too circuitous.

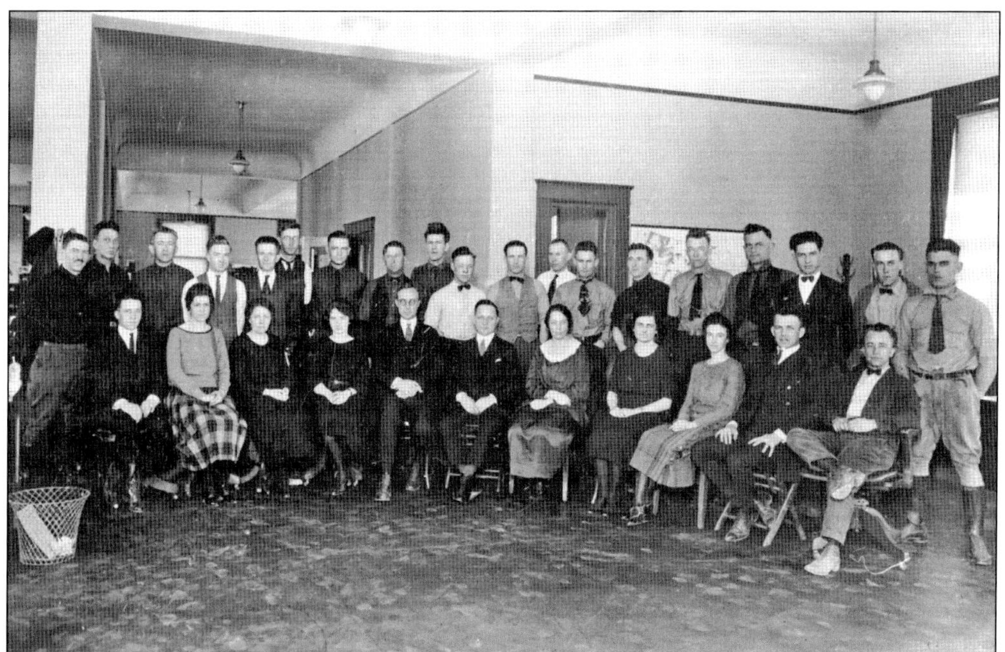

This is a highway department group photo from 1922. A key part of the team from the earliest days of the highway department, yet one whose work does not photograph well, is the Right-of-Way Division, which is responsible for acquiring highway-related property. This includes not only the roadway itself but also land for maintenance stations, material pits, radio towers, rest stops, and access rights to the various properties.

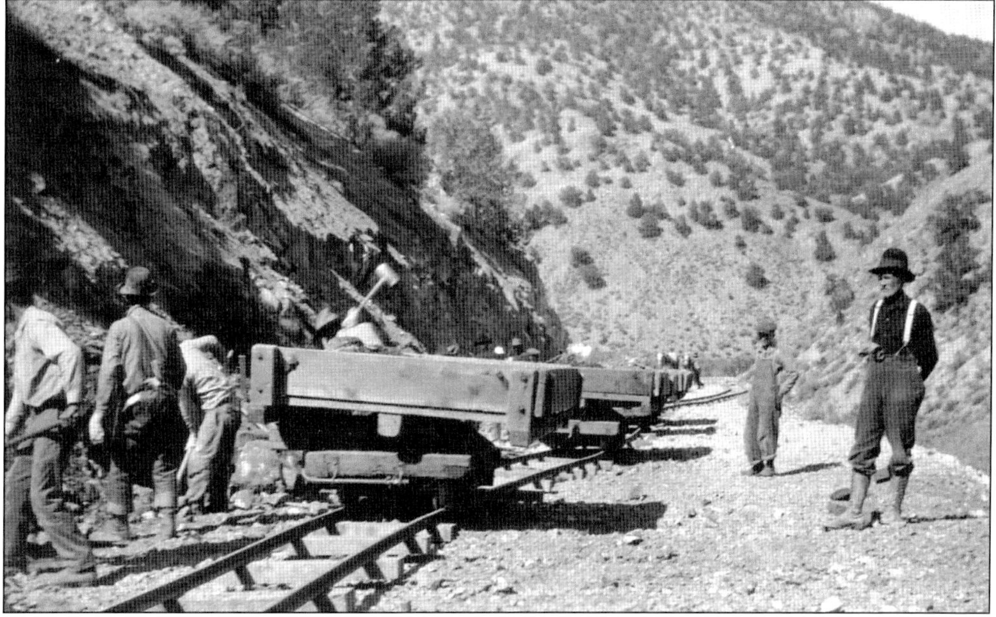

This 1923 photograph shows workers constructing the road through Carroll Summit. The work was backbreaking, particularly the last two miles through the summit itself, which were carved largely out of unforgiving rock. In all, workers graded 11.81 miles of road between Eastgate and the Lander County line.

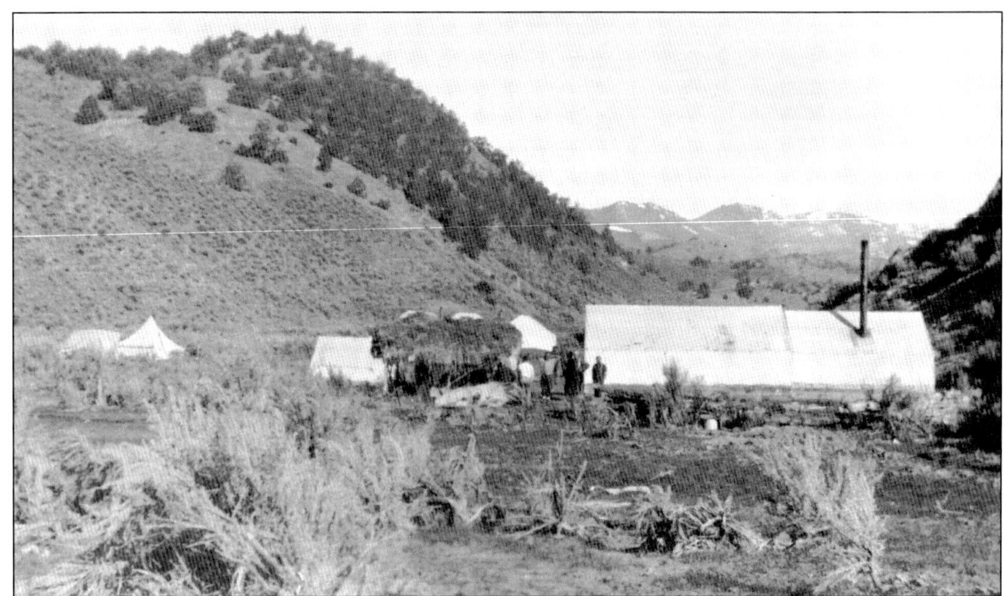

According to a 1925 statement made by the highway department, "There is no more beautiful mountain scenery in the State of Nevada than that along the State Highway Route through Campbell Creek and Eastgate Canyons." Hopefully workers agreed because, before the age of numerous hotels throughout the state, crews had to camp near the job site. Pictured is a Campbell Creek construction camp in 1923.

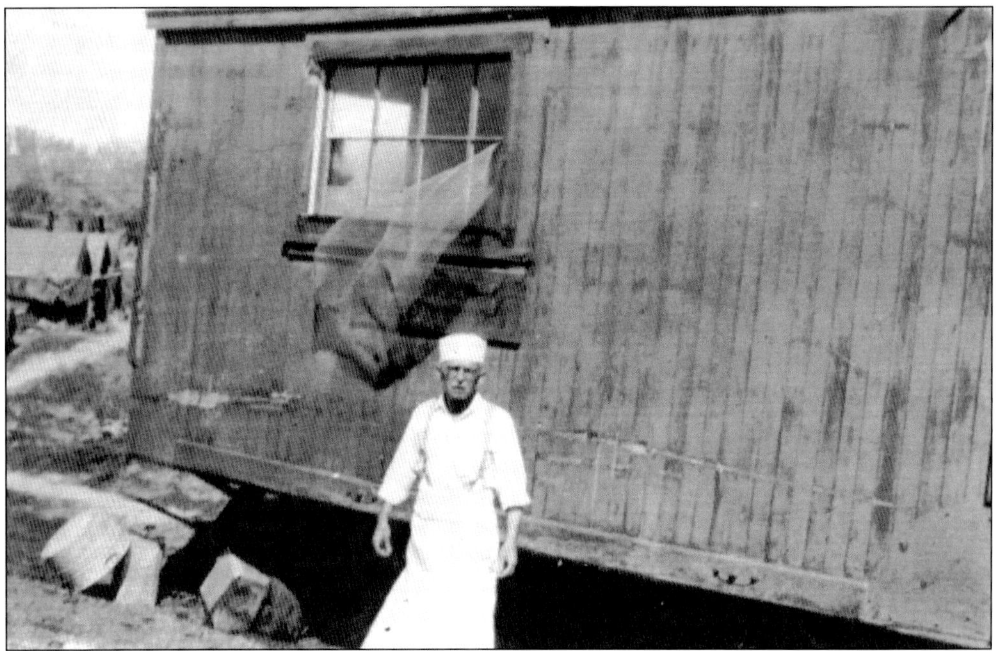

Acknowledging the discomforts, the highway department issued this statement in 1925: "Extreme heat and cold, isolation and poor living conditions are factors . . . but men of high type have been obtained who do their work well and cheerfully under these conditions. When we look behind the scenes we discover many things, and to those whose employment under the Department means more than a living no small measure of praise and encouragement is due."

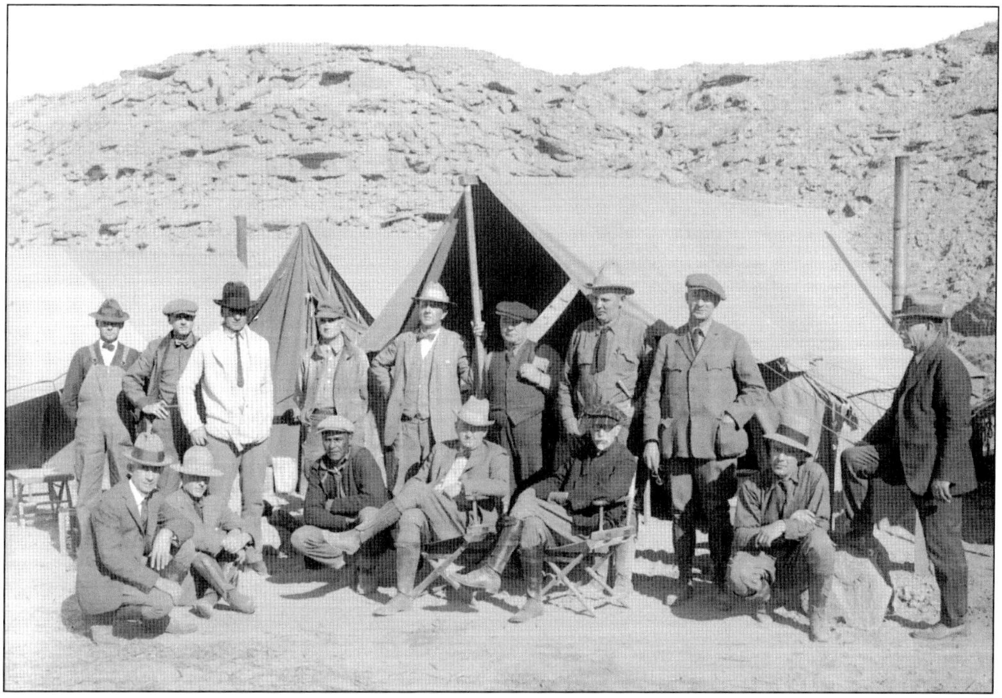

During the years of 1923 and 1924, the survey department located 804.41 miles of potential highway routes. Office engineers were also busy as they created a method of standardizing design plans, as well as a method for figuring out exact material quantities rather than estimates. The new procedures allowed contractors to bid projects more precisely and removed the need for wiggle room when it came to charging the state for services.

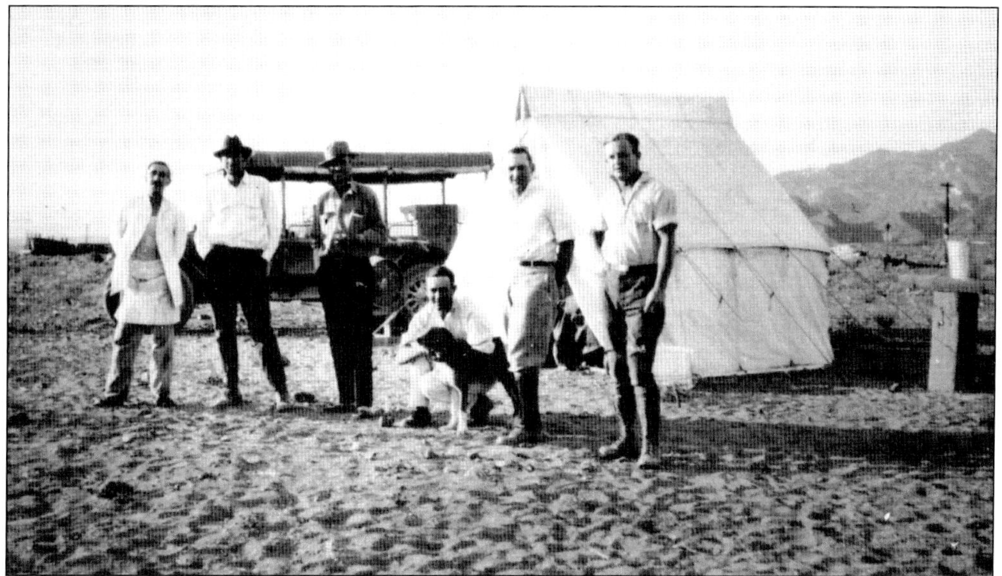

Shown here is another survey crew working at Coaldale in 1925. From left to right are Henry Thompson, the cook; P.R. Pawles, the transitman; R.W. Windele, the chief of the party and location engineer for the department; G.T.C., duties unknown; A.M. Merritt, duties unknown; and Rod McLeod, the stake artist. The dog's name has been lost to time.

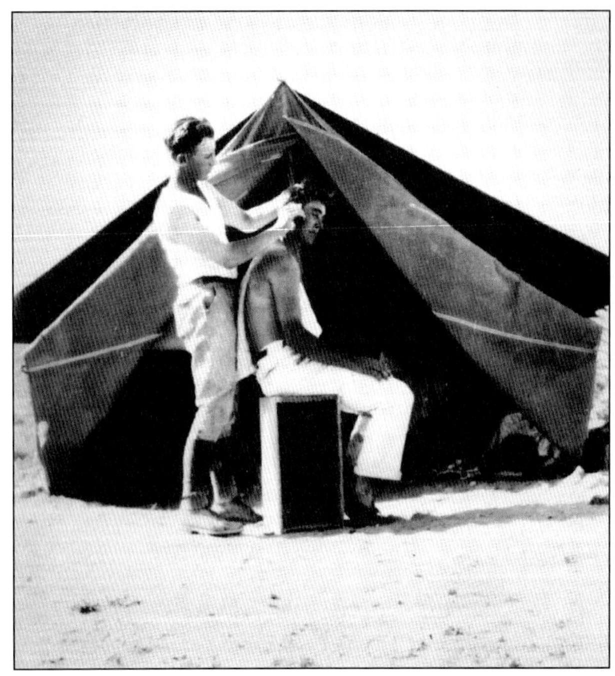

This shot is from the same 1925 Coaldale survey camp. Without the modern-day infrastructure that has built up along the Silver State's roadways, not to mention the commuting ease that came with good roads, camping was a must. Given the amount of time crew members had to spend with each other, fellowship among these coworkers was even more important than in a typical office group.

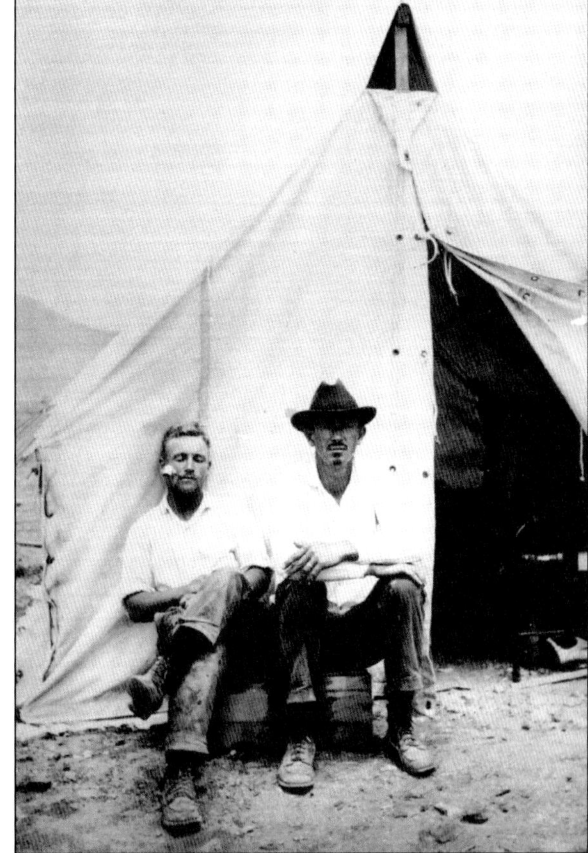

Pictured here are P.R. Rawls (left) and Francis Slader, also of the 1925 Coaldale crew. This image of the two men likely relaxing after a day of hard work, coupled with the previous photograph showing the simple act of giving someone a haircut, truly showcases the camaraderie such living conditions can foster.

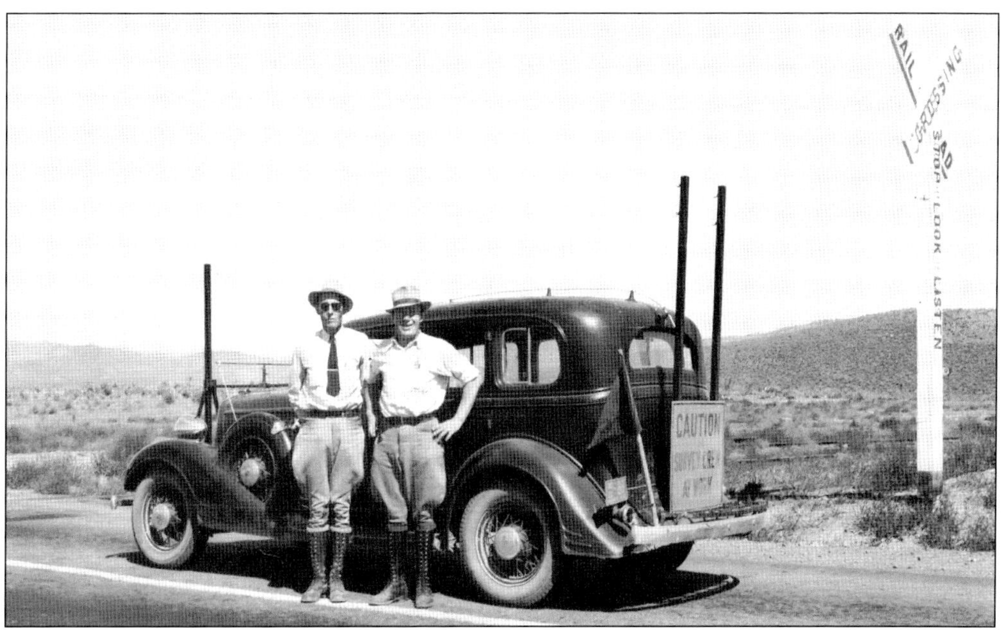

This is a survey crew from about 1936. With a growing highway system to contend with, the highway department created the Planning and Survey Division in 1935. The division was in charge of three phases of highway planning: inventory, mapping, and traffic. As the highway system grew even further, the division added road life, local fiscal considerations, special studies, and photogrammetry to its duty roster.

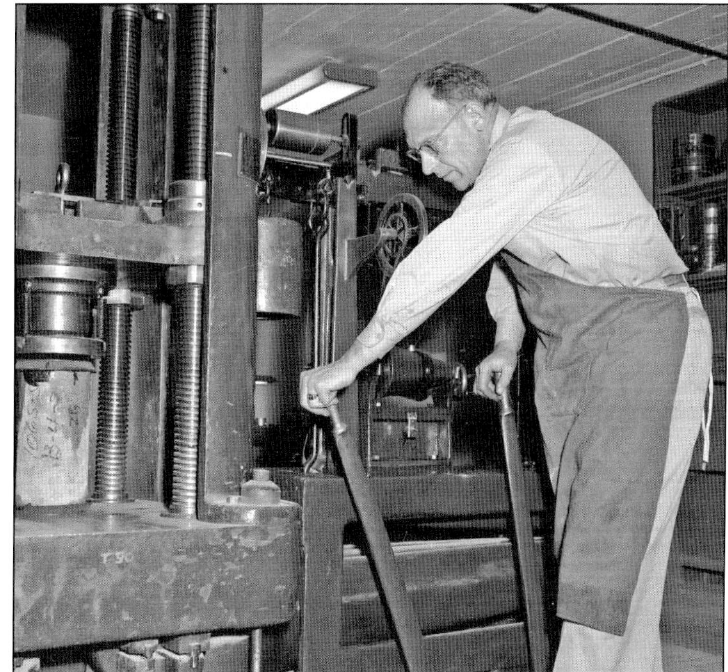

Another vitally important group within the highway department, and also one that has been around since the very early days, is the Materials Testing and Research Division. Pictured here is a division worker testing the strength of a Portland cement sample around 1958. The division as a whole was tasked with controlling and accepting all materials used in highway construction and maintenance.

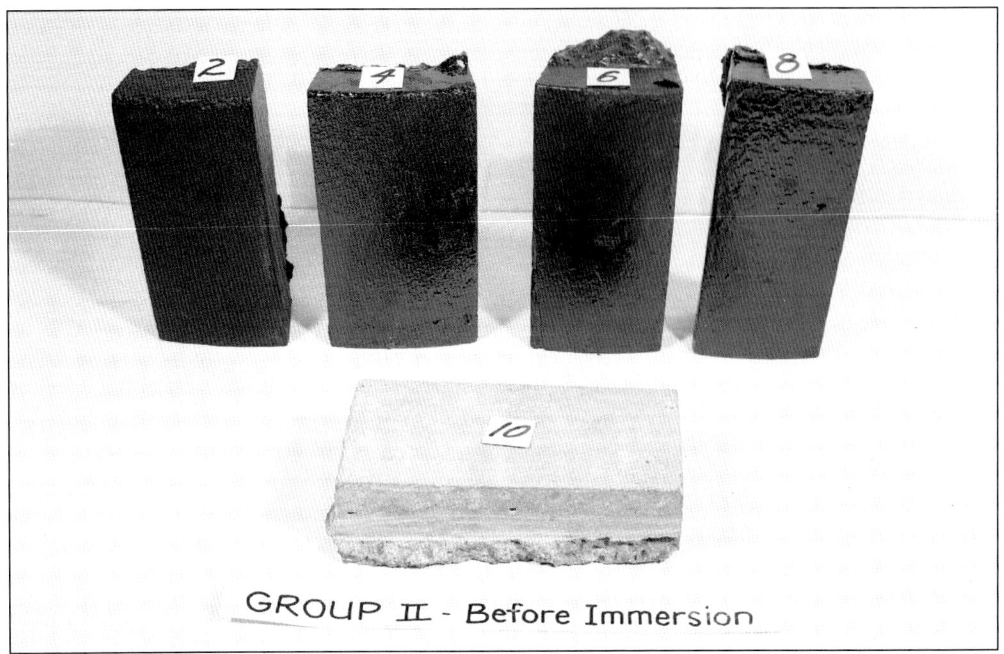

Some of the duties assigned to the Materials Testing and Research Division included finding material sources, testing materials to design a roadbed fitted to a particular stretch of road in terms of traffic and weather patterns, and training personnel to test and inspect materials processed on a job site.

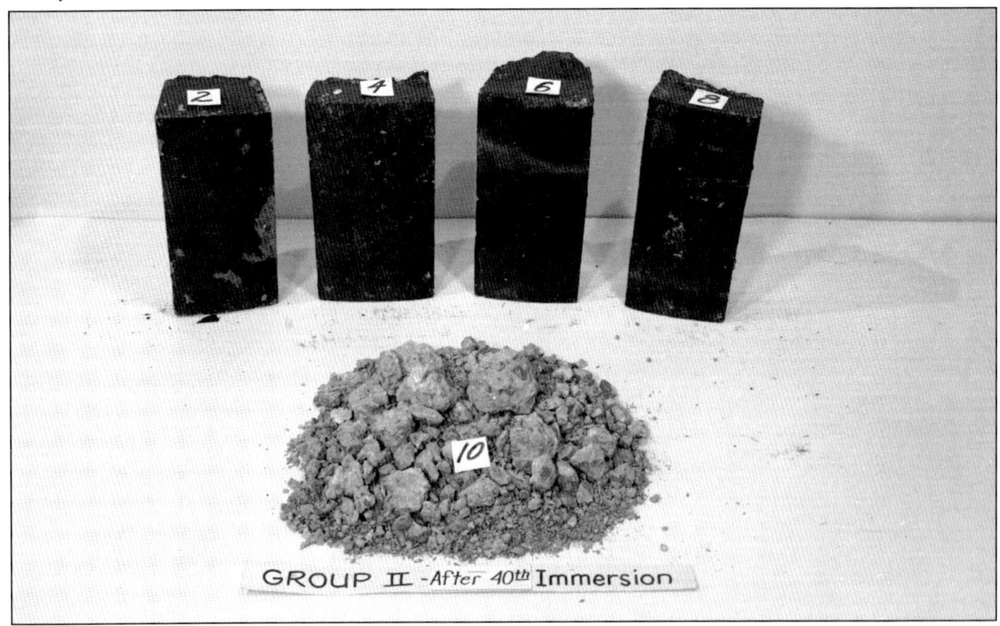

The Materials Testing and Research Division was also responsible for inspecting and testing all prefabricated materials included in road construction and maintenance, investigating any trouble spots along the roadways and determining corrective measures, and researching ways of improving testing equipment and methods. Finally, the division was tasked with researching old and new products to ensure each product was being used in the most efficient way.

This is another member of the Materials Testing and Research Division around 1958. As the highway department wrote, "Base and surface aggregates [are] weighed and sieved for quality. Materials used in road construction are continuously checked for specification conformity." The division also got new equipment the same year, including "a new 4-tube Maybolt Furol Viscosimeter, [and] a new water-bath with magnetically operated temperature control."

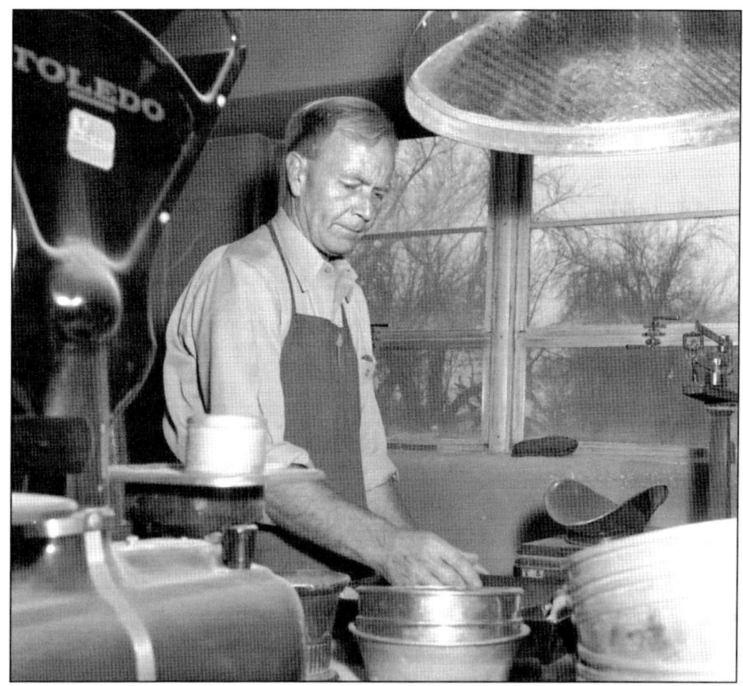

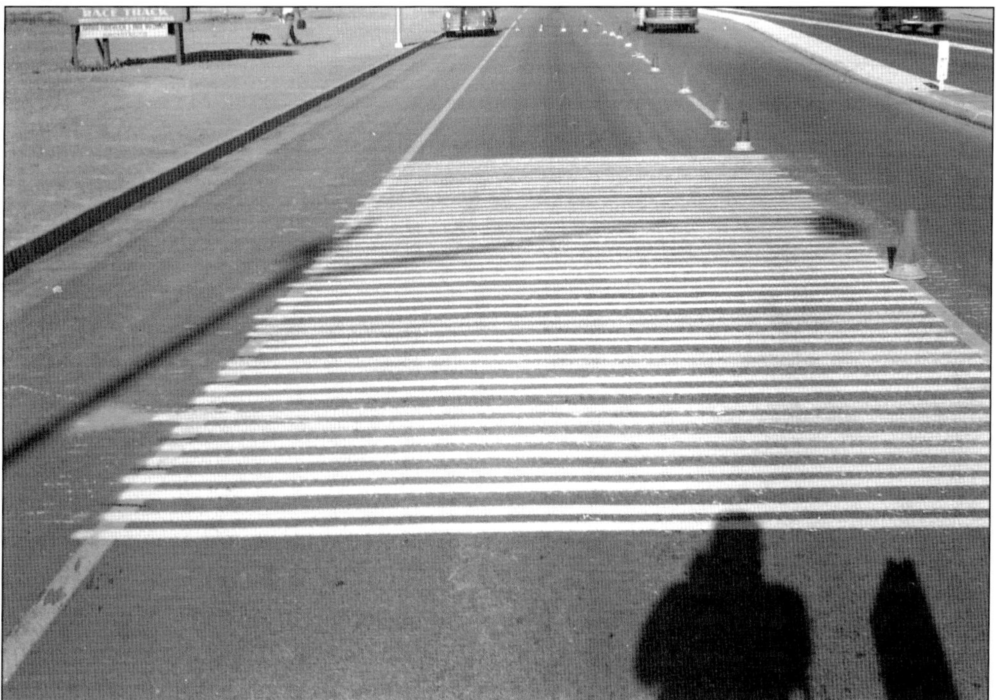

The Materials Testing and Research Division also ensured the quality of paint used in striping. Pictured here in 1952 is a striping test set up in Las Vegas, wherein the division tested samples of paint manufactured by various companies. After rigorous field and laboratory testing, the division would report which paints passed muster and those companies would then be invited to bid on that season's paint supply.

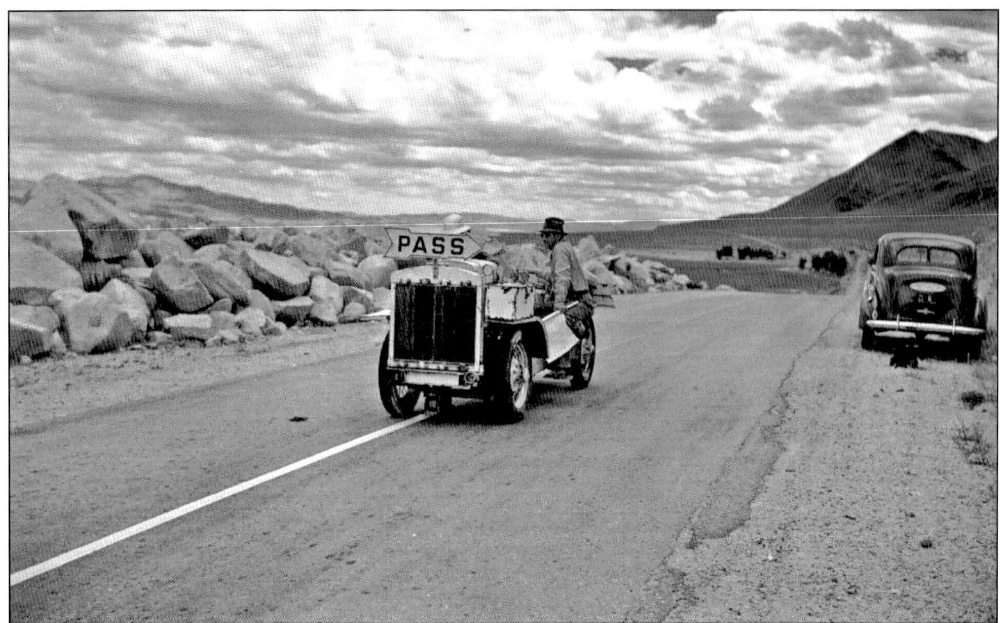

By the mid-1930s, the highway department had acquired the Seagull striping machine. The Seagull broke all Nevada striping speed records when crews were able to stripe 27 miles of highway in six hours, rather than the two and a half days it would have taken with previous machines. Dubbed "the flying painter," the machine was self-propelled, with a cruising speed of over 50 miles per hour.

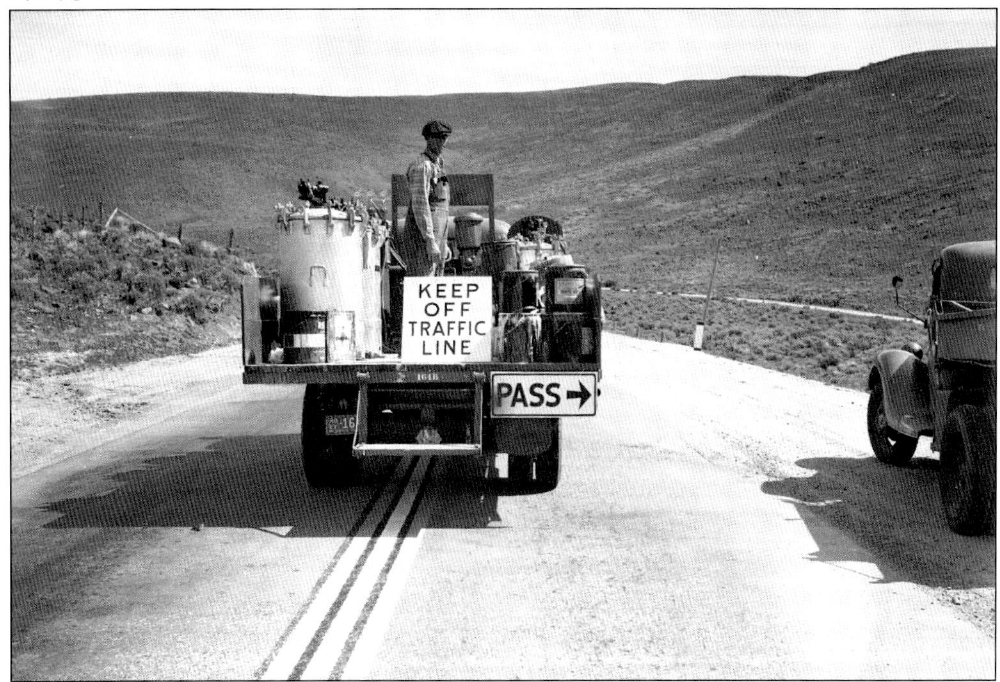

The Seagull was safer to operate than its predecessor because of its greater maneuverability, which allowed the operator to pull off the road quickly should the need arise. The machine also included a paint shutoff system so it could be moved away from the centerline without affecting the stripe. The quick-drying paint could be driven on five minutes after the stripe was painted.

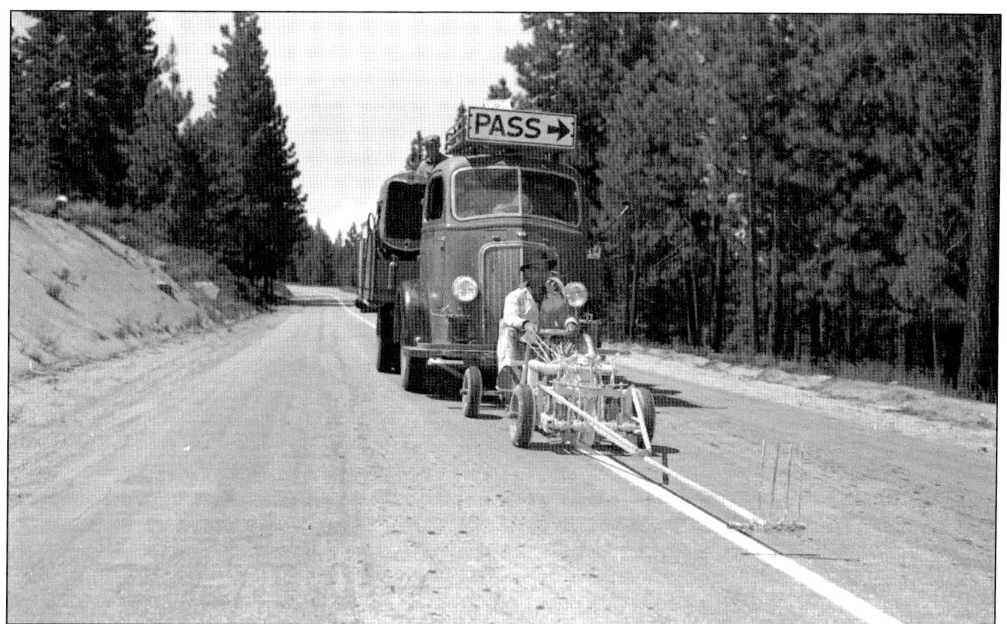

This early striping machine took two people to operate—one to pilot the striper and one to drive the truck that pushed the striper down the road. Because the striper was so small and low to the ground, there was a real risk that drivers trying to pass the striping team would cut back into the lane too soon and hit the machine.

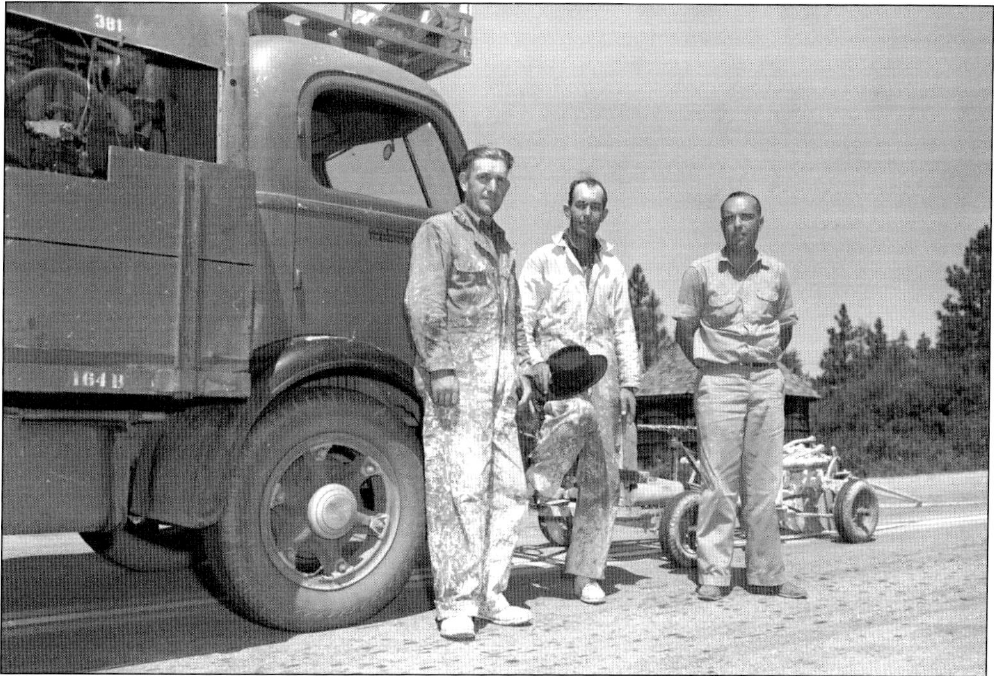

The striping crew shown above performed an essential role in maintaining safe roads throughout the state. From June 1935 and into 1936, the crew's efforts were focused on US 91 (now Interstate 15), where they painted 71 miles of traffic stripe. The final goal was to paint an additional 85 miles so that the road was painted from state line to state line.

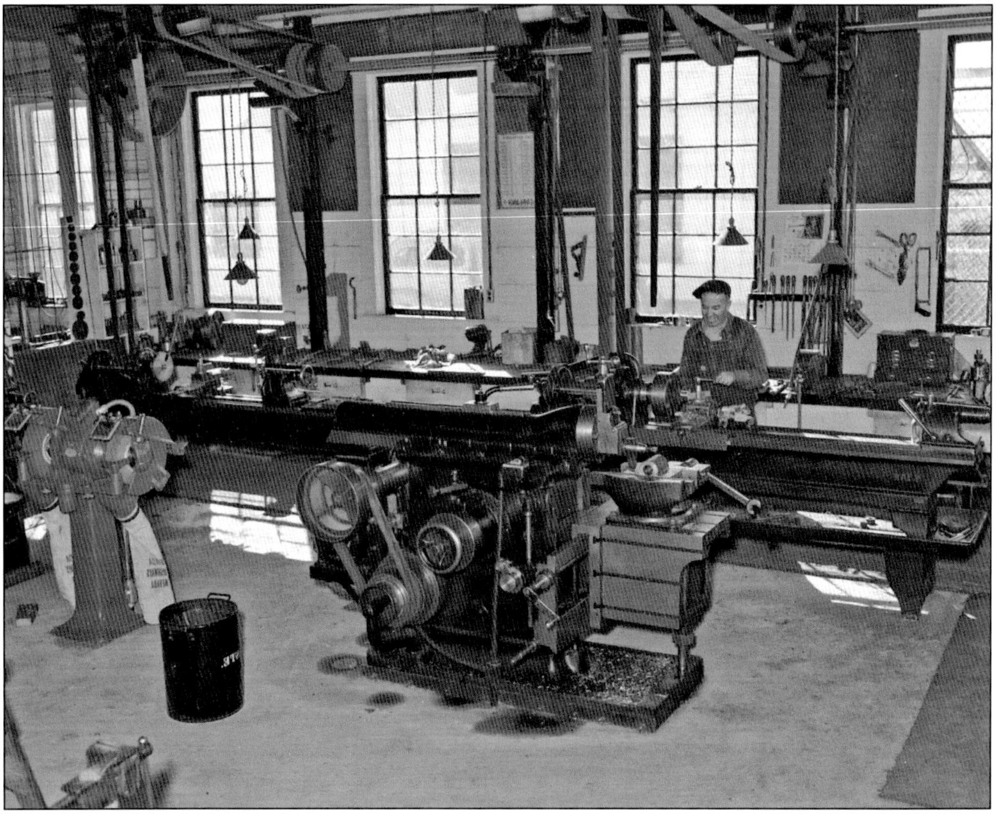

Pictured here in the 1930s is the Reno shop, where equipment was stored and repaired. The Equipment Division was in charge of buying, distributing, maintaining, and storing all equipment and supplies used in building and servicing the highways. Also tasked with building new equipment, division workers built five combination scarifier and road drags, an oil distributor, a pile driver, a 15-ton trailer, a water tank trailer, and a concrete mixer in 1929–1930.

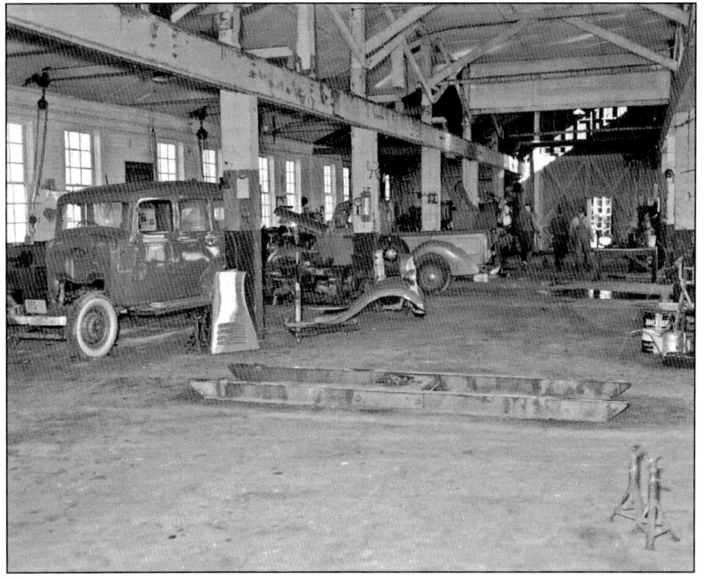

This is an interior shot of the Reno shop in the 1930s. Initially, the Reno shop was tasked with housing, repairing, and maintaining all state equipment. However, having everything headquartered in Reno was eventually not cost effective given the size of the state. Therefore, as the regional divisions were established and good roads were built, repair and storage shops within the divisions were built as well.

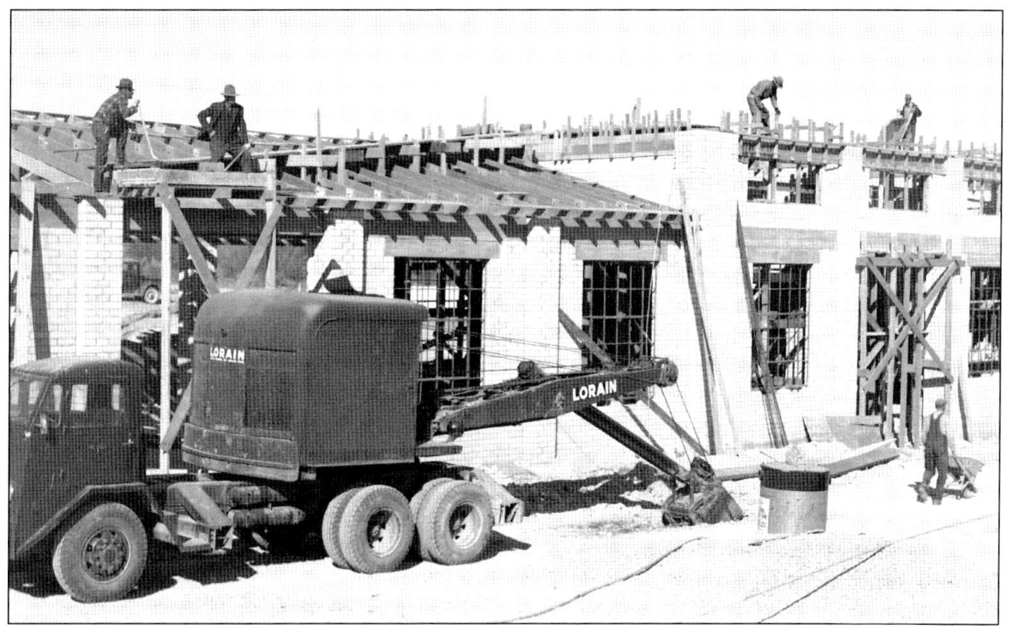

Pictured here is the 1950s construction of the Las Vegas yard. Given how large the state is, it soon became more economical to have regional divisions that handled construction and maintenance. By 1929, the highway department had created five divisions: Division 1 was based in Las Vegas, Division 2 was in Reno, Division 3 was in Elko, Division 4 was in East Ely, and Division 5 was in Tonopah.

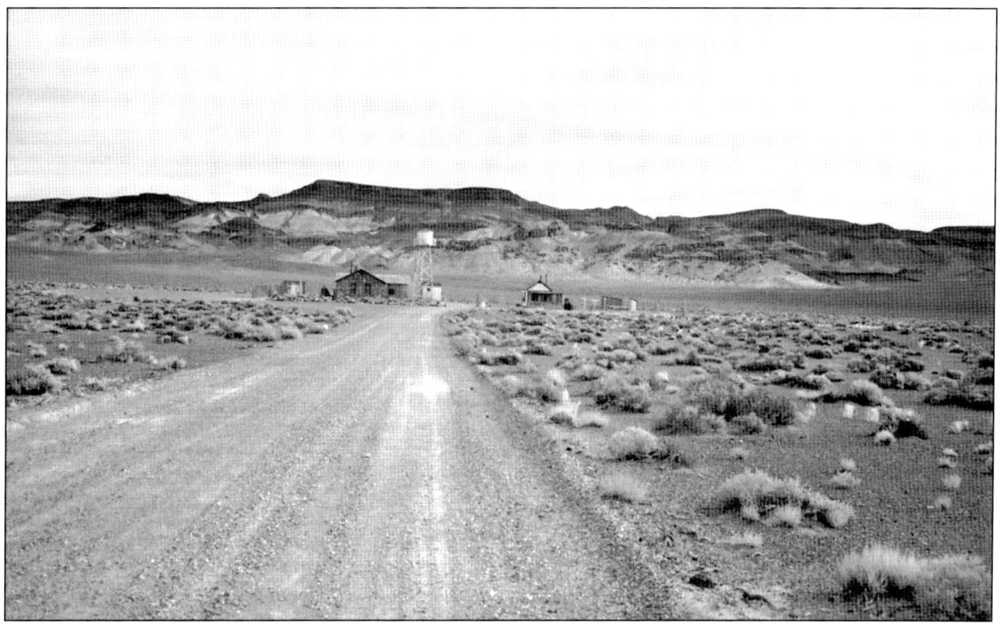

Maintaining roads through a state with few population centers required building maintenance stations in the remote corners of Nevada. In the 1920s, maintenance stations were usually small wood-framed cabins that were described as "camps." By the 1930s, there was a need for more comfortable housing and larger equipment sheds. The isolated maintenance station seen here was home to two or three families.

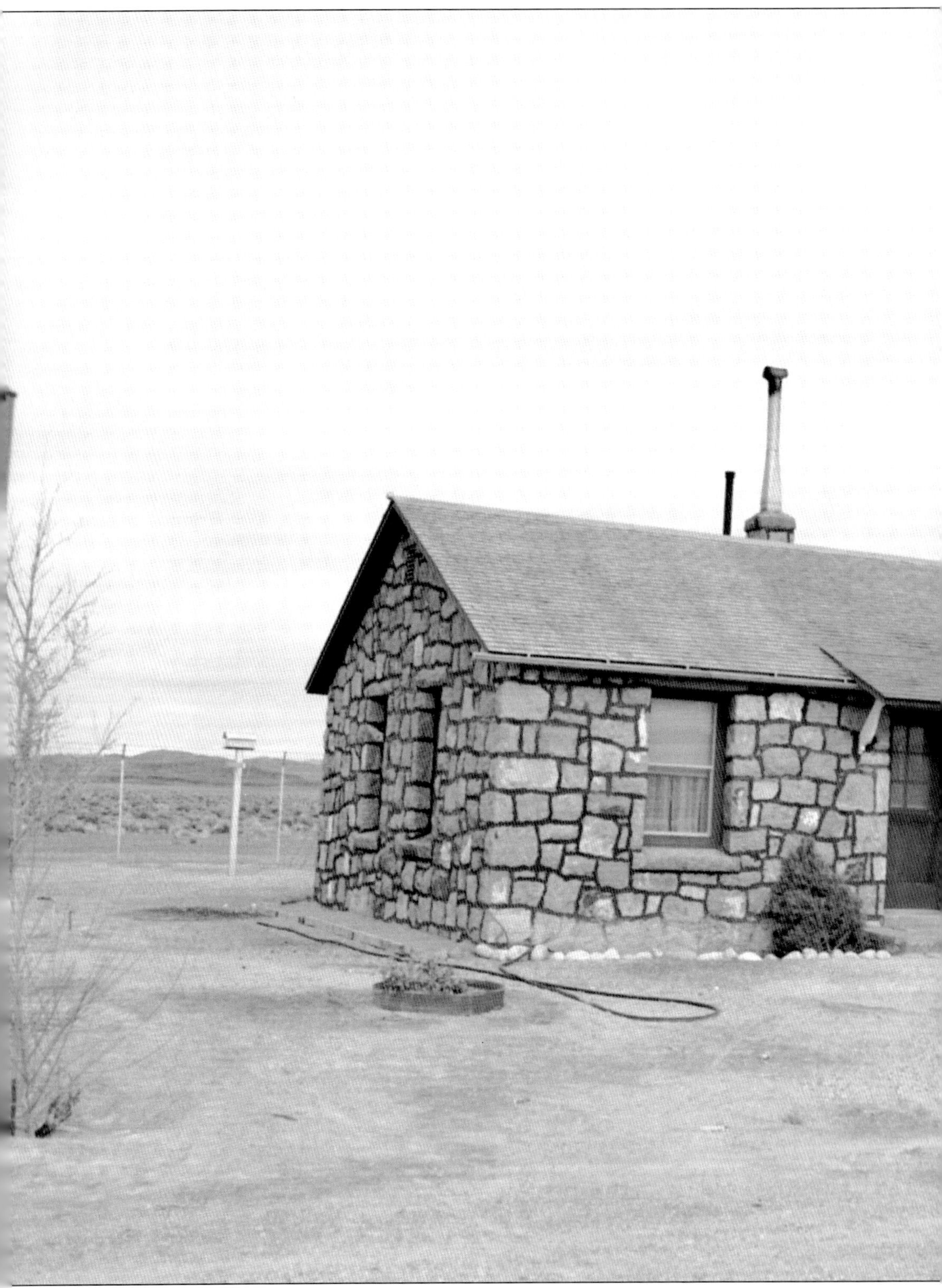

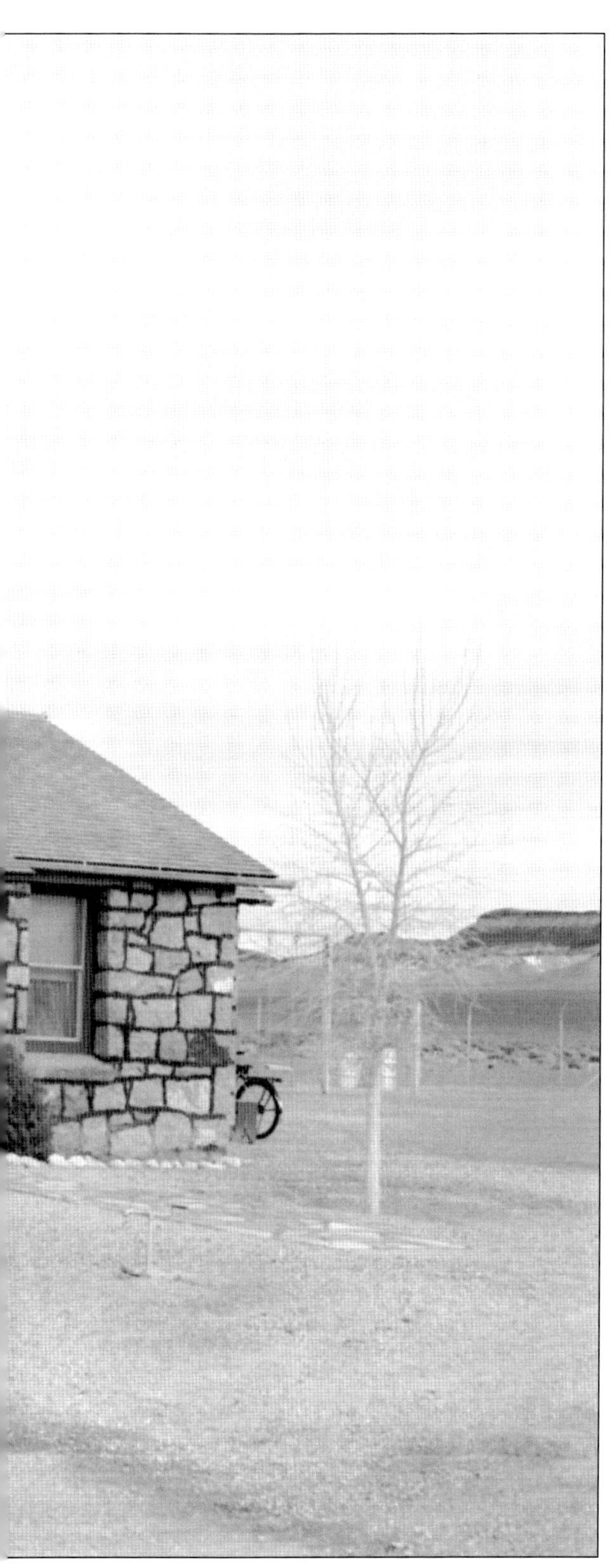

A swing set in the background and a bike leaning against the side of the house suggest that a family with children lived in this maintenance station house. Like all station houses, this one was designed by the highway's architecture department. It is a little different from most houses constructed with this plan because it uses local stone instead of wood. The stonemason used blacking in the mortar to accentuate the pattern of the roughly shaped stones. The home's landscaping was necessarily sparse. The only available water source was a well, and the water was stored in a water tower. One can only hope this remoteness inspired a sense of freedom and camaraderie instead of loneliness.

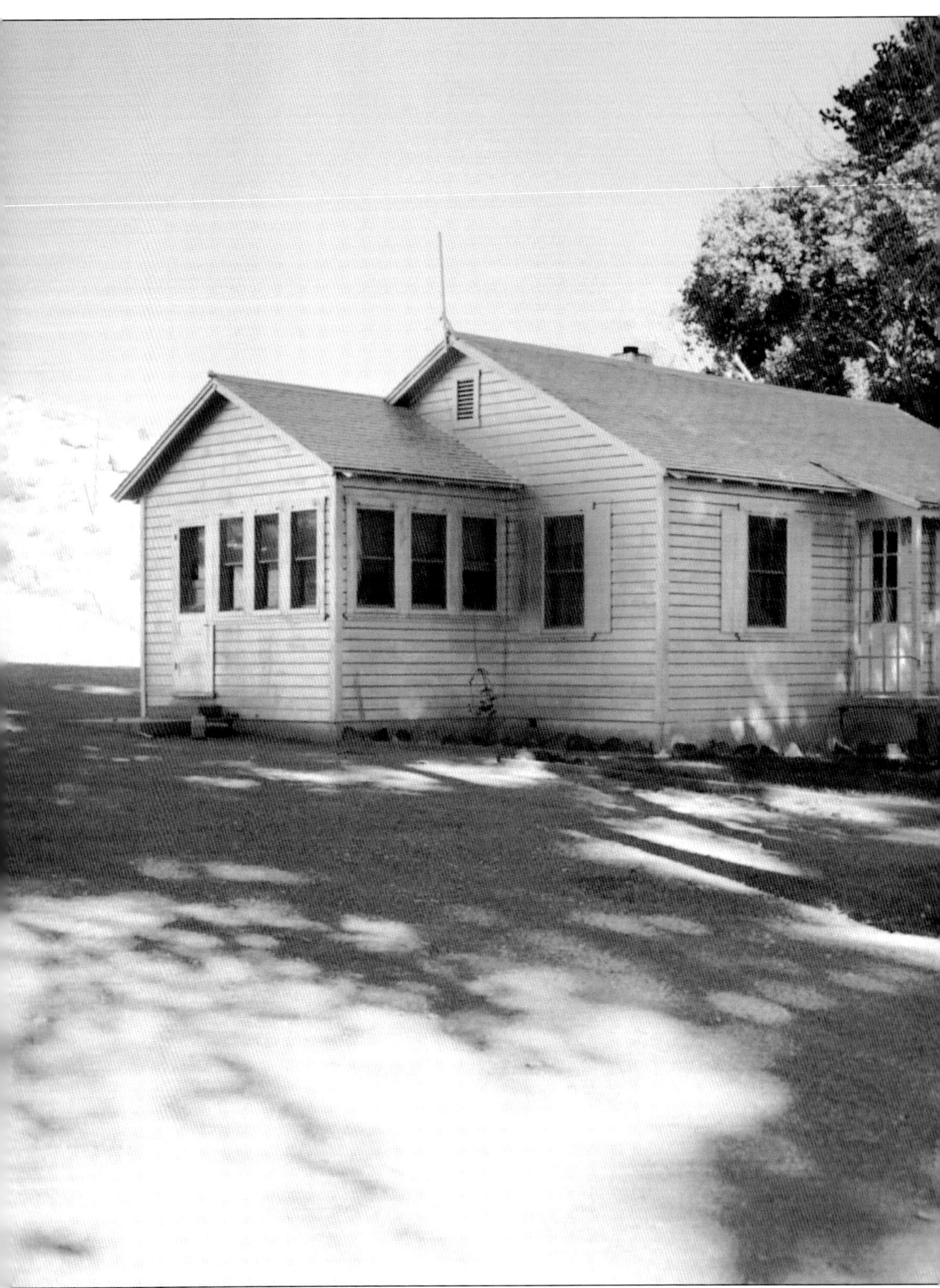

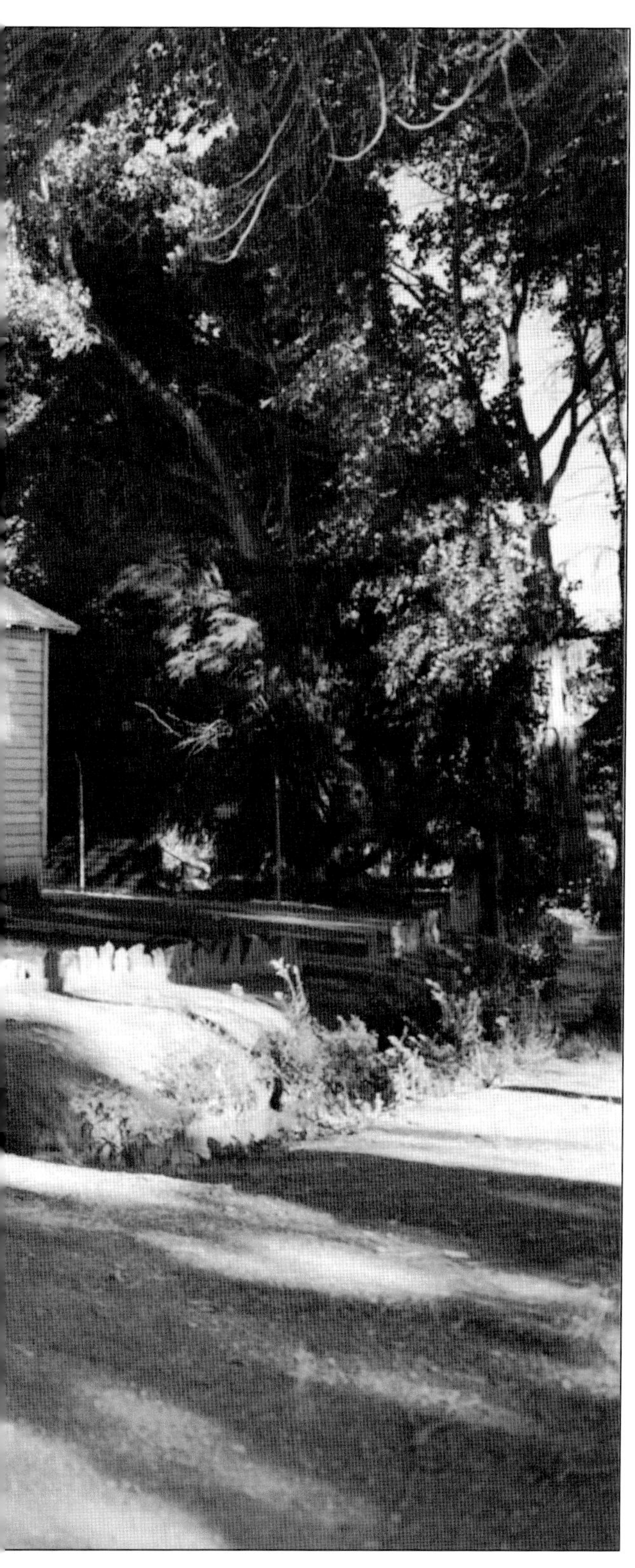

In the 1950s, the highway department embarked on a statewide effort to improve the maintenance stations built in the 1920s and 1930s. The 1955–1956 highway department biennial reported, "A number of maintenance stations built in the Department's early days now require enlargement and modernization. Numerous storage and shop buildings constructed at that time will not accommodate the ponderous snow removal and maintenance equipment of today." This little cottage represents one of the "up-to-date" maintenance station houses provided for highway employees and their families. Rural maintenance stations usually comprised two residences, multiple equipment sheds, an equipment shop with an office, a well, and a gas pump.

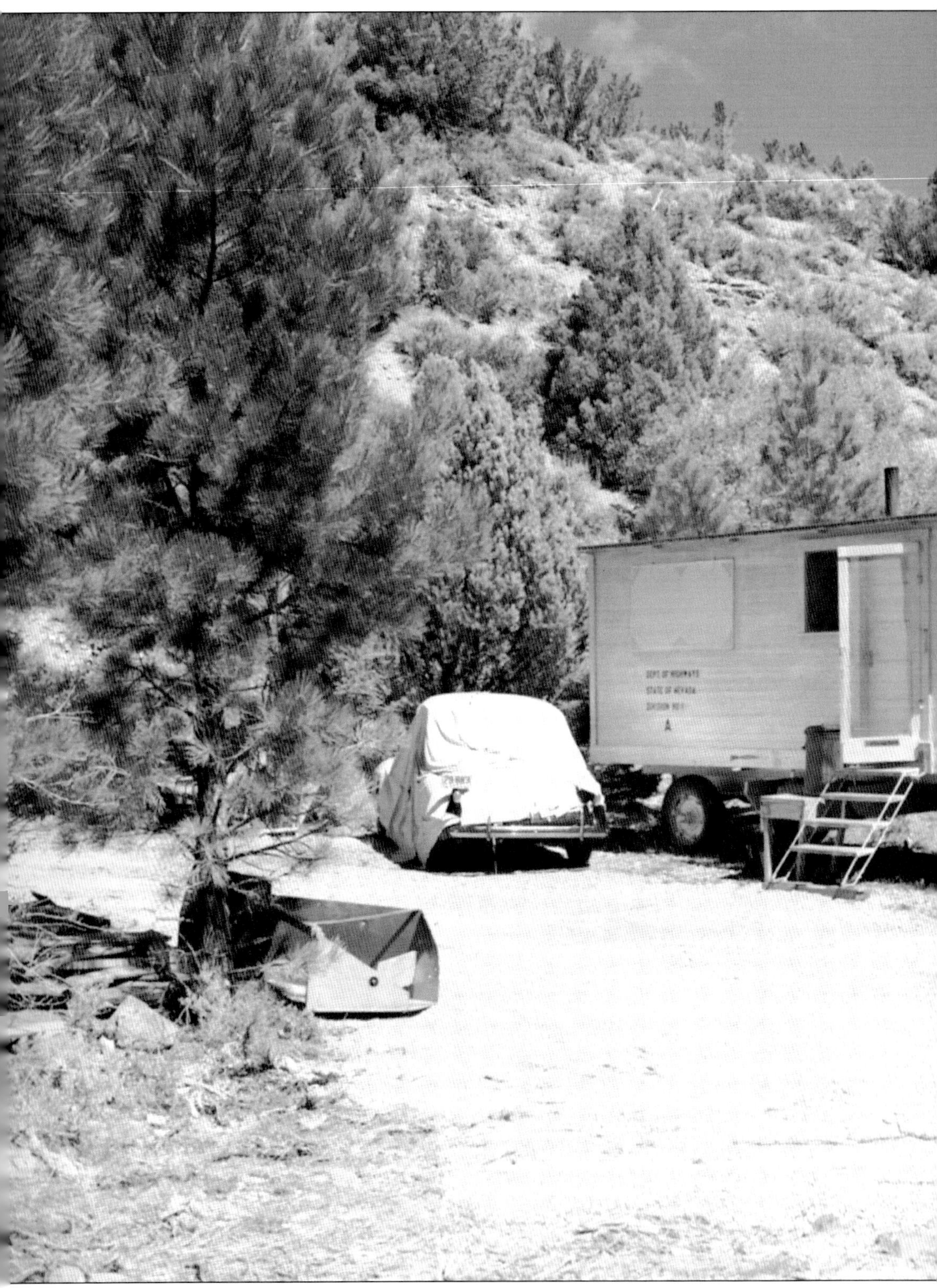
DEPT OF HIGHWAYS
STATE OF NEVADA
A

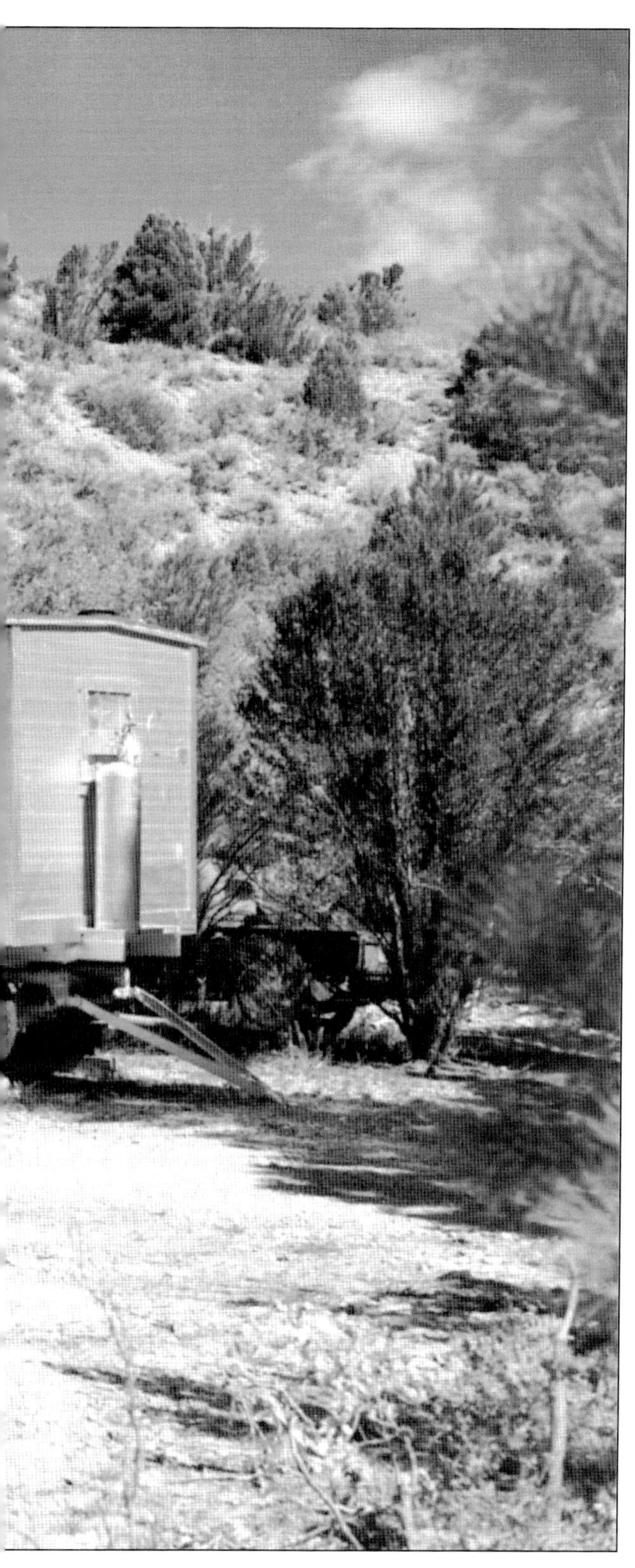

The maintenance stations stored heavy equipment, such as snowplows, grading machines, and oiling trucks. They were also a good place to park the portable laboratory when not in use. The portable lab could be towed to construction sites to test the quality of the road-building material in the field. The 1934–1936 highway department biennial describes the first portable lab: "A novel fire-proof portable testing laboratory mounted on a trailer chassis with pneumatic tires was designed and built for the testing department. This equipment is apparently unique among the highway departments of other States, since articles regarding its design and usefulness have appeared in various construction publications."

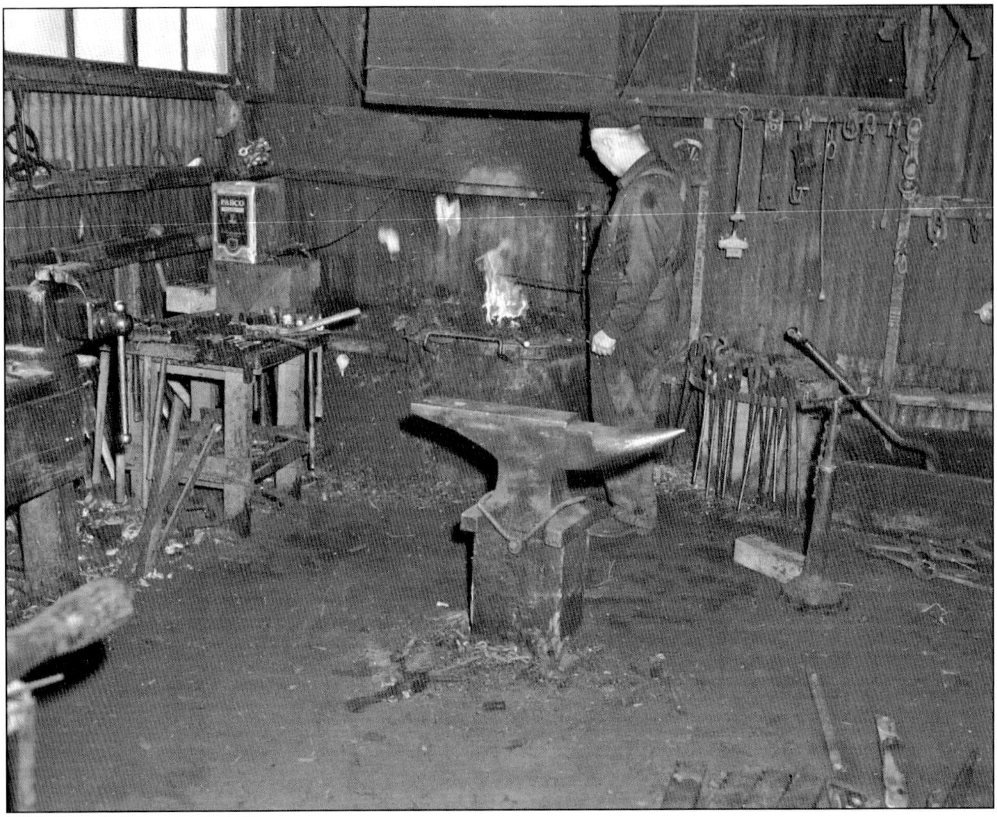

The Tonopah maintenance station included a blacksmith shop. Many of the highway department's early blacksmithing tools were inherited as World War I military surplus and might have still been in use when this picture was taken in the 1940s. Skilled metal fabricators were essential for repairing and constructing highway equipment. The maintenance workers usually designed and built their own specialized equipment, such as paint stripers and road-oiling sprayers.

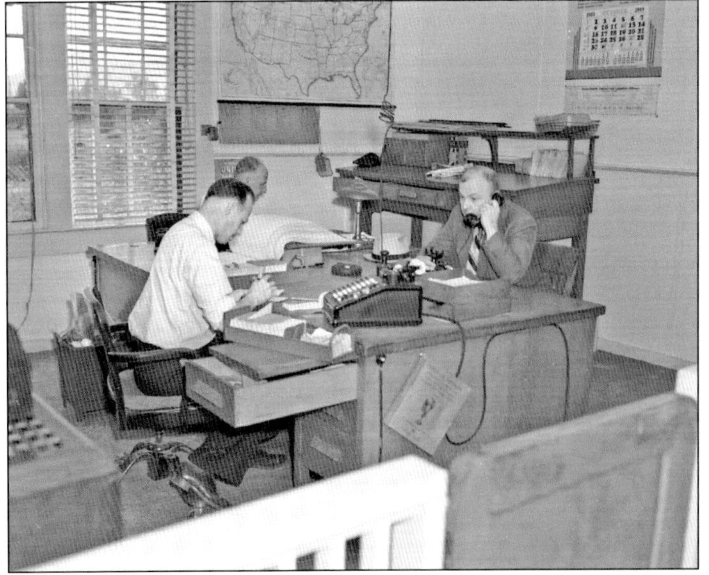

Here are workers in the Reno shop around 1939. Effective in 1928, the Equipment Division created a system in which each piece of equipment had a rental rate that the division would charge to each engineering division requesting its use. The idea was that the rental charges would offset repair, replacement, and depreciation costs while also creating a fund from which new equipment could be purchased.

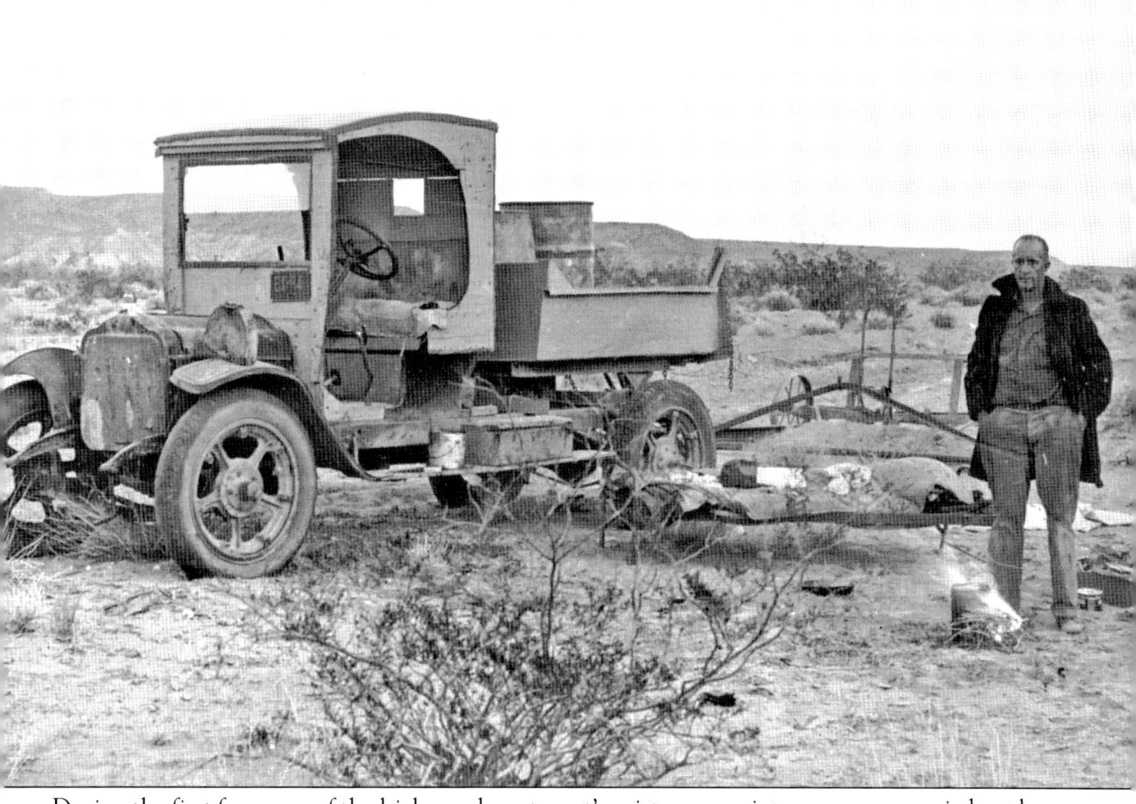

During the first few years of the highway department's existence, maintenance was carried out by an individual known as a patrolman. Like the one shown here, the patrolman was put in charge of a specific section of road and was expected to keep it in good repair. Given the enormity of what the department was undertaking in creating thousands of miles of road that it had to keep in good, safe driving condition in perpetuity, it is no wonder that looking for new and better methods to accomplish this task was a constant conversation. In 1921–1922, the department enacted new policies, stating that it would only maintain roads within the highway system and that maintenance was to start as soon as a road was built. Other policies ensured there was always room in the budget for maintenance, and when costs became too high or when traffic justified it, highways would be reconstructed with a better pavement than what had been used previously.

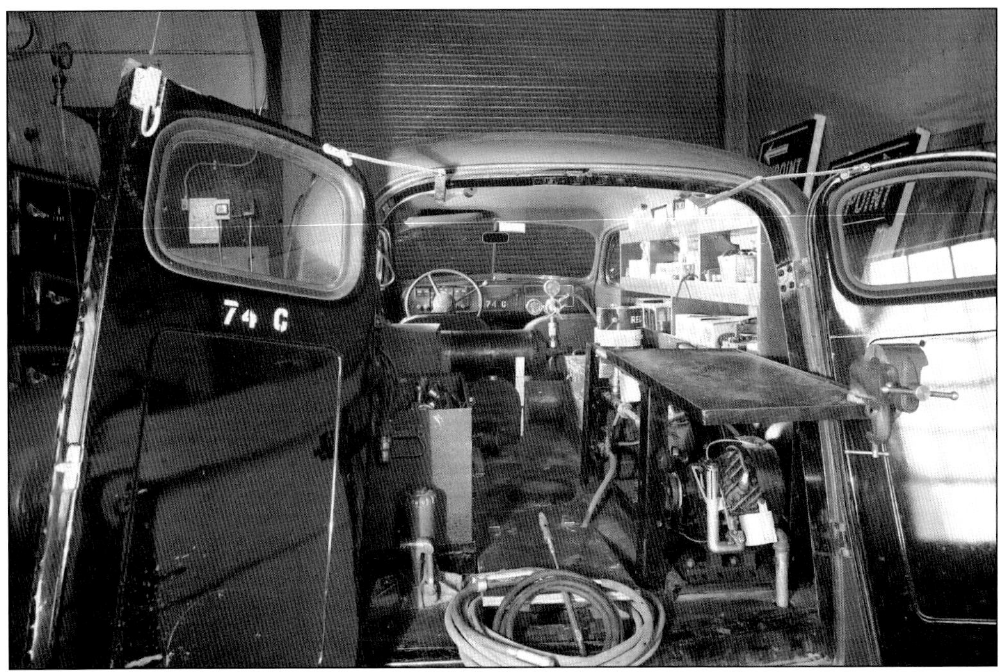

This is the interior of a mid-century maintenance car, which came well equipped with the tools of the trade, and by the late 1950s, the operator was really going to need it. As the highway department lamented in 1958, maintenance costs were "spiraling" and were only going to get worse. The new interstate system was going to require maintaining overhead lighting systems, installing bigger signs, and adding more landscaping.

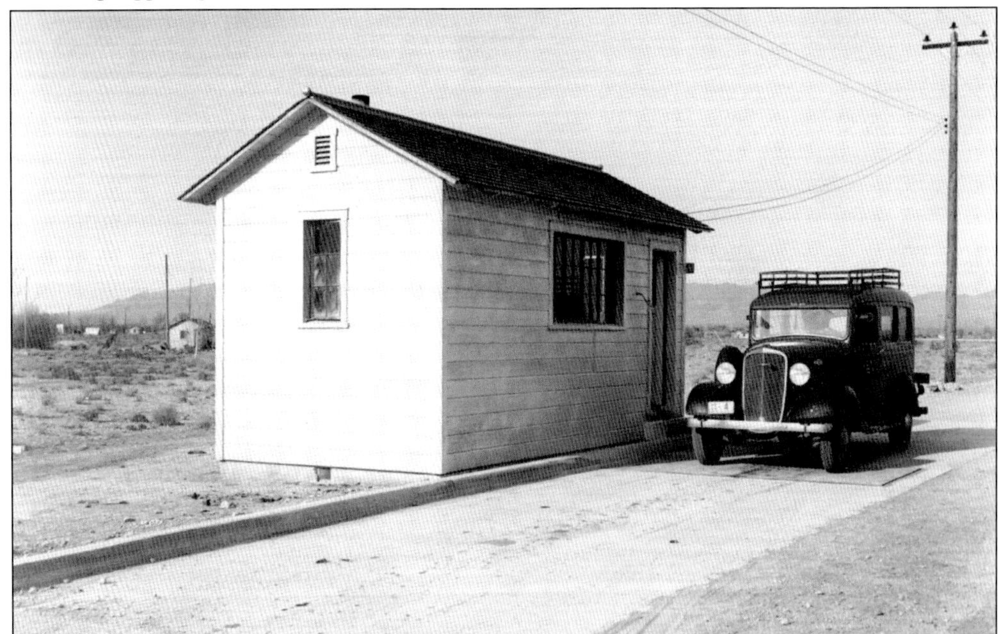

Pictured here is the exterior of the Las Vegas Loadometer station around 1936. It was one of 36 stations placed throughout the state to weigh trucks and busses and record a variety of information about the vehicle and its load.

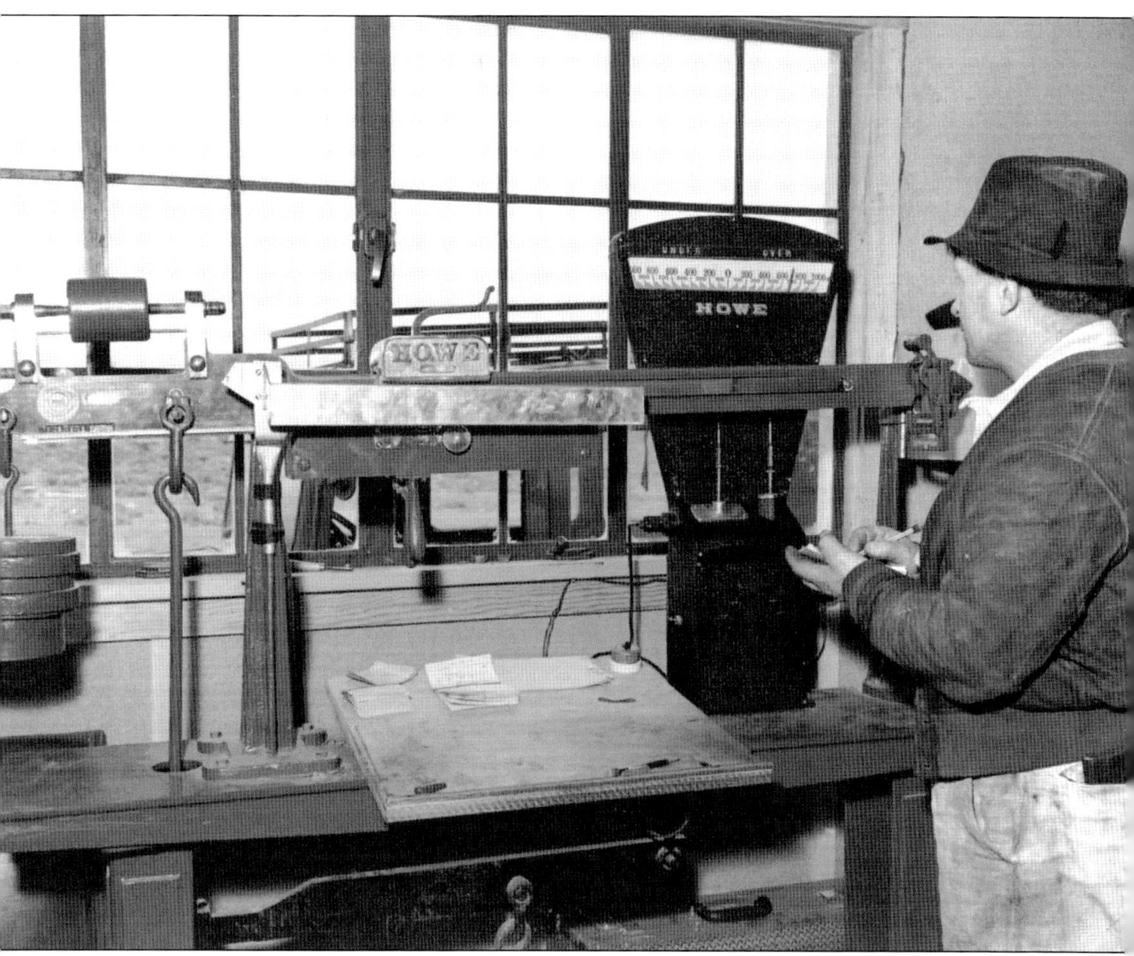

Here is the interior of the Las Vegas Loadometer station pictured on the opposite page. The station operator was not only responsible for recording vehicle weights, but was also tasked with recording the state in which the vehicle was registered and whether the vehicle was registered as commercial or private. The documentation included the vehicle license plate number, how much weight the vehicle was officially rated as being capable of carrying, where the driver was coming from, where the driver was going, and what the driver was hauling. The stations were operated day and night, and despite a seemingly long list of data to record, the process took about three minutes from start to finish. Overall, the point of the program was to gather real-time statistics on the volume and types of heavy loads traveling via Nevada's highways. By knowing the number of vehicles, an average weight, and an approximate origin and destination of the heavy loads, the highway department could ensure that it was designing and building roads capable of handling the real traffic they carried.

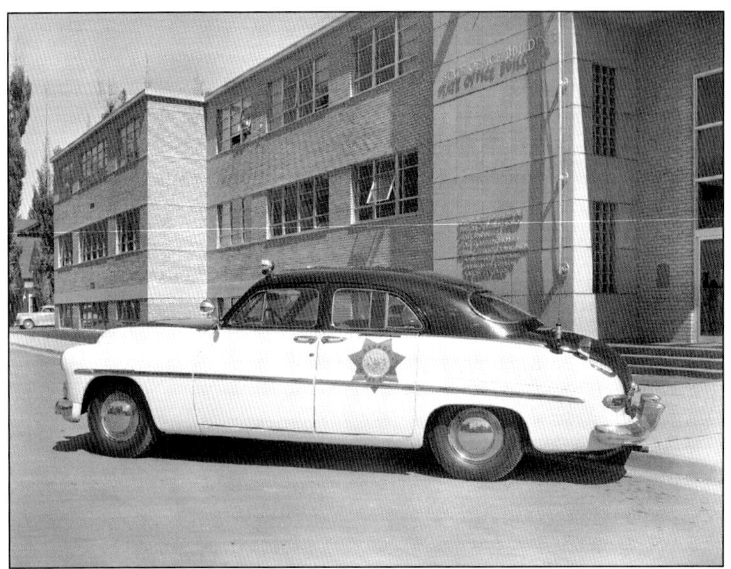

The highway patrol was originally part of the highway department. The first patrolman started duty on June 26, 1923. By 1936, there were seven patrolmen, along with district offices in Las Vegas, Reno, Wells, and Elko. The patrol force continued to grow, and on July 1, 1949, it was removed from the highway department and placed under the Public Service Commission.

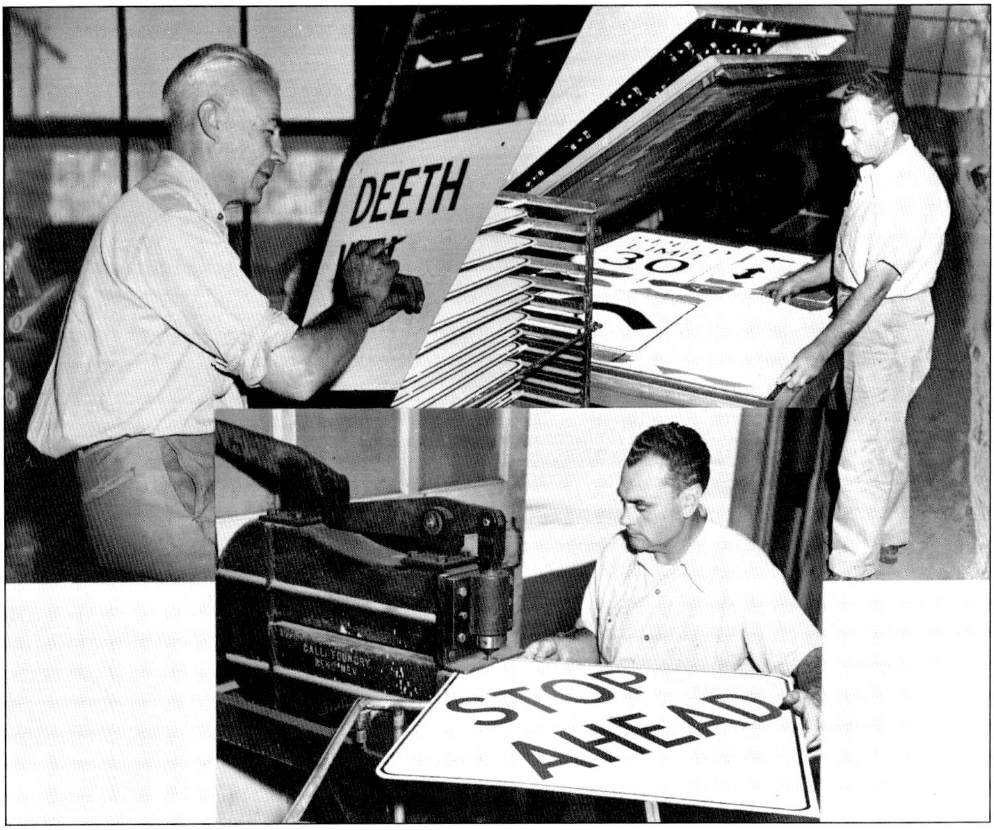

This collage shows sign shop workers around 1952. As the highway department described it, "Painting signs for the benefit of the traveling public is on mass production in the Highway Department's sign shops in Reno. Some signs are hand painted, while others are machine made, using Scotchlite application. After the signs are fabricated, holes are punched for ease of mounting on sign posts."

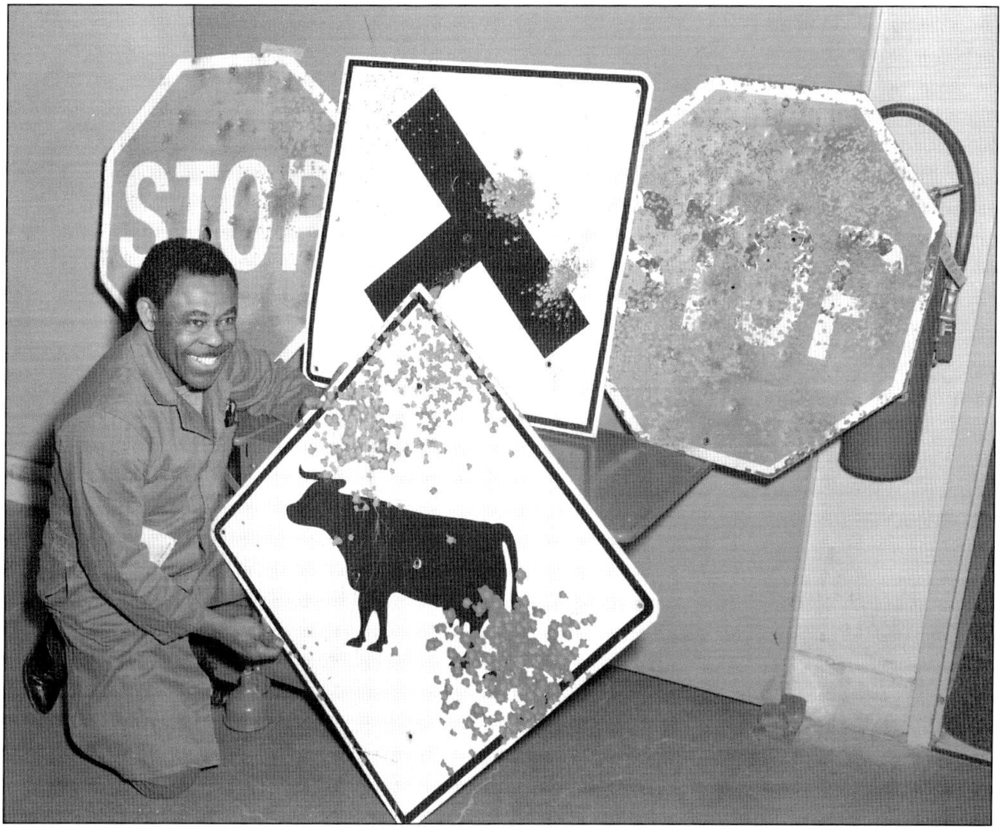

In the 1950s, the highway department reported that most signs were lost through shootings. In an attempt to save the signs, the department provided targets to the traveling public. Using the lids of five-gallon buckets, workers painted bull's-eyes with the words "Save Signs" and attached the targets to the road signs. Allegedly, the enterprise attracted nationwide attention, but it also reduced the shooting of signs.

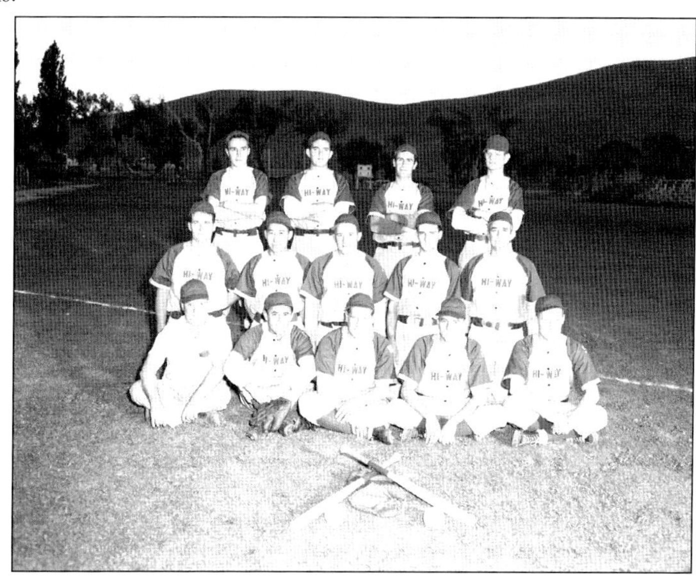

In addition to keeping the roads—and signs—safe for all Nevadans, members of the highway department also liked to showcase their team spirit by playing on the department's baseball team. Featured here is a shot of the "Hi-Way" baseball team taken in 1949. No record of their performance has yet been found, but we are sure they "steamrolled" the competition!

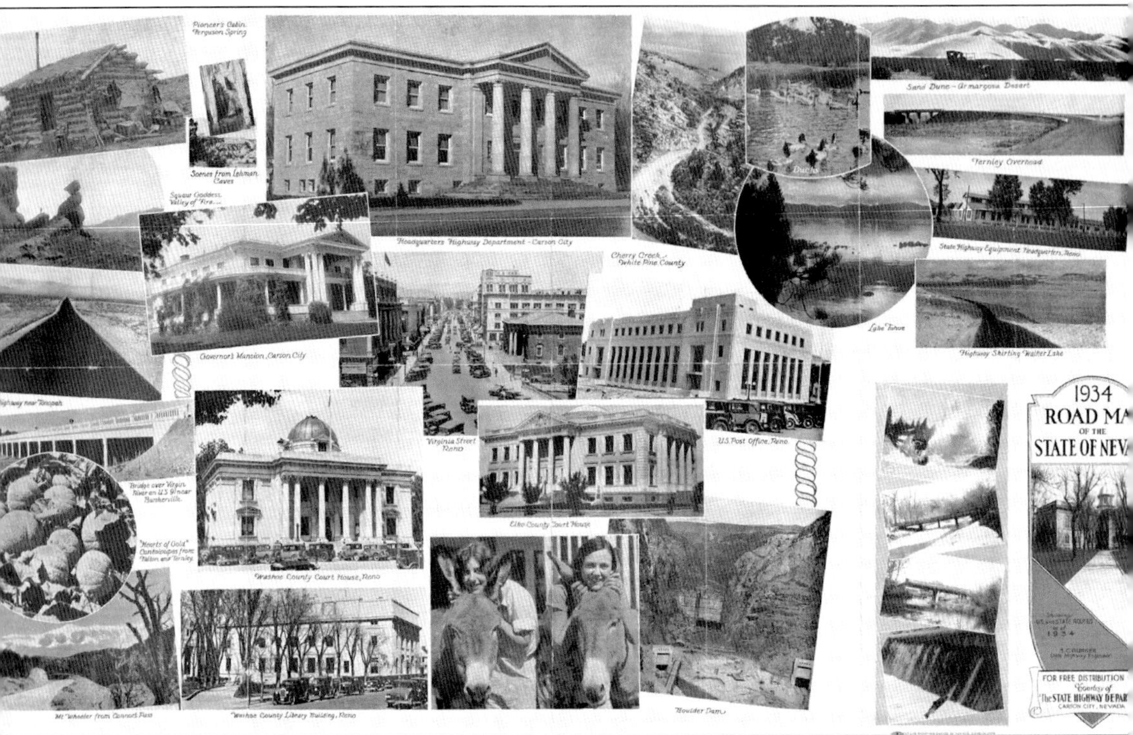

Starting in the early 1920s, the highway department was tasked with creating highway maps and tourist information for the traveling public. Because the department had employees spread all over the state, it was uniquely qualified to provide timely information about the far reaches of Nevada. Information provided by employees was compiled at headquarters and put into tourist bulletins that were issued every two weeks during the peak season. The hugely popular bulletins were distributed to many large touring bureaus in the United States. The highway maps, which were also very popular, were generally issued every year or two. As time went on, fun and colorful information beyond basic road locations was included with each map. For instance, this collage is actually the back of the 1934 highway map. Other maps included useful information, such as Nevada's motorist laws. As was stated on the 1939 map, "No person under 12 years of age is permitted to drive a motor vehicle in Nevada." The age requirement has since been changed.

In the early 1950s, the highway department began studying the feasibility of using radio communications in its construction and maintenance endeavors. The department acquired radio equipment tuned to frequencies assigned to Nevada, and workers mapped coverage by setting up a portable base station in various locations, then traveling throughout the state in radio-equipped cars. Relay stations were established on Winnemucca Mountain and Emigrant Pass.

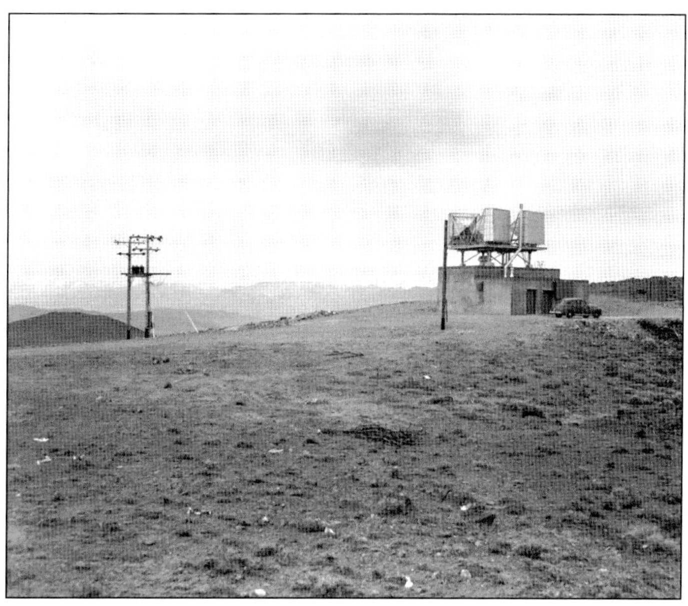

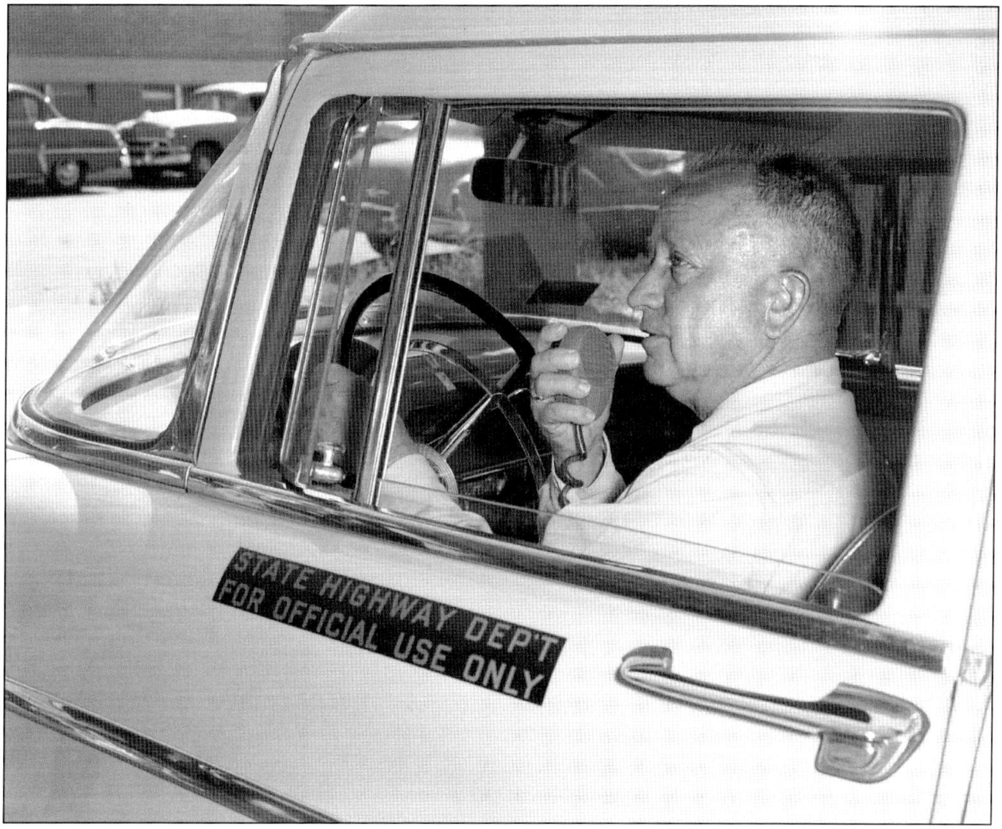

In three short years, the highway department had the system up and running, with base stations installed in each of the five districts. Four repeater stations were completed, 10 maintenance stations were radio equipped, and 200 mobile units were installed in various vehicles. Here, W.T. Holcomb, assistant state engineer, tests out the system in a highway department vehicle.

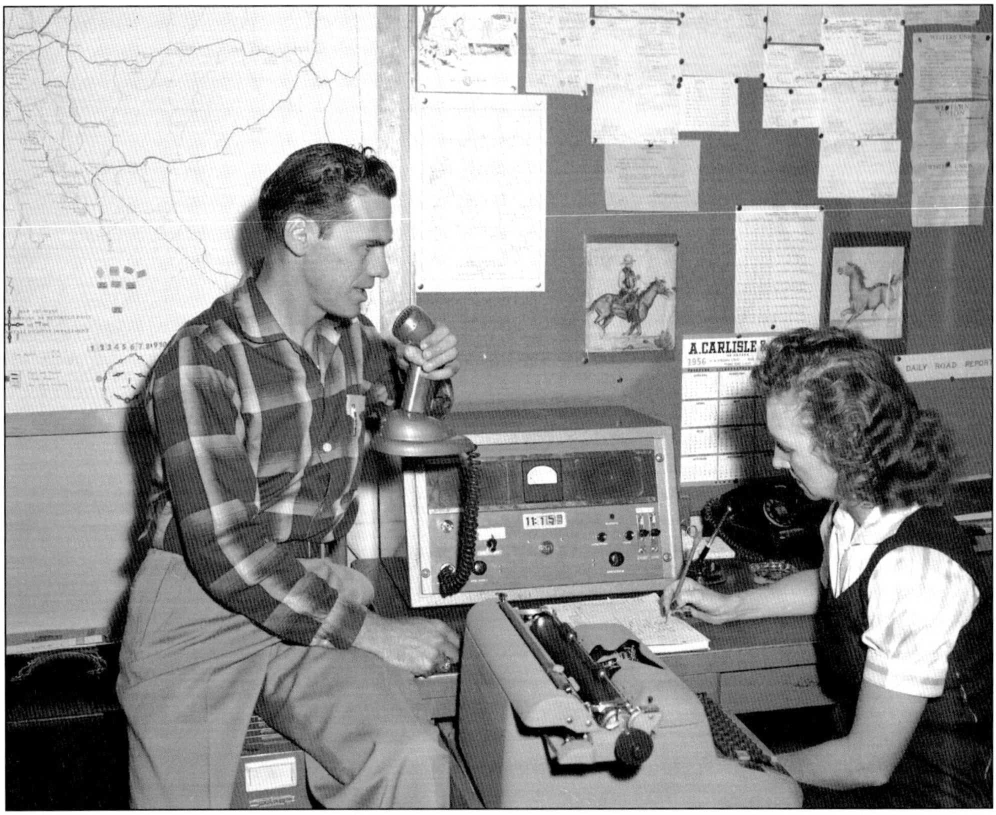

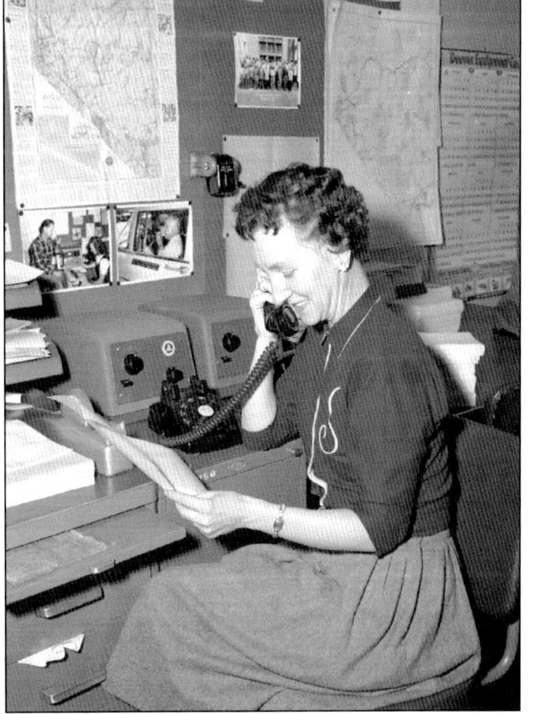

By the late 1950s, the system had established 233 mobile units, 8 repeater stations, and 27 base stations. The radio system was extremely useful in many ways, not the least of which was when a vehicle broke down in a remote area. The system was also incredibly useful in winter months when communications personnel would compile road condition reports that were then provided to the public through a telephone answering machine.

The public relations office was rekindled in the early 1950s, and by the late 1950s, the highway department had a dedicated Public Information Program. The program was largely fueled by the nationwide unpopularity of the impending interstate system, which necessitated an intense public awareness campaign. Featured here is a communications worker; note the photographs tacked to the board above the phone.

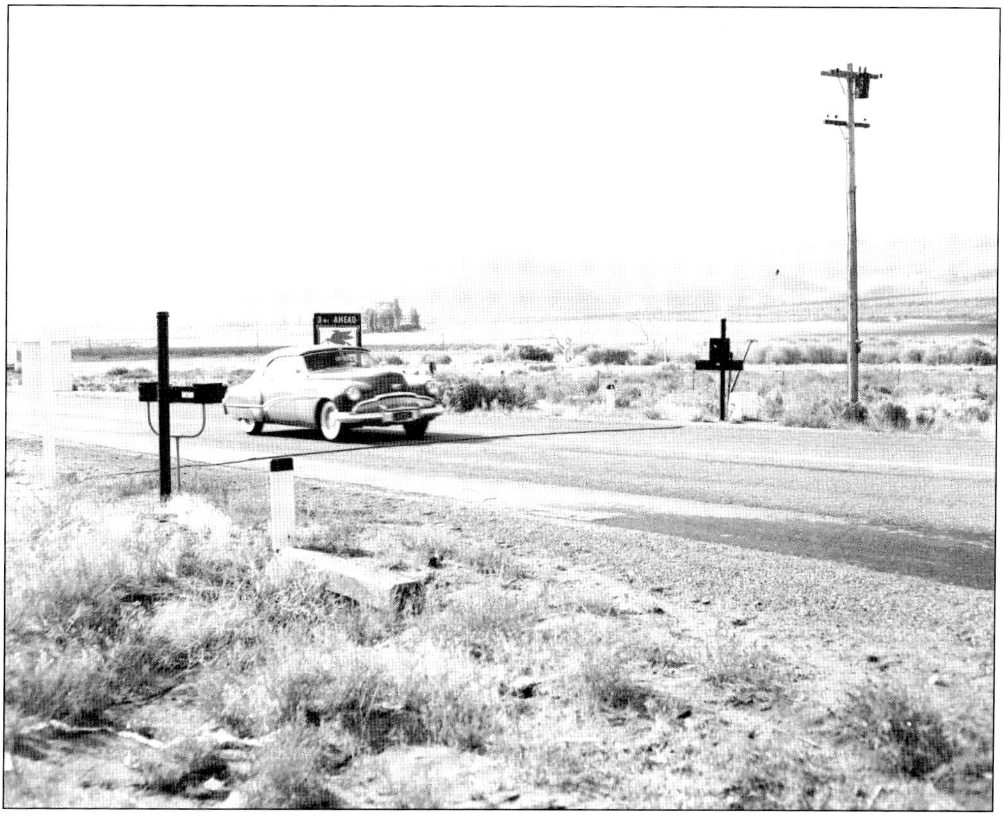

Pictured here is an IBM traffic recorder from 1952. The highway department's IBM section saw substantial growth in the 1950s as the department recognized the advantages of machine computation. The department stated, "Speed of operation is evidenced by the example of an earthwork problem, solved by IBM in less than three days as opposed to the some three months the problem would require of a skilled engineer to complete."

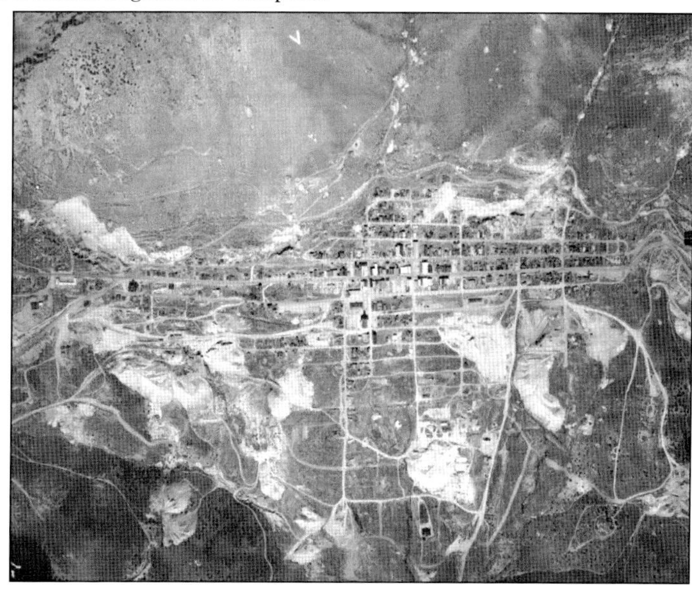

This is an aerial photograph of Virginia City. Aerial photography and mapping was done by the Photogrammetry Unit of the Planning and Survey Division. The Photogrammetry Unit was created in the late 1950s, and the capabilities and tools have since grown to the point that the highway department now has a Locations Services Division that includes specialists in GIS, LiDAR, Geodesy, and CADD mapping, among others.

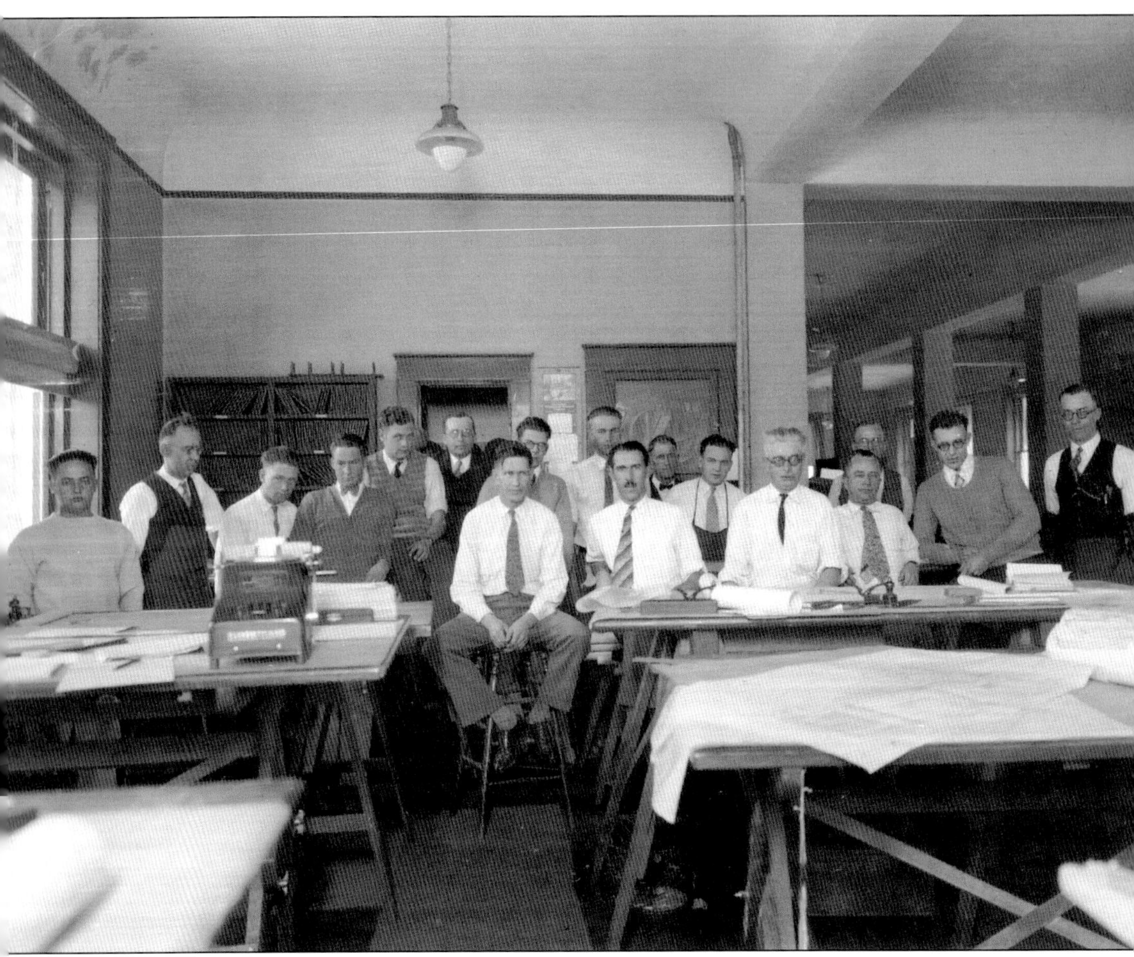

The highway department has grown exponentially since this group shot was taken in 1929, and the divisions themselves have gone through numerous permutations and changes in the intervening years. In fact, the department has grown so much that it now has three regionally based districts, and each district has its own engineering team. The districts are based out of Las Vegas, Reno, and Elko, and all three are responsible for overseeing projects within their territory. Currently, there are also three well-equipped and strategically located maintenance stations. Located in Ely, Tonopah, and Winnemucca, these enhanced stations support the smaller outlying stations. Finally, there are now new divisions and sections that were never contemplated in 1917, but because of population growth, traffic increases, and radical changes in technology, they have become critical parts of the process. This chapter could not encompass them all, but their contributions cannot be diminished.

Three

In the Wake of a Road

How Highways Irrevocably Change a Landscape

Traveling through a small Nevada town can be like driving into a time warp. The residue of another era is sensed instinctively. By slowing down and really looking at the roadside landscape, it becomes more apparent what is actually eliciting that feeling. A row of narrow storefronts perched on the edge of the road, enameled signs nailed to a convenient post or tree, the pattern of wood utility poles along the roadside—these little details are the physical remnants of history that tell the story of what happens in the wake of a road. The roadside landscape represents the coevolution of hard-surfaced roads and automobiles, a combination that spawned an entire industry of travel-related inventions: gas stations, garages, drive-through diners, auto courts, billboards, and the peculiar roadside attraction.

When cruising through Genoa, look beyond the fancy new decorative streetlights. Look for the 1919 radial wave light fixtures suspended from a splintery utility pole. In Yerington, a sharp eye will be rewarded with the discovery of the original street curbs made from redwood planks. And the next time you pull over to take a pit stop along a deserted section of US 50, look for a half-buried concrete pillar inscribed with an "N" for "Nevada" that once marked the highway's right-of-way.

Nevada's earliest east-west highways were the Victory Highway (US 40) and the Lincoln Highway (US 50). The main north-south highways were the Bonanza Highway (SR 39 and SR 52), the Roosevelt Highway (US 6), and the International Four States Highway (US 93 and US 91). Many alignments of Nevada's first roads can still be driven today and are some of the best routes to take to observe the accumulation of road history.

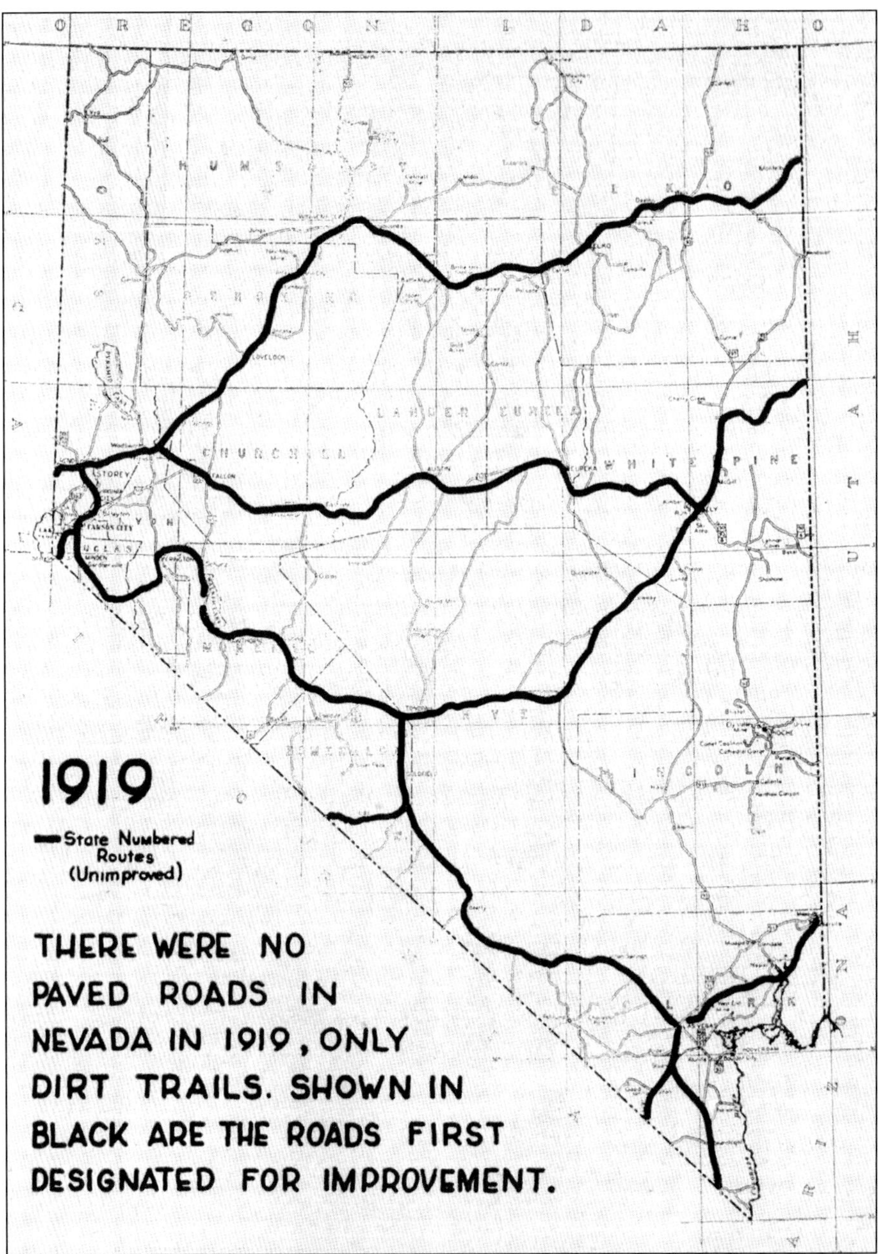

A map showing the condition of roads in 1919 illustrates that motorists could not just get from here to there. Shortly after the formation of the highway department, most of the state could still only be accessed by foot, hoof, or rail. In Nevada, towns often developed where the mineral resources were found, usually in some remote mountaintop totally unsuitable for a townsite. Nevertheless, communities of hundreds and sometimes thousands of fortune-seekers would spring up in unlikely places. The town came first, and the road came second. If the strike managed to hold out, a road or railroad spur would eventually be built to the town. For all the nostalgia of the independent, self-reliant miner, settlers were still dependent on canned food, store-bought tools, manufactured fabric, and imported lumber from faraway places, all transported via roads, the lifelines of the community.

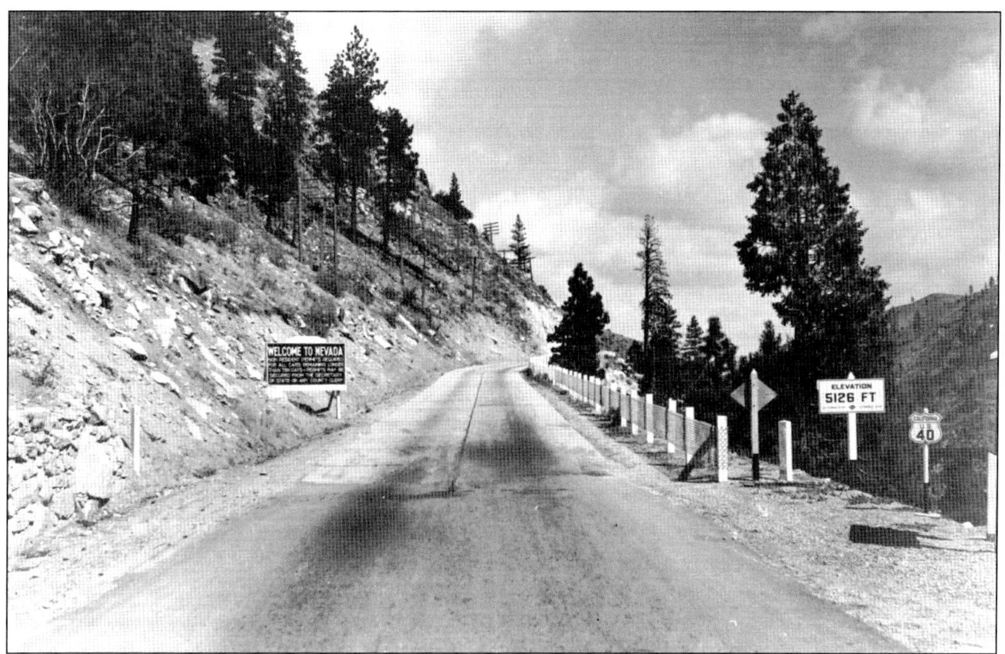

The Victory Highway and one alignment of the Lincoln Highway shared the road from Verdi to Fernley. The crossing from Verdi, California, to Verdi, Nevada, was marked by the start of a concrete road and a sign with the message, "Welcome to Nevada. Nonresident permits required for all cars remaining longer than ten days—Permits may be secured from the Secretary of State or any county clerk."

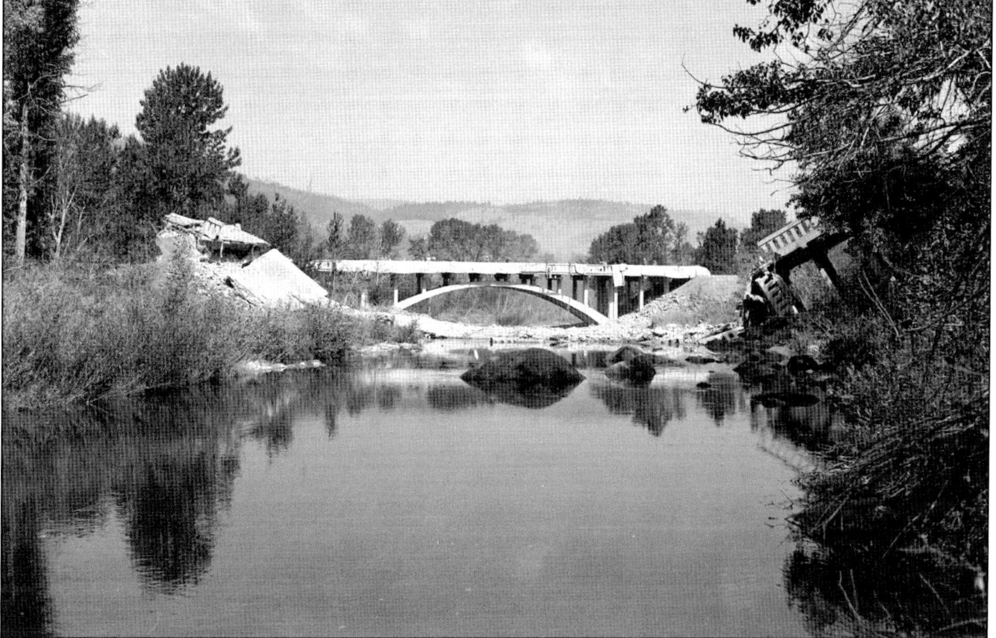

A 141-foot-long bridge just east of Verdi carried the Lincoln Highway and Victory Highway over the Truckee River. Seen here in 1939 is the newly completed open-spandrel bridge. The remnants of the previous mid-1920s bridge are in the foreground, in the process of being demolished.

Form 13 Rev.

STATE OF NEVADA
DEPARTMENT OF HIGHWAYS

MEMORANDUM

October 23, 1961

To JACK PARVIN, District Engineer

From JOHN E. BAWDEN, Deputy State Highway Engineer
Subject:

Attached is a picture of an old drainage structure west of the checking station near Lawton's. It clearly shows "Lincoln Highway" and is one, if not the only one, left in existence. It may be desirable to salvage the portion indicating the "Lincoln Highway" if at all possible.

Would you check and see if it is reasonable to consider salvaging these markers; especially before the new freeway construction may destroy them.

John E. Bawden
Deputy State Highway Engineer

JEB:mr
Attach.

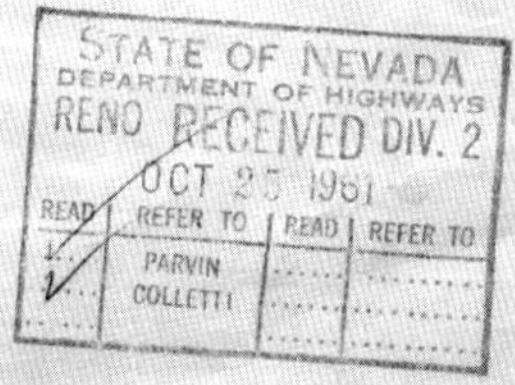

Ou Purpose Is to Build and Maintain Highways, Not Spend Money

A set of unique Lincoln Highway bridge rails located between Verdi and Reno were almost destroyed when US 50, now part of Interstate 80, was widened in the 1960s. The concrete railings spelled out "Lincoln" on one side of the bridge and "Highway" on the opposite side. Fortunately, John E. Bawden, deputy state highway engineer, recognized the historic significance of the bridge and decided to save the railings. This memo from October 23, 1961, asks the district engineer to "check and see if it is reasonable to consider salvaging these markers; especially before the new highway construction may destroy them." The logo at the bottom of the memo clarifies, "Our Main Purpose is to Build and Maintain Roads, Not Spend Money."

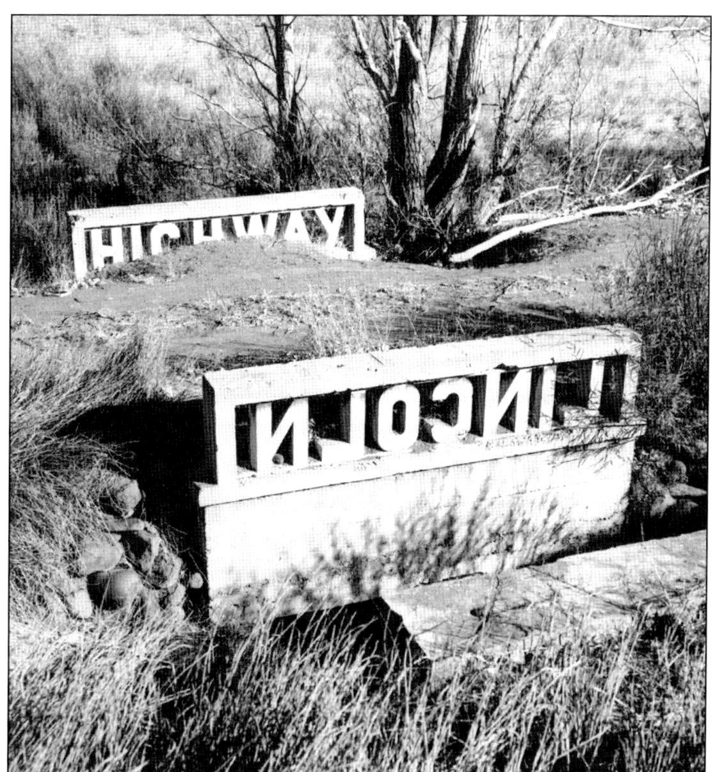

These unique concrete bridge rails originally graced a bridge between Verdi and Reno. Anton F. Neidt designed the concrete rails, which were constructed in 1914. Neidt was a contractor specializing in concrete work and highway paving. The railings were preserved, and today they can be seen at a pullout on eastbound Interstate 80, approximately one mile west of the bridge's original location.

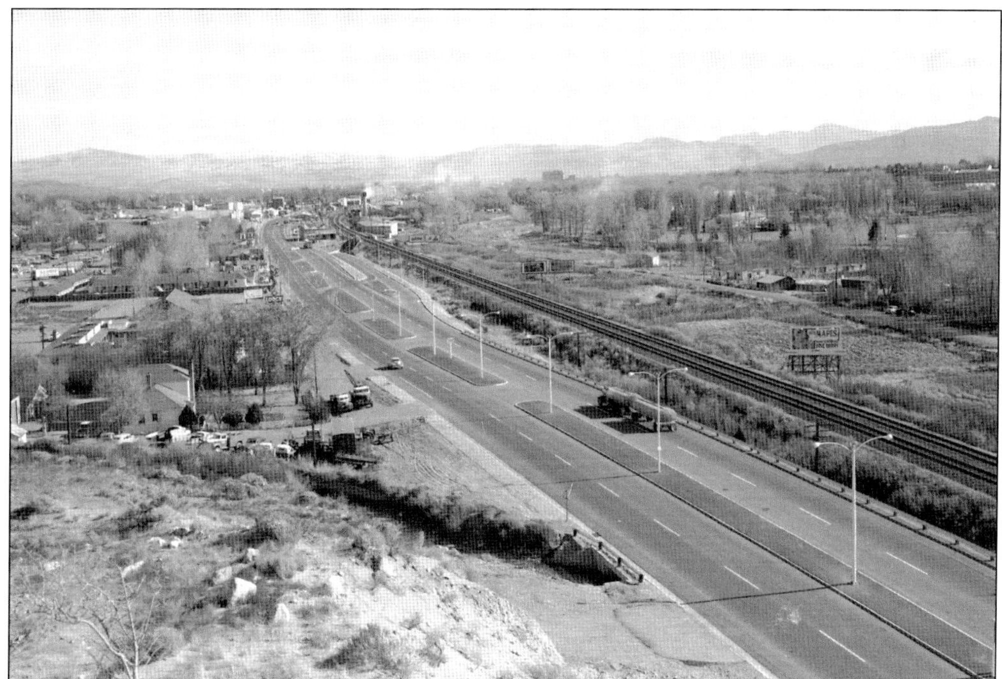

From Verdi, the Lincoln Highway and Victory Highway traveled to Reno and Sparks along Fourth Street. The western approach to Reno is seen here in 1955. The former two-lane road has just received a makeover with a divided four-lane highway illuminated by double cobra-head streetlights.

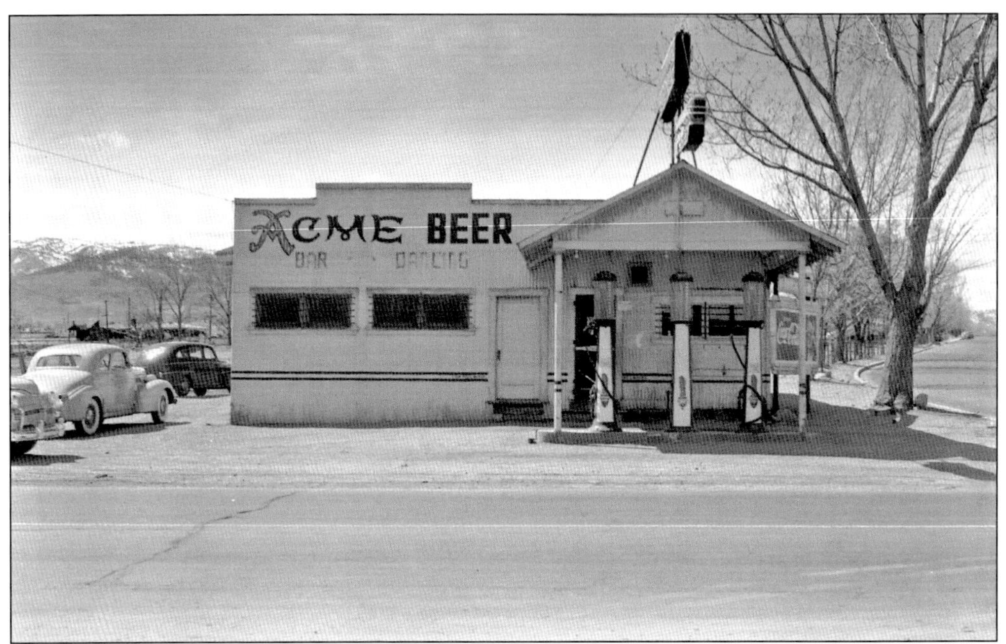

Beer, dancing, and gasoline—there is a little something for everyone at Dougherty Service Station in Reno, run by Roger and Rose Dougherty. Gas station architecture evolved as companies started designing stations to represent a corporate identity. But the Doughertys' station, with its corrugated metal siding, barred windows, and simple gabled canopy over the visible gas pumps, appears to have escaped corporate architects.

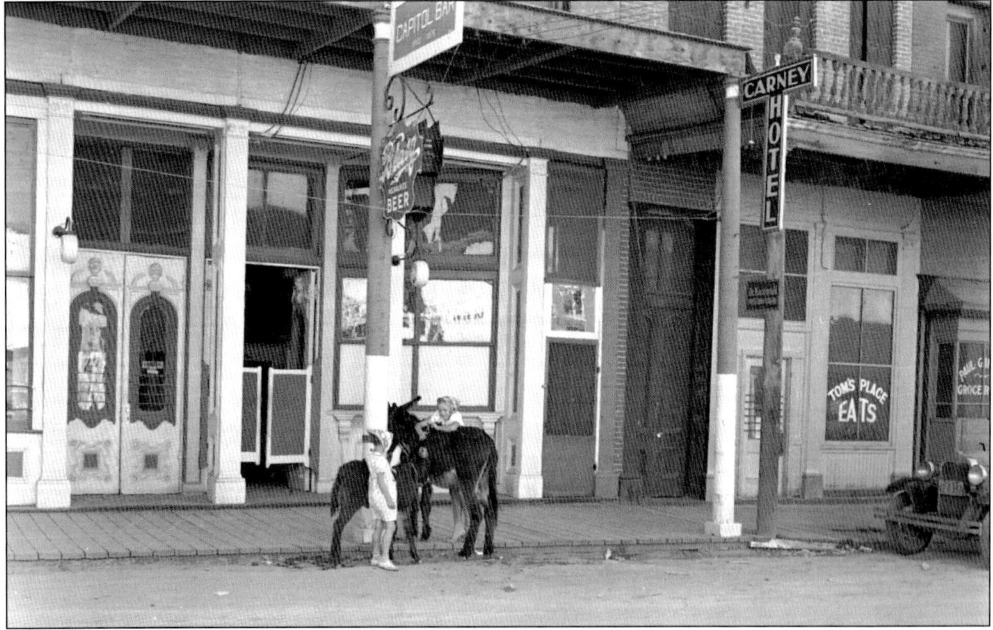

A short detour from the Lincoln Highway in Reno, Geiger Grade (Route 341) took visitors to the mother lode of Comstock gold and post–Comstock gold tourism—Virginia City. In 1939, two girls on C Street find the Virginia City residents scruffy but friendly. The anachronistic swinging saloon doors on the Capital Bar were added to satisfy tourists' expectations of an Old West town.

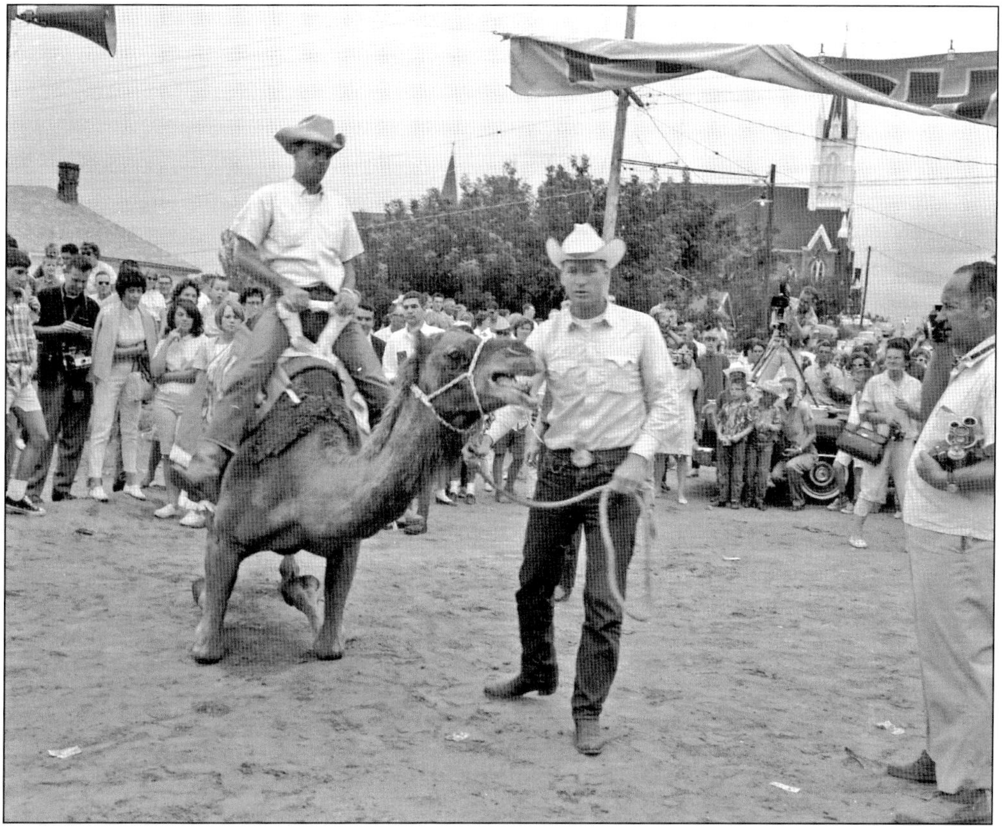

Camel and ostrich racing has been a tourist draw in Virginia City since 1959. These forms of racing started as a facetious story announcing a camel race down the main street of Virginia City and got out of hand when people actually showed up with camels. By 1965, the races were well established. Today, hundreds of people take the serpentine road to Virginia City to attend the races.

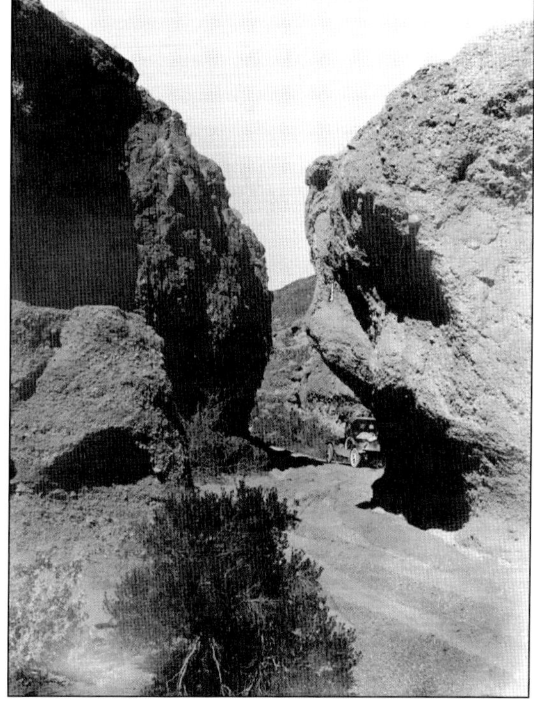

From Virginia City, returning to the Lincoln Highway via Route 17 (now Route 341) meant passing through Devil's Gate. This natural bottleneck marked the boundary between Lyon County and Storey County. The gate was later widened to accommodate an improved road through Silver City, Gold Hill, and Virginia City.

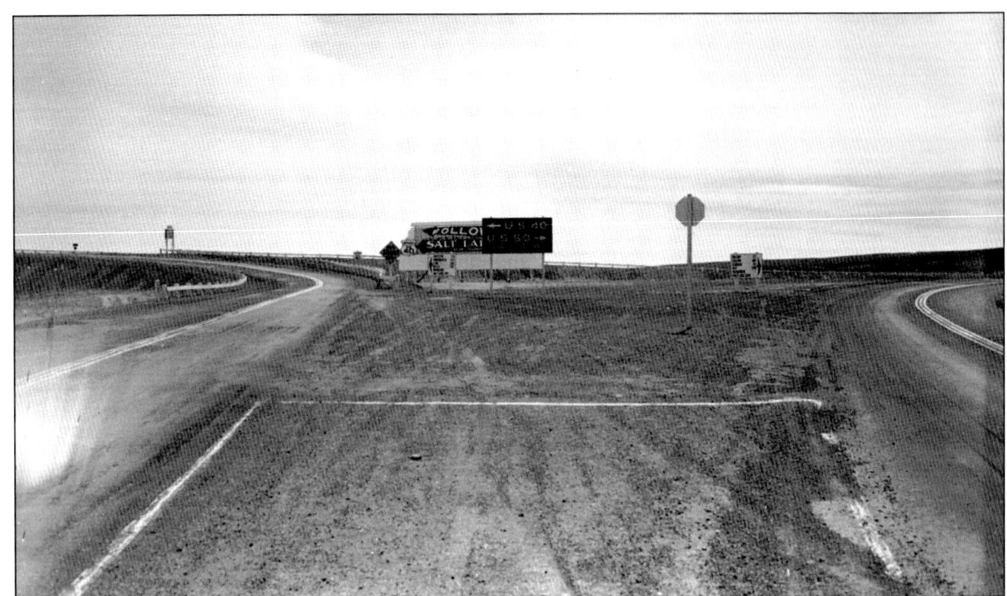

The Lincoln Highway and Victory Highway parted ways in Fernley, an agricultural and railroad town. The Victory Highway headed northeast toward Lovelock, and the Lincoln Highway continued east toward Hazen and Fallon. The critical junction is seen here in 1950. A stout timber guardrail protects drivers on the sharp curve.

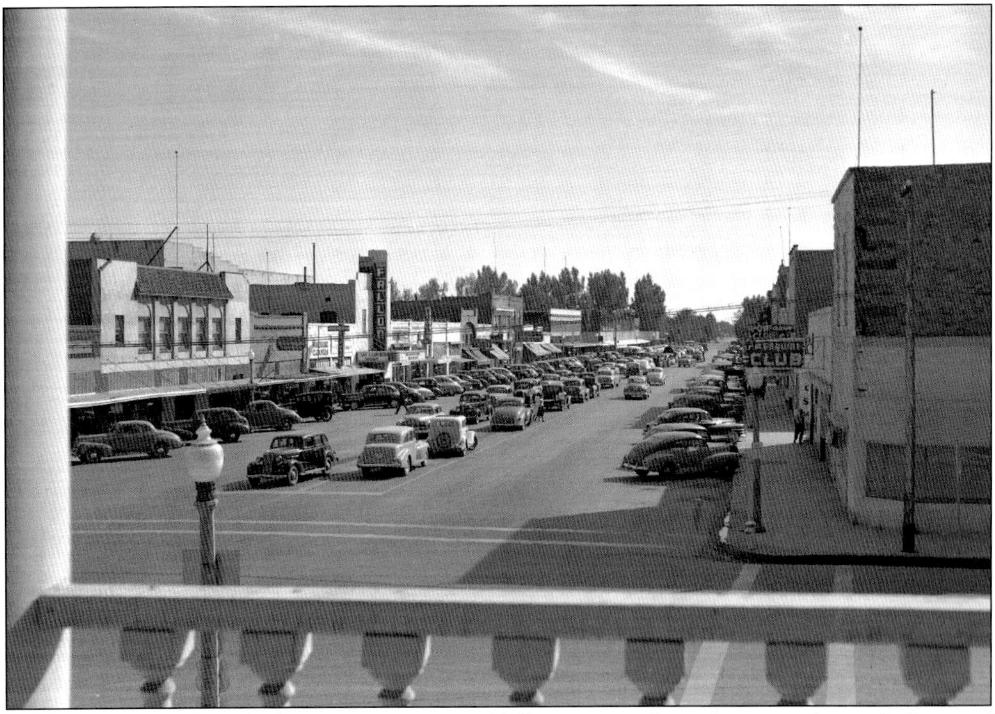

This c. 1950 photograph shows Main Street in Fallon as seen from the second-story balcony of the Churchill County Courthouse. The population of the town was small, but it played host to all the ranch families in Lahontan Valley for fairs, rodeo events, and trading. Thus, the streets were originally laid out extra wide to accommodate parking down the center of the street.

Lincoln Highway travelers would pass by the neoclassical Churchill County Courthouse in Fallon. The 1919–1920 highway department biennial explained, "The city of Fallon is a thriving and rapidly growing community and is the hub of the Newlands Reclamation Project, and we felt that, because of the rapid development of this territory, Churchill County should have first consideration for road improvements."

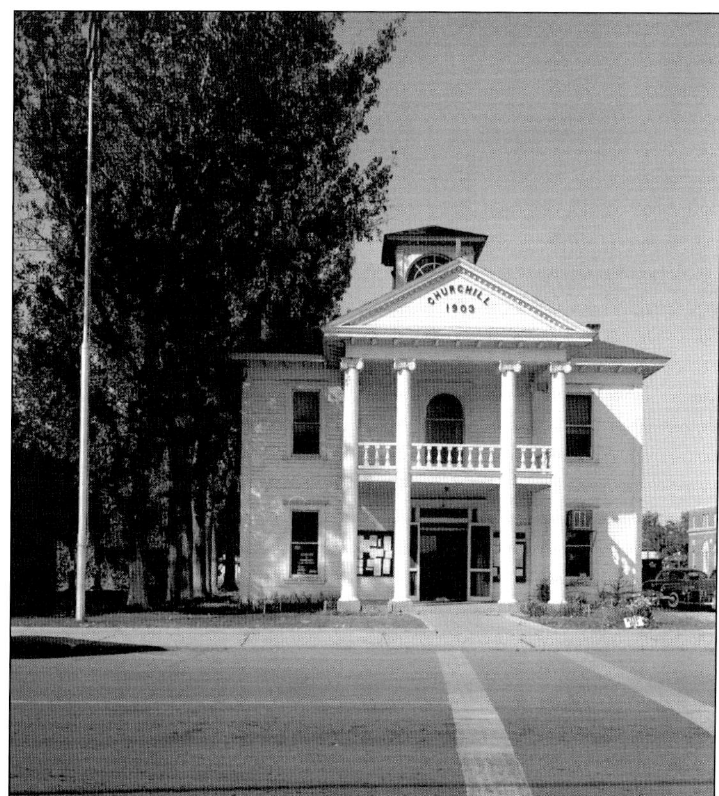

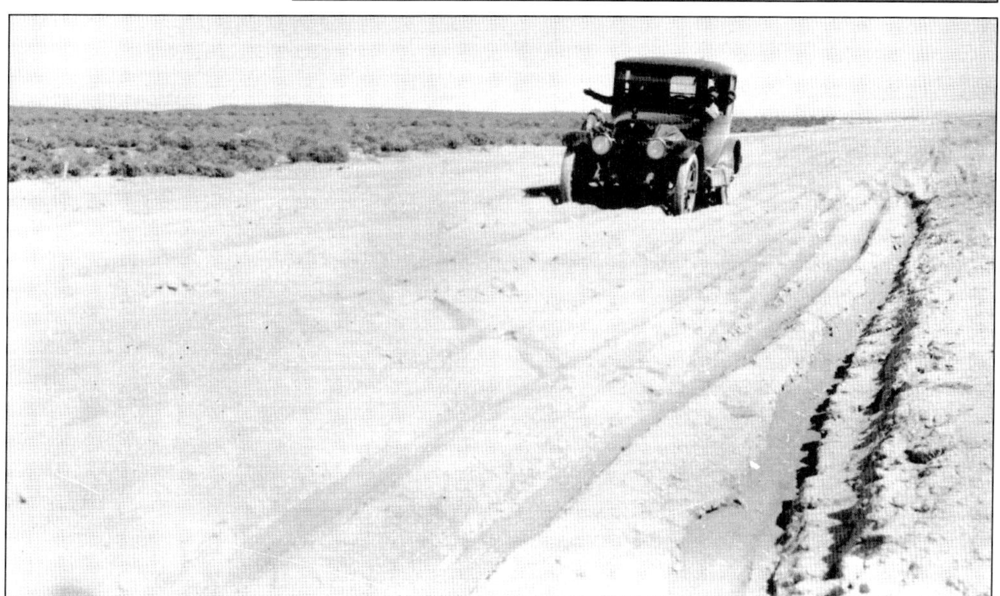

Western Nevada's sandy roads, like this unidentified section of the Lincoln Highway pictured in 1920, plagued early travelers. Some drivers recommended letting a little air out of the tires to keep the wheels from sinking into the soft soil. Of the 12,182 miles of roads in Nevada, including county, toll, and private roads, only 262 miles were "surfaced" with oil or gravel, according to a 1914 federal report.

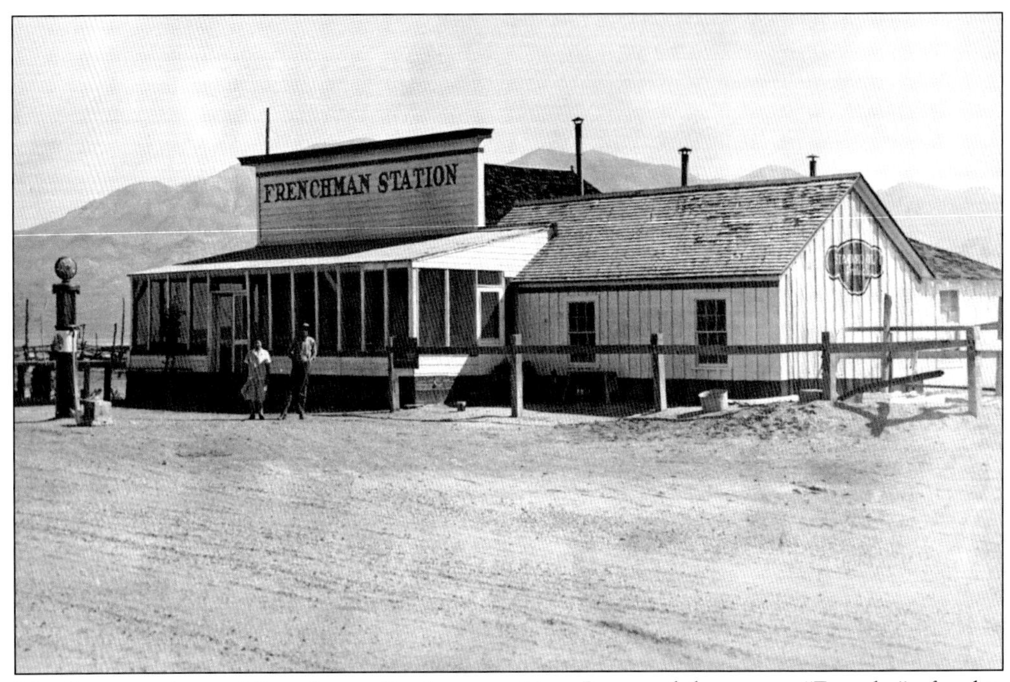

The first proprietor of Frenchman Station was Aime Bermond, known as "Frenchy" after his homeland. Frenchman Station originally served freighters and stagecoaches traveling to the Wonder and Fairview mining camps. By 1930, when this photograph was taken, Frenchman had become a rest stop for hot, wind-whipped motorists. The sign painted on the gable advertises "Standard Oil Products," and the visible gas pump stands at the ready.

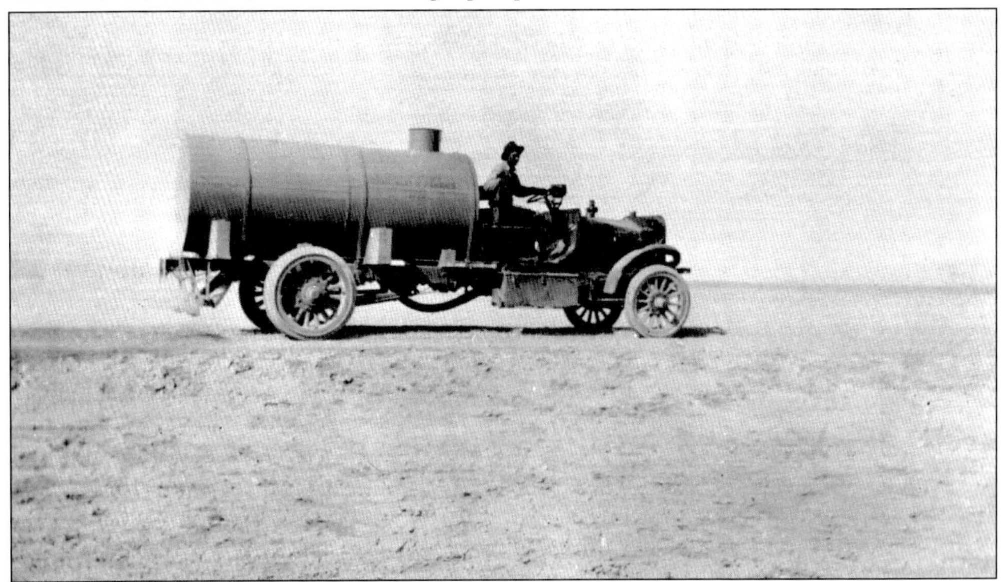

A water truck marked "Nevada Department of Highways" sprinkles water over the Frenchman's Flats section of the Lincoln Highway in Churchill County in 1923. Water sprinkling helped the road compact into a solid, uniform surface. This treatment was part of regular maintenance for gravel roads. The Lincoln Highway Association donated $10,000 to grade and gravel five miles of Frenchman's Flats. The highway department completed the work under budget in October 1922.

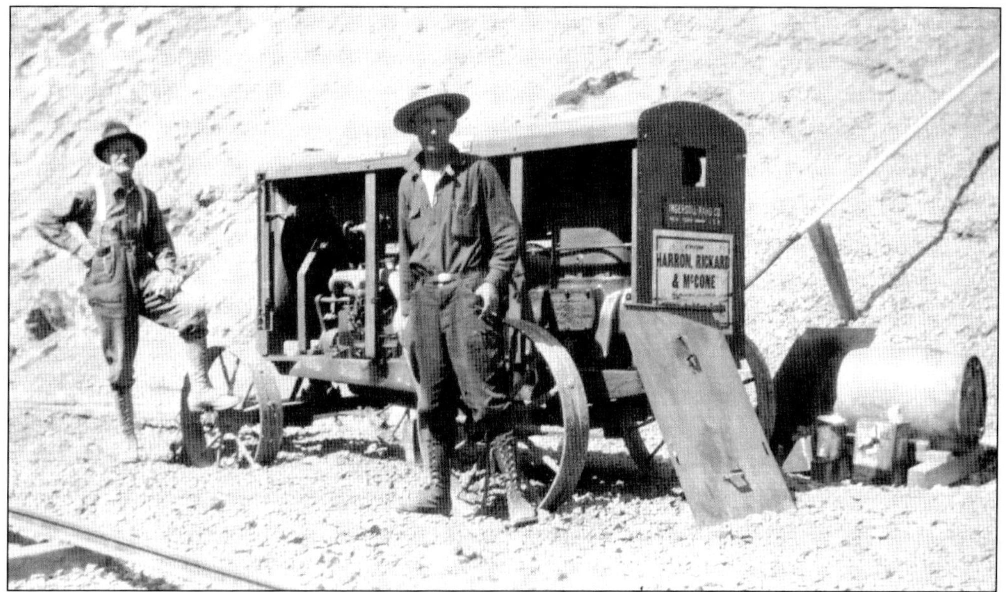

San Francisco mining company Harron, Rickard & McCone provided the enormous gasoline-powered air compressor for construction on the Lincoln Highway through Carroll Summit. Jackhammers and air chisels could be run by the machine, augmenting the work done by hand. The Lincoln Highway Association and the highway department preferred the Carroll Summit route over the long stretches of alkali flats faced by motorists taking the alternate route through the Reese River Valley.

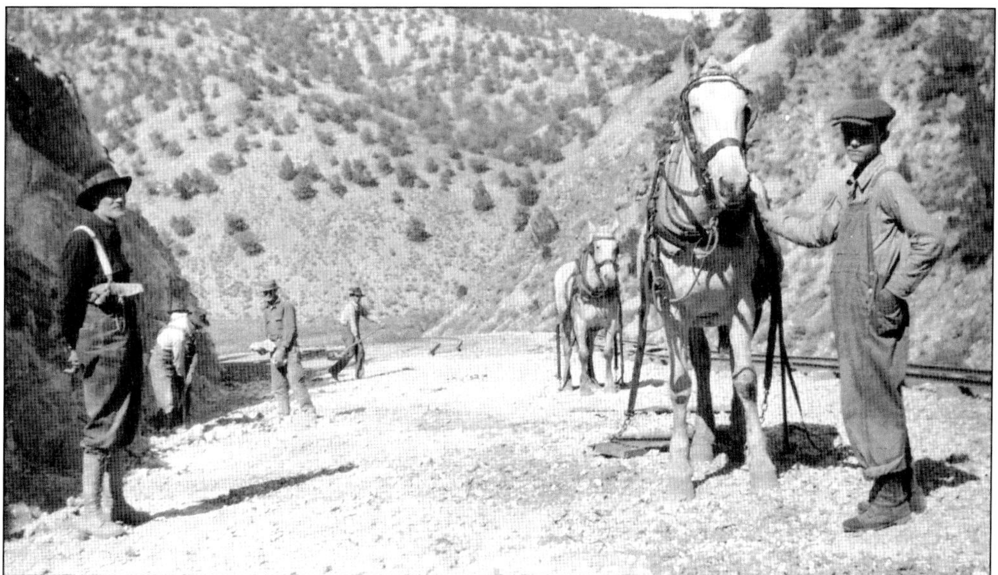

The Caroll Summit construction supervisor stands at left while a boy holds the reins of a draft horse. The highway department used horse teams to construct roads for the new automobile well into the 1930s. The contribution of child labor is less documented, though this image shows that children did help build Nevada's early roads. Motorists can still drive Carroll Summit, a scenic 7,452-foot-high pass, on what is now named Route 722.

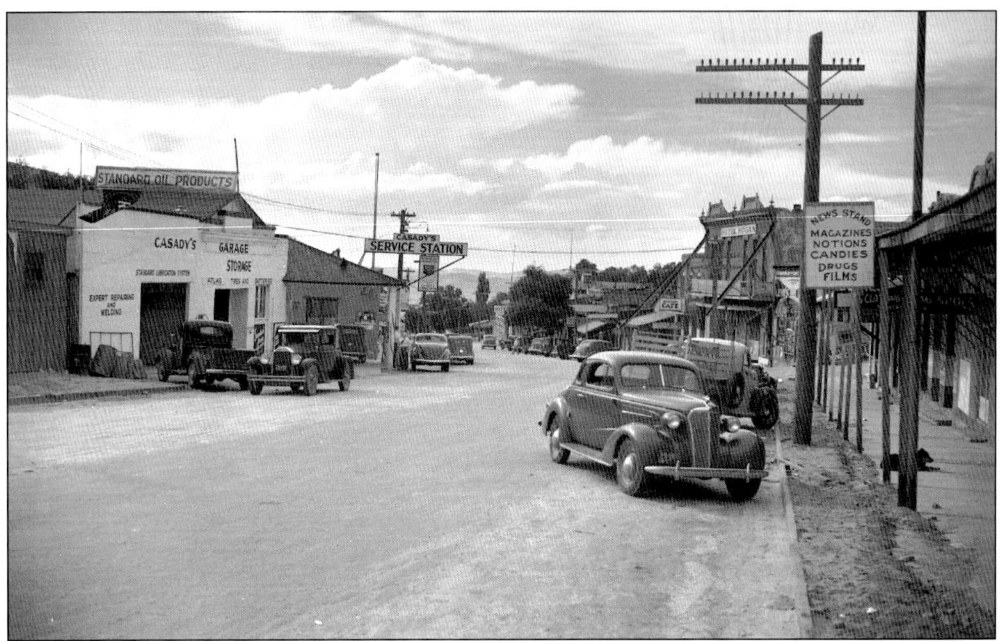

From Carroll Summit, the Lincoln Highway descended into Pony Canyon and brought travelers to Austin, a silver-mining town founded in 1862. Seen here in 1940, the town has transitioned from mule trains to automobiles, with a garage and service station.

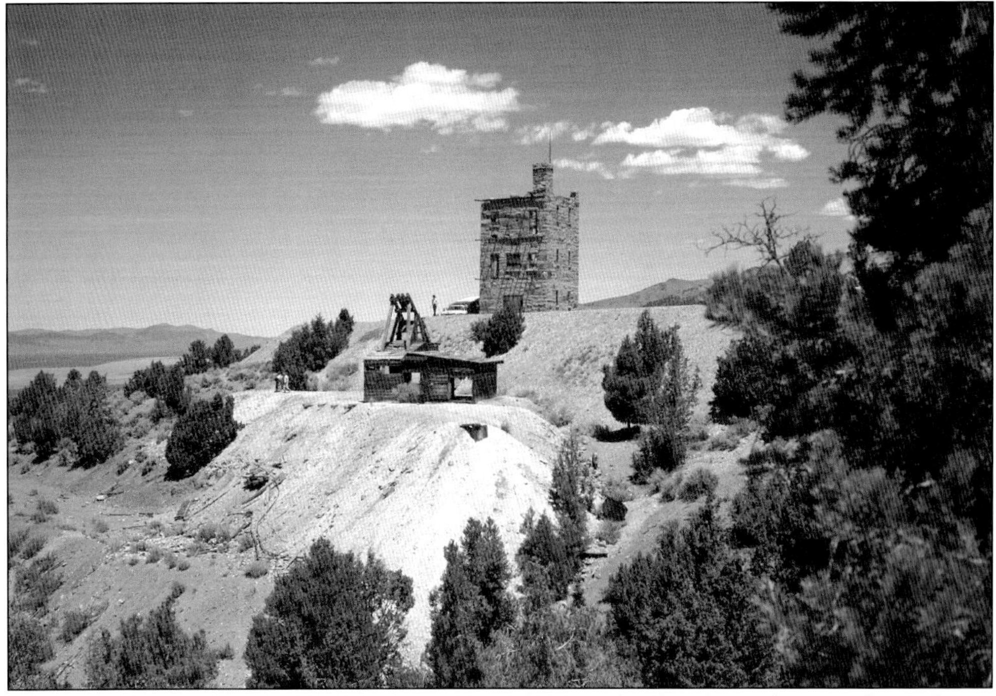

Overlooking the Reese River Valley, Stokes Castle was a landmark on the Lincoln Highway. Anson Phelps Stokes built the eccentric stone tower as a vacation home in 1896–1897. His family lived in the home for only a little over a month. It had been abandoned and fallen into disrepair by the time highway travelers were greeted by the unusual building.

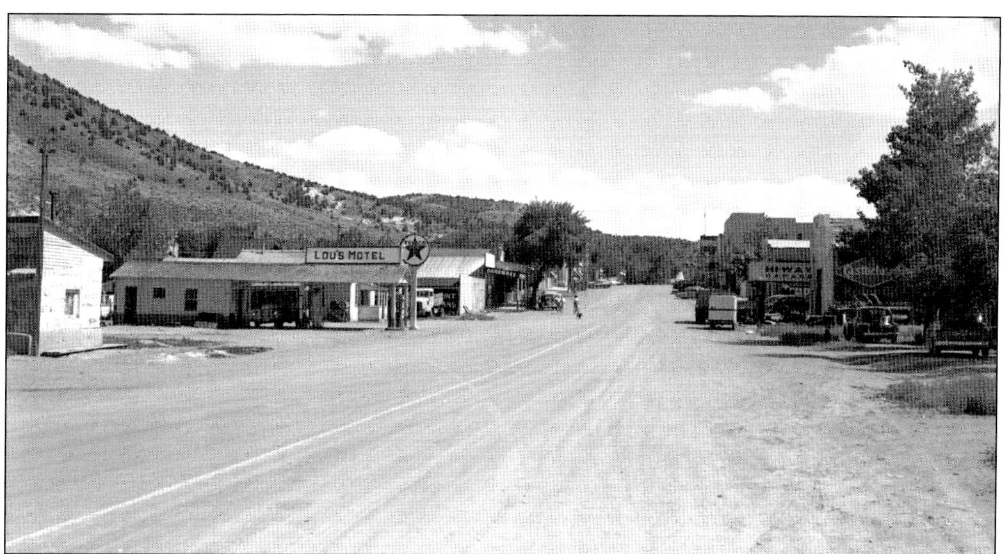

From Austin, the Lincoln Highway traveled to the silver-mining town of Eureka, known as the "Friendliest town on the Loneliest Highway," though there are few to choose from. In the 1950s, the Hi-Way Garage, Lou's Motel, and gas pumps at the edge of town served travelers.

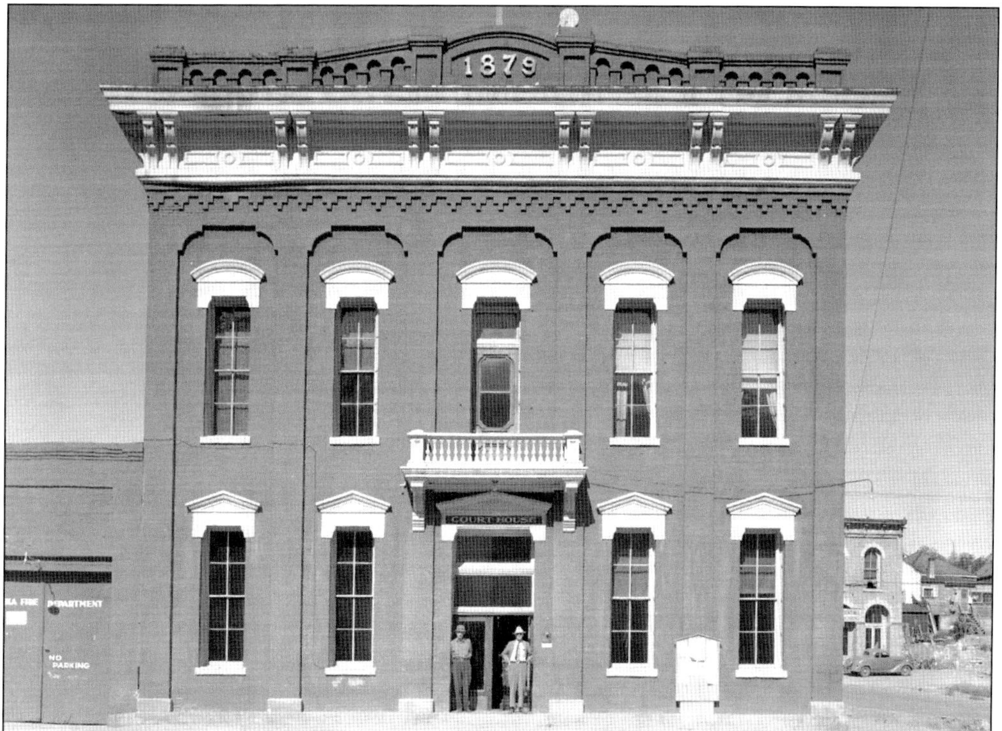

General Motors Company (GMC) funded construction of 22 miles of the Lincoln Highway near Eureka. Hard-surfaced roads that were a delight to cruise across in the latest model of car were in the best interest of automobile manufacturers. Not to let their good deed go unadvertised, a bronze plaque giving credit to GMC was placed near the White Pine–Eureka County line. Today, the plaque stands by the 1879 Eureka County Courthouse, seen here in the 1950s.

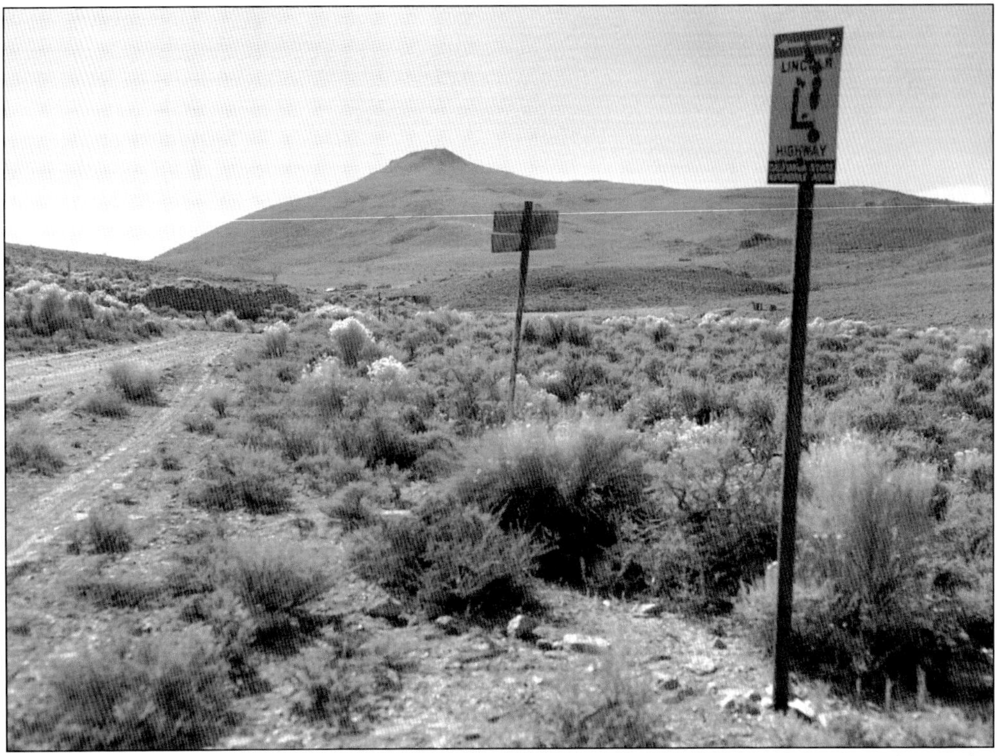

From Eureka, the original route of the Lincoln Highway made a loop through Hamilton. The Lincoln Highway Association agreed to donate $7,500 if the road that traveled through the dwindling town of Hamilton was rerouted to the north, through Antelope Summit. Construction on the new 10-foot-wide gravel road was started in July 1922. The bypass added further insult to this once booming mining town that served as White Pine County's first county seat.

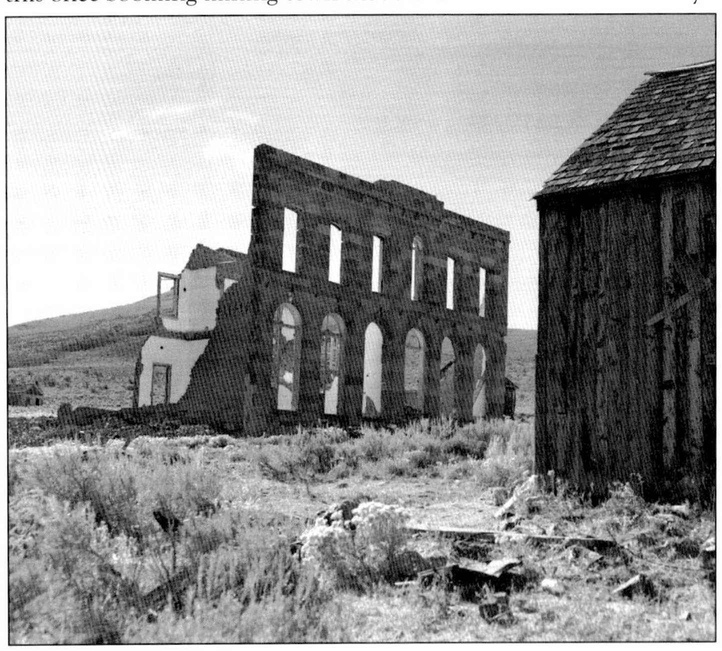

By the time the Lincoln Highway route reached Hamilton in 1913, the town was already a ghost of its former self. In the summer of 1869, the town sported a population of about 12,000 people, but successive fires and depletion of the ore was the end of the town. The remaining ruins of the stone J.R. Withington Building are seen here in 1969.

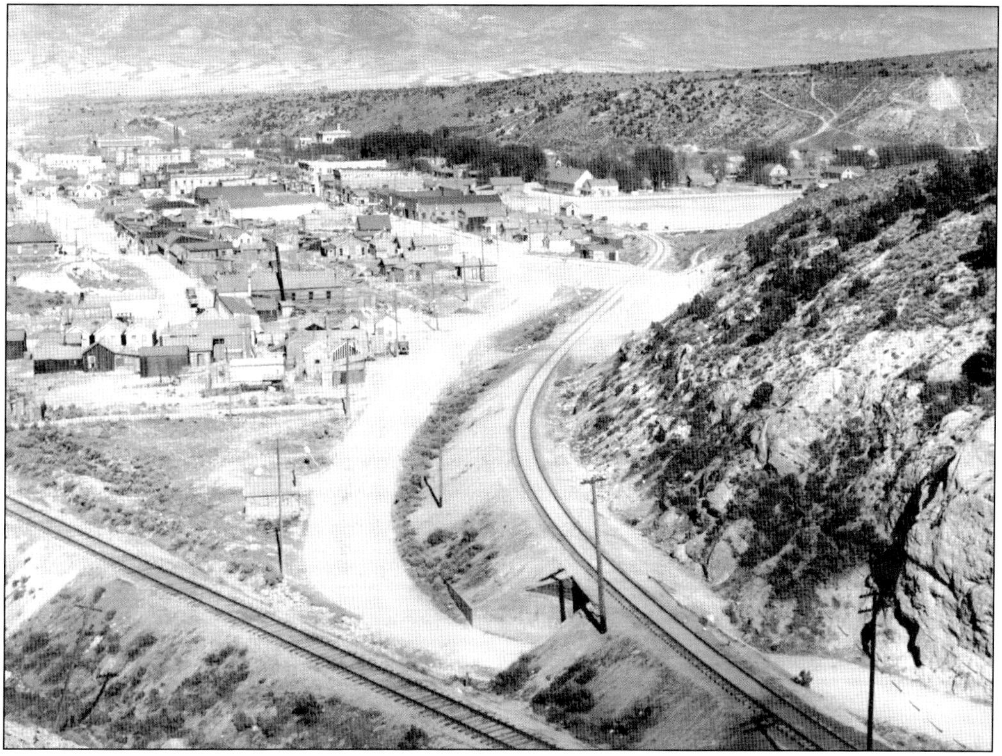

For eastward travelers on the Lincoln Highway, the last big Nevada town was Ely. Taken in the early 1920s, this photograph of the western entrance into town shows the original road traveling under the railroad tracks. The dashed lines drawn along the lower right of the photograph indicate where the hill would be cut and the new "Hyway" built.

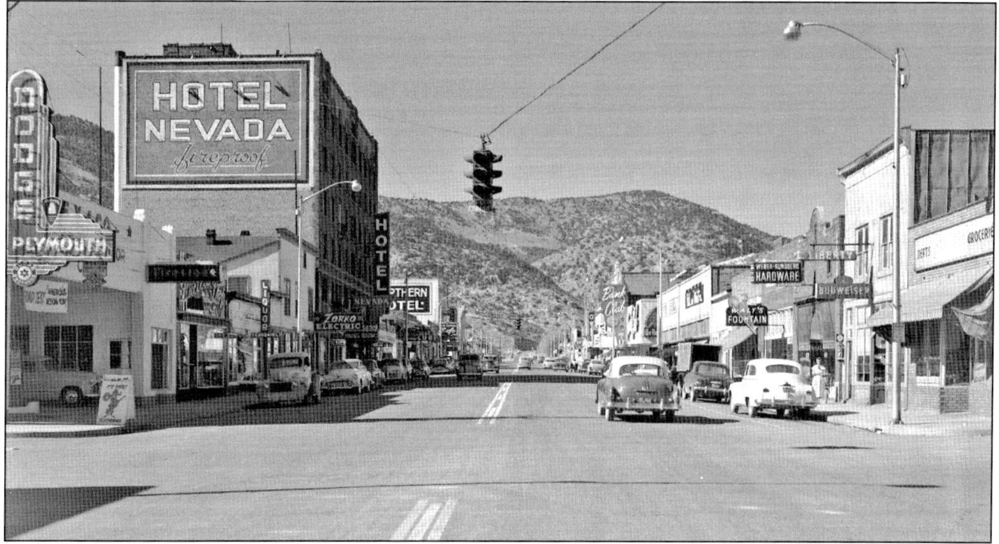

Ely started as a Pony Express stop in 1864 and boomed in 1906 when copper deposits were discovered nearby. The new craze for telephones and electricity required copper wire, and lots of it. The mines around Ely were happy to supply it. Starting in 1929, Lincoln Highway travelers could stay at the "fireproof" Hotel Nevada, seen here in 1953.

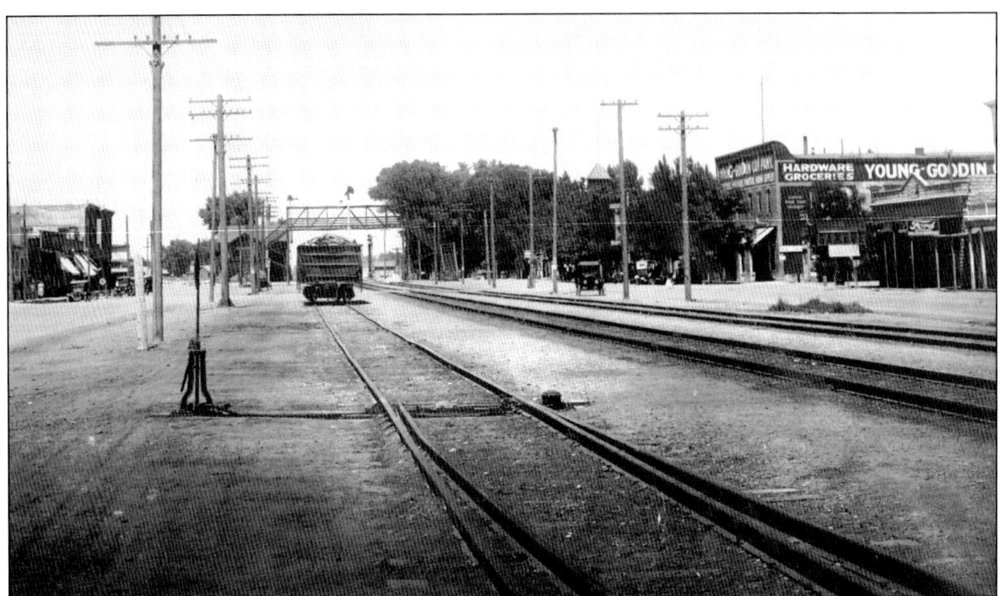

The Victory Highway traversed a more northerly route than the Lincoln Highway. The journey across the state from Verdi to Wells followed a much older transportation corridor. It was first traveled by American immigrants on the California Trail and later by the transcontinental railroad line. The railroad tracks cut through the middle of Lovelock, the Pershing County seat, on the Victory Highway.

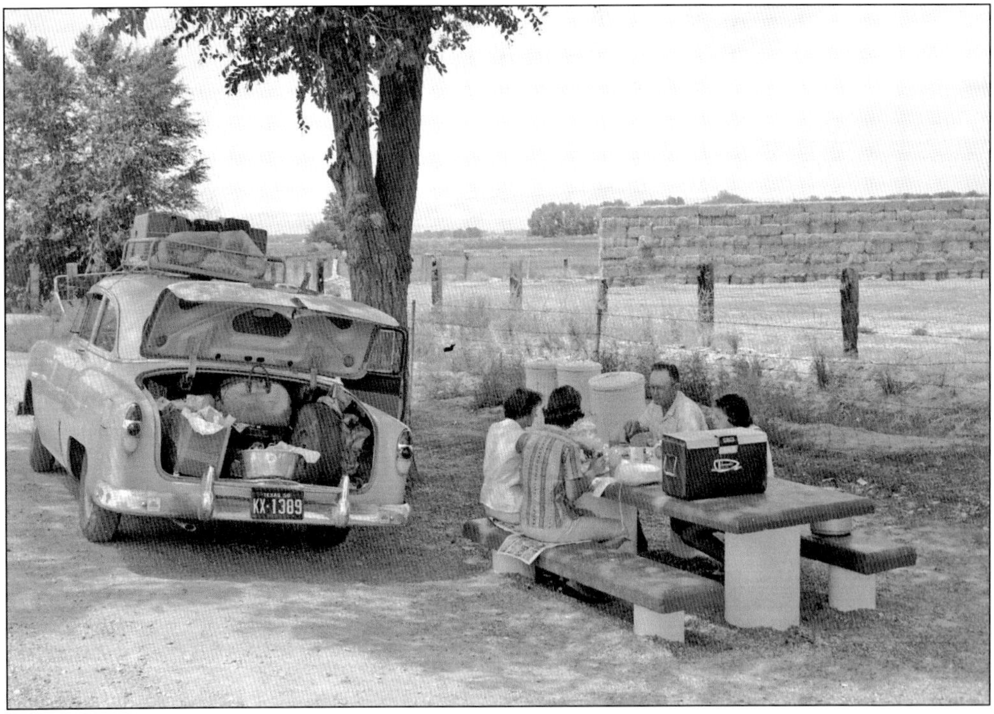

A picnic table, three trash cans, and a tree make for a spartan but satisfactory roadside rest stop for a Texas family picnicking near Lovelock around 1958. The wall of hay attests to the valley's agricultural success, made possible by irrigation from the Humboldt River.

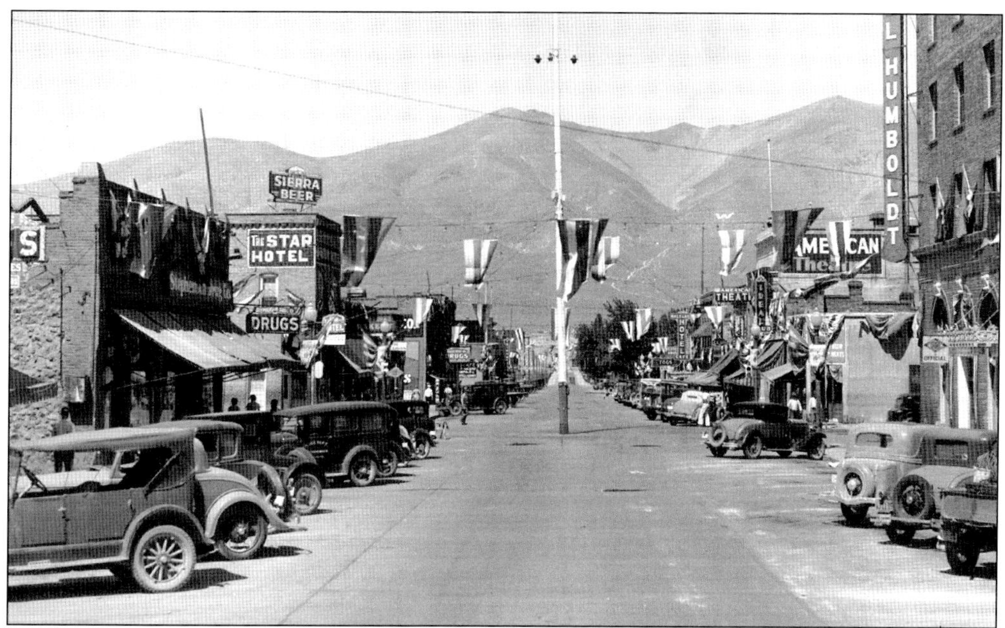

From Lovelock, the Victory Highway traveled to Winnemucca. Automobiles line South Bridge Street in Winnemucca in the 1930s. On September 26, 1930, the *Reno Evening Gazette* commented, "The number of self-propelled vehicles in the state shows that there are 22,386 pleasure cars, 5895 in commercial use and fifty-nine motorcycles . . . Taking pleasure vehicles alone, this would give the state one for every four inhabitants, which is a rather good showing."

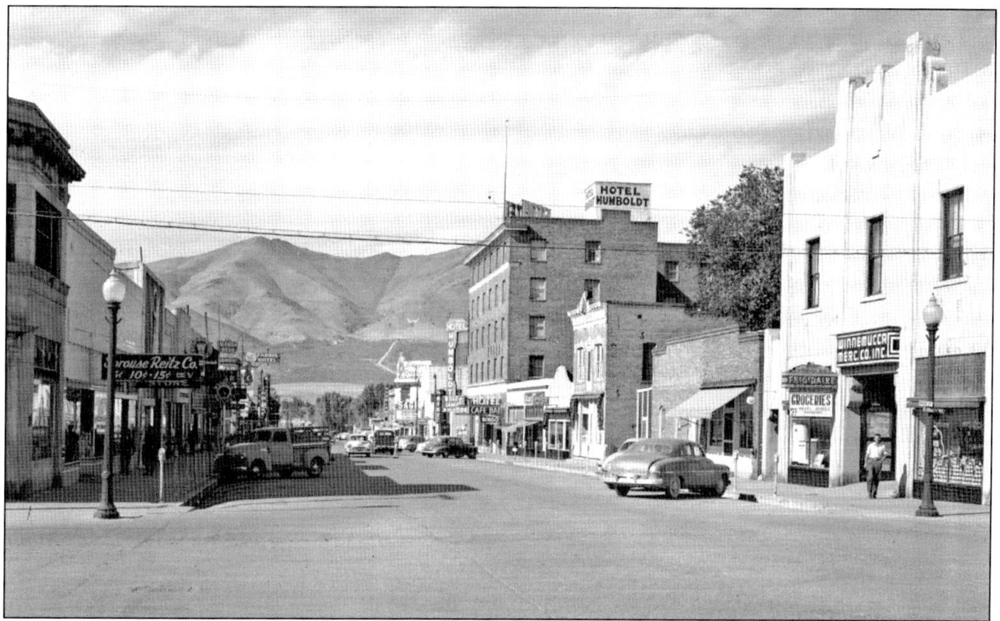

This is the same view of Winnemucca as the previous photograph. Over 30 years, the town had matured. The single streetlight suspended above the intersection was replaced with rows of streetlights on poles. The dirt road evolved into a paved road with all the accoutrements of a city: concrete curbs, gutters, sidewalks, and metered parking. The five-story Humboldt Hotel can be seen in the background. Completed in 1923, the hotel had 100 rooms.

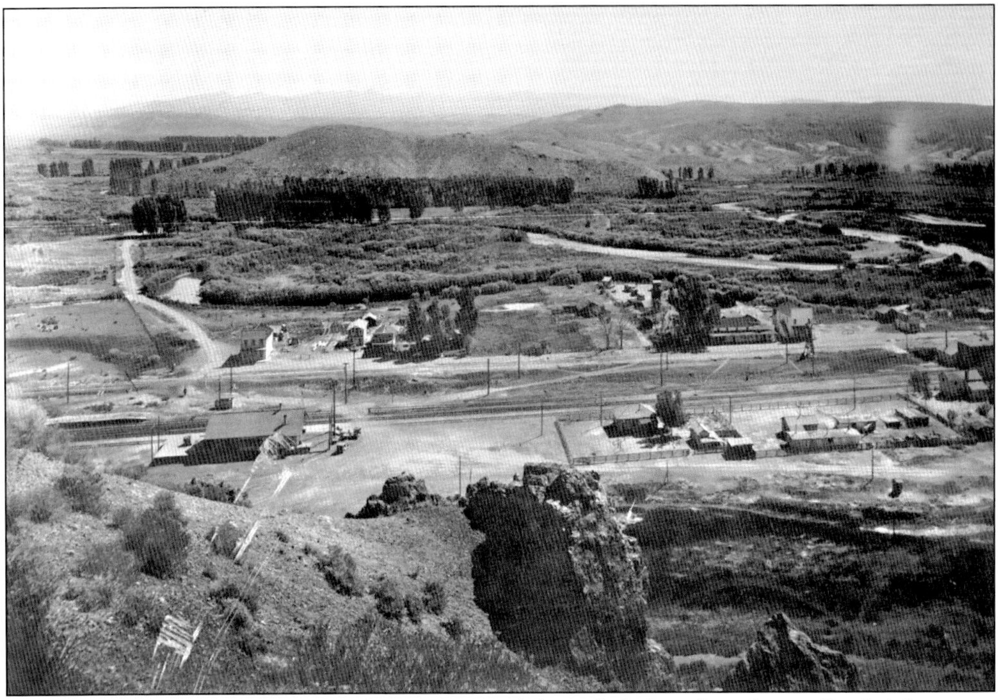

After Winnemucca, the Victory Highway continued through Golconda and on to Battle Mountain. In the early 1920s, Battle Mountain was little more than the Central Pacific Railroad depot (left), a few wood-framed businesses, and homes. Between 1925 and 1926, the highway department paved 0.31 miles of the Victory Highway through town.

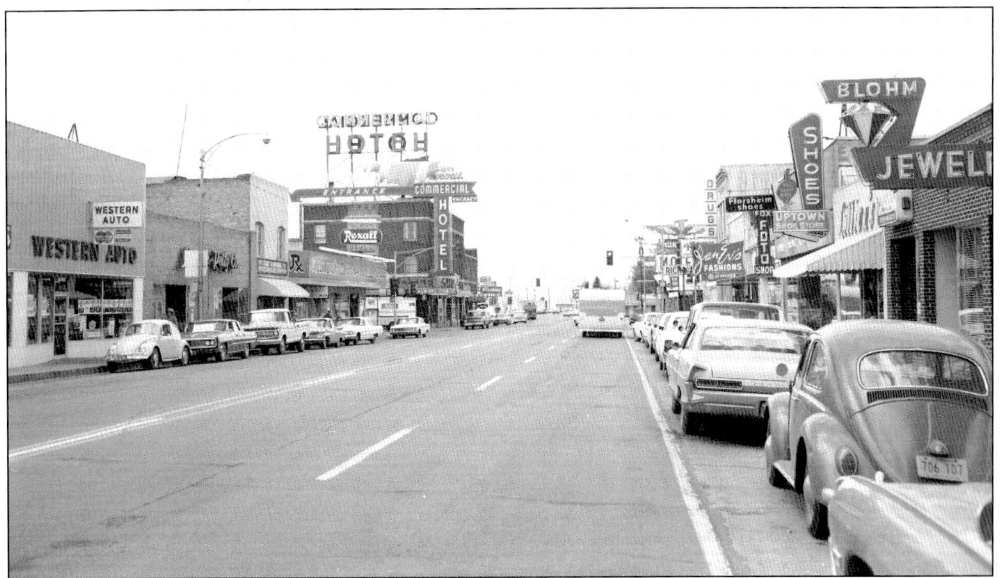

The next town on the Victory Highway was Elko. At night, the town lit up with neon signs advertising everything from jewelry to shoes. Illuminated neon signs worked great for catching the eye of motorists speeding down the road. One company, the Young Electric Sign Company (YESCO), was responsible for designing and constructing the majority of the historic neon signs in Nevada.

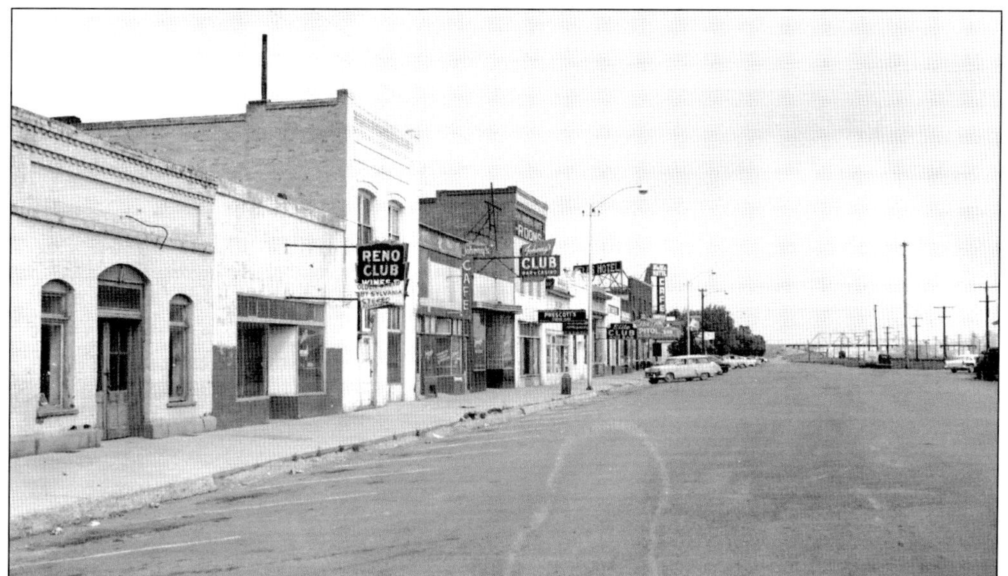

Like many old towns along US 40, Wells owes its existence to the Central Pacific Railroad. A railroad town already had many of the businesses and infrastructure for travelers that the subsequent automobile tourist would need. In the 1960s, Wells offered the thirsty traveler a full assortment of bars and clubs.

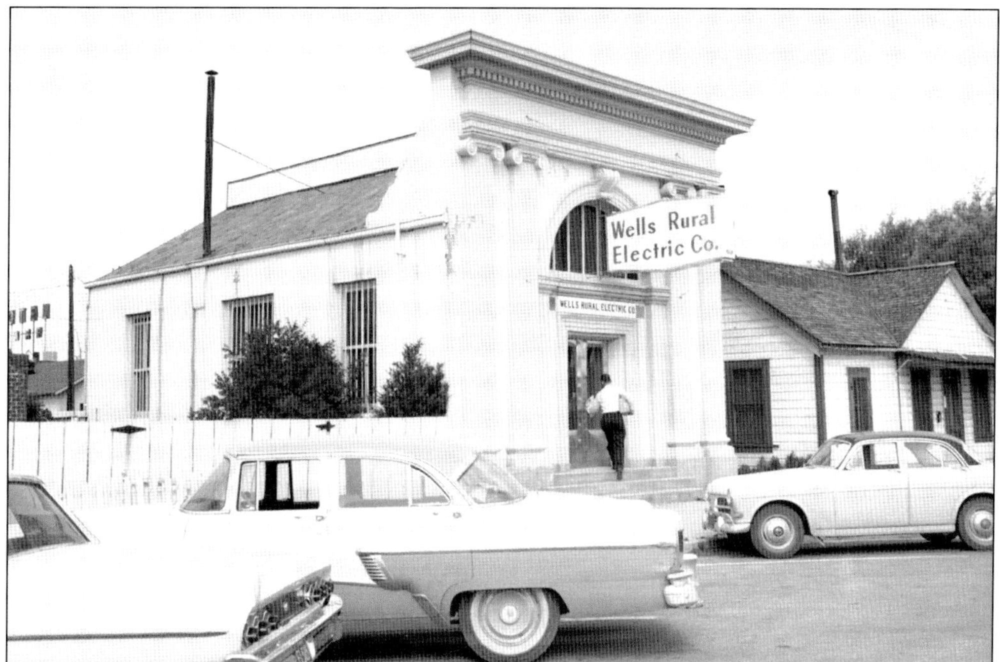

Grandeur, on a tiny scale, could be found at the Wells Rural Electric Company. The electric company was housed in the former Wells Nevada Bank building on Seventh Street, seen here in the early 1960s. In 1927, the communities of Wells, Deeth, and Starr Valley received power from the state's first fully automatic hydroelectric plant. Electrical lines were handy navigational devices for early Nevada motorists. From Wells, travelers proceeded to Wendover, the easternmost Nevada town, on the Victory Highway.

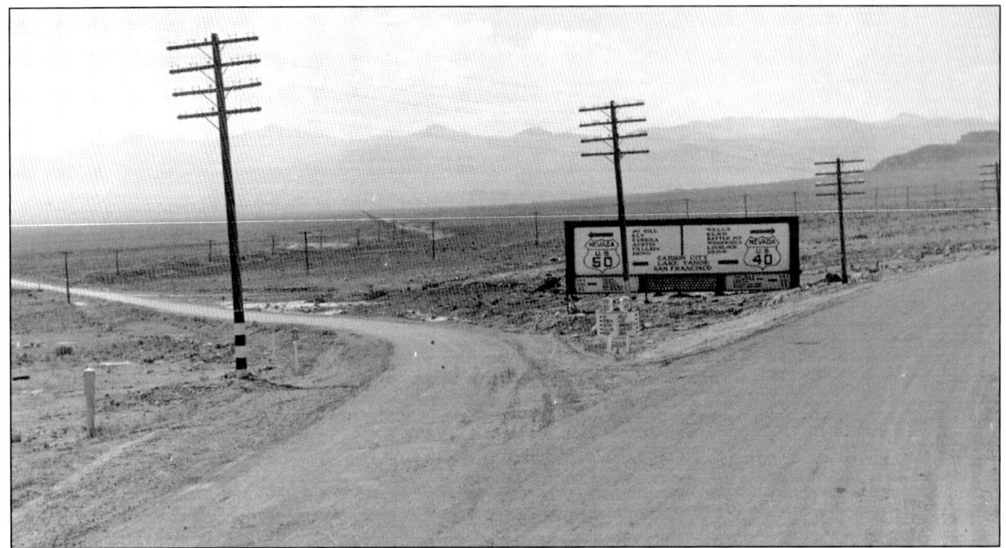

The fork in the road near Wendover directs westward travelers with easy-to-read, standardized signs. An earlier effort to mark the road can be seen at bottom left. The concrete post is a Lincoln Highway marker. Directional signs were crucial to navigation. With fewer than 92,000 people living in Nevada in 1930, there were few opportunities to ask for directions.

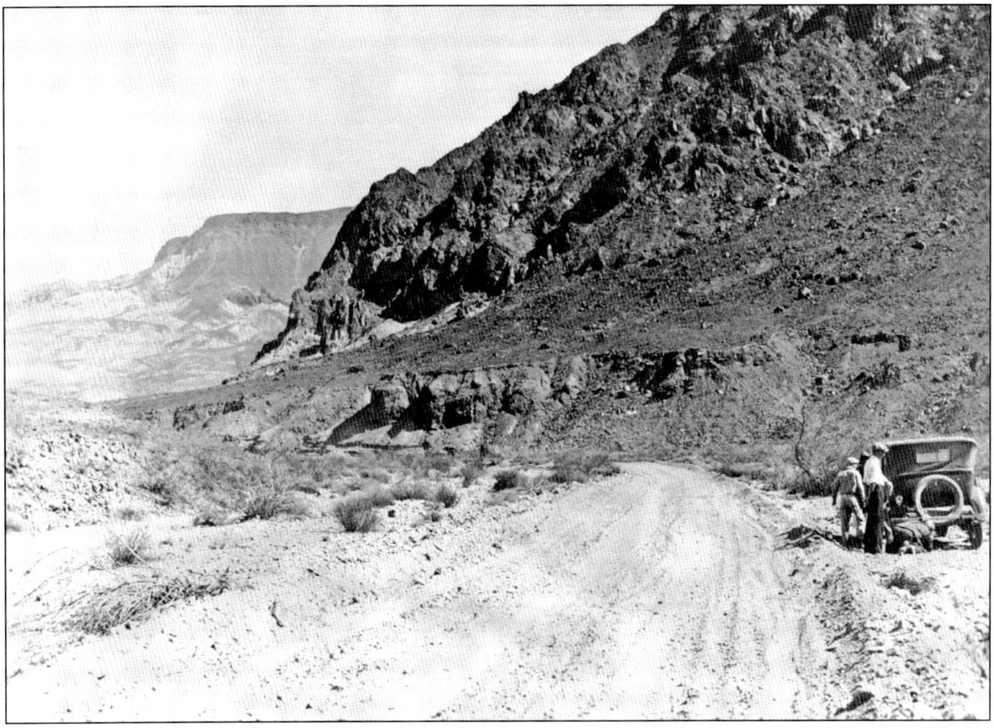

A tire change in southern Nevada was a frequent occurrence in the 1920s. Traveling from north to south in the Silver State was decidedly less straightforward than west-to-east travel. Branching roads eventually brought travelers through Nevada's southern settlements. Prior to the construction of Boulder Dam, there was not much incentive to go south. Clark County, home of Las Vegas, was not even included in the 1917 highway bill.

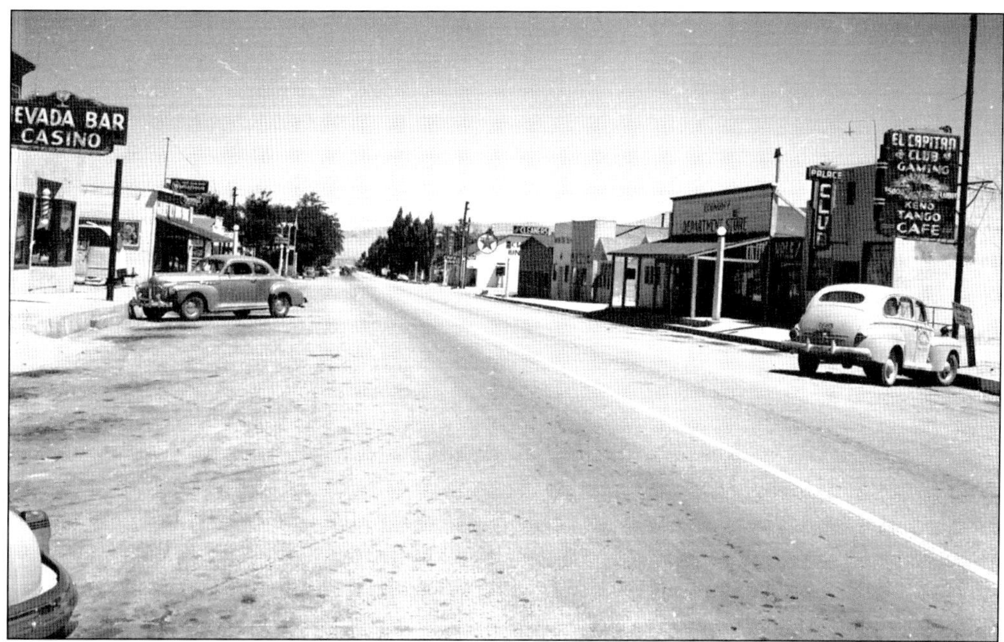

In the 1950s, Hawthorne on Route 3 offered a variety of cafés and clubs for travelers. But business was not open for everyone. Nonwhite travelers faced unique logistical problems. A number of annual travel guides were published to help African American tourists find auto courts, garages, restaurants, and gas stations that would serve them. One of the most popular guides was the *Negro Motorist Green-Book*, published from 1936 to 1966.

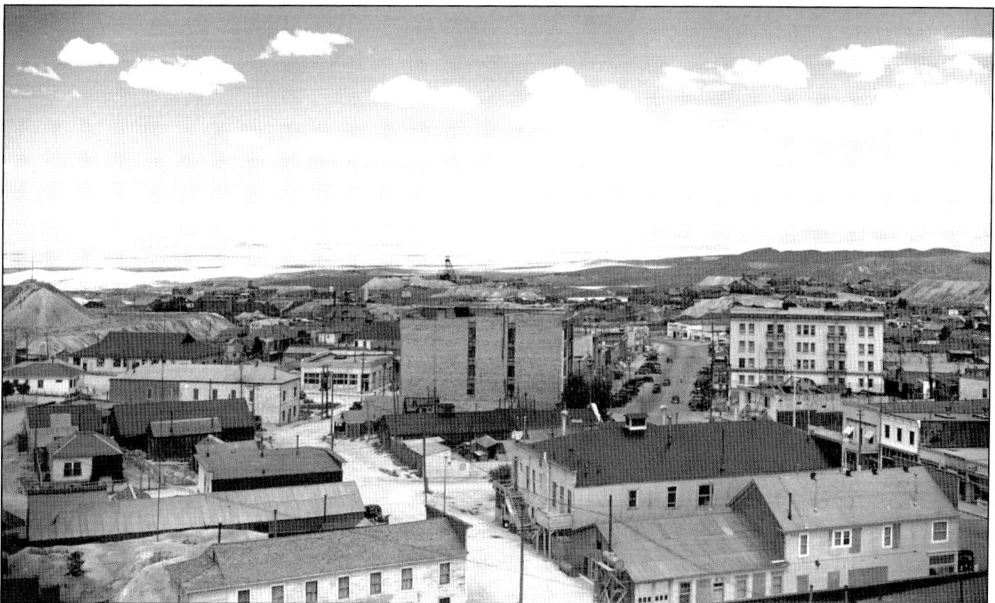

Tonopah in the 1960s still shows the haphazard town planning of a silver-mining town. Route 3 (US 95) is flanked by the five-story Mizpah Hotel on the right and the equally tall State Bank & Trust building on the left. The other streets meander according to the topography and the whim of the original town surveyor. Sometimes Nevada's highway alignments had to jog to line up with the main street of a preexisting town.

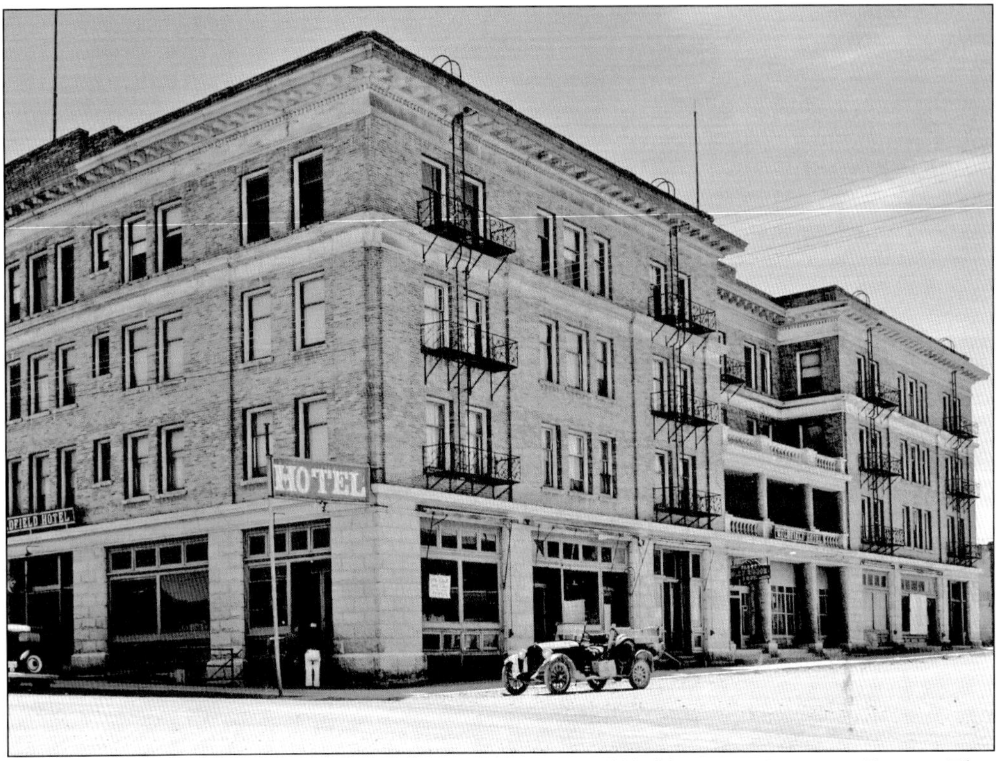

Route 3 joined Route 5 at Lida Junction and led from Goldfield to Las Vegas, via Beatty. This alignment was later subsumed by US 95. In the early 1900s, the Goldfield Hotel hosted early travelers and adventurers in lavish style. The road outside might have been little more than a rutted dirt path, but inside the hotel were crystal chandeliers, an elevator, gilded columns, and European chefs.

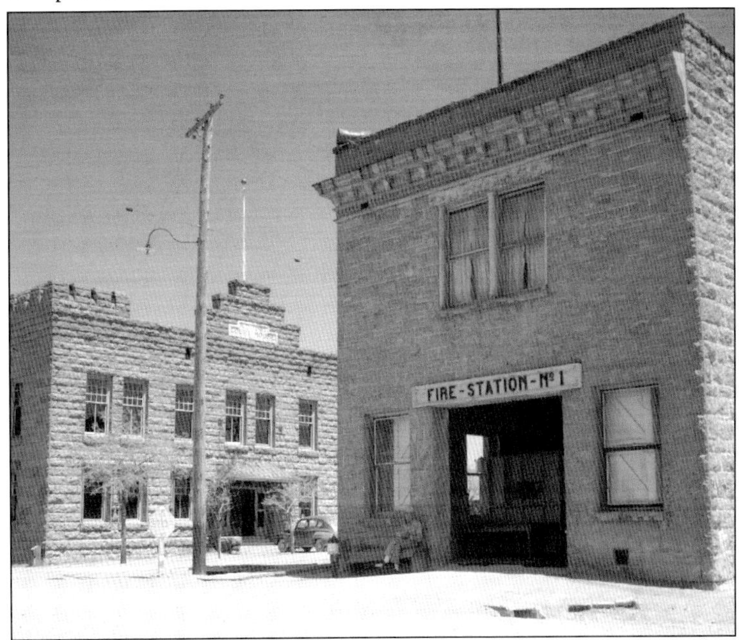

Route 5 (US 95) runs between the crenellated Esmeralda County Courthouse and the fire station, seen here in the 1960s. Streetlights in Goldfield amounted to a radial wave light fixture attached to utility poles, probably installed in the 1920s. From 1906 to 1910, Goldfield was the largest city in Nevada.

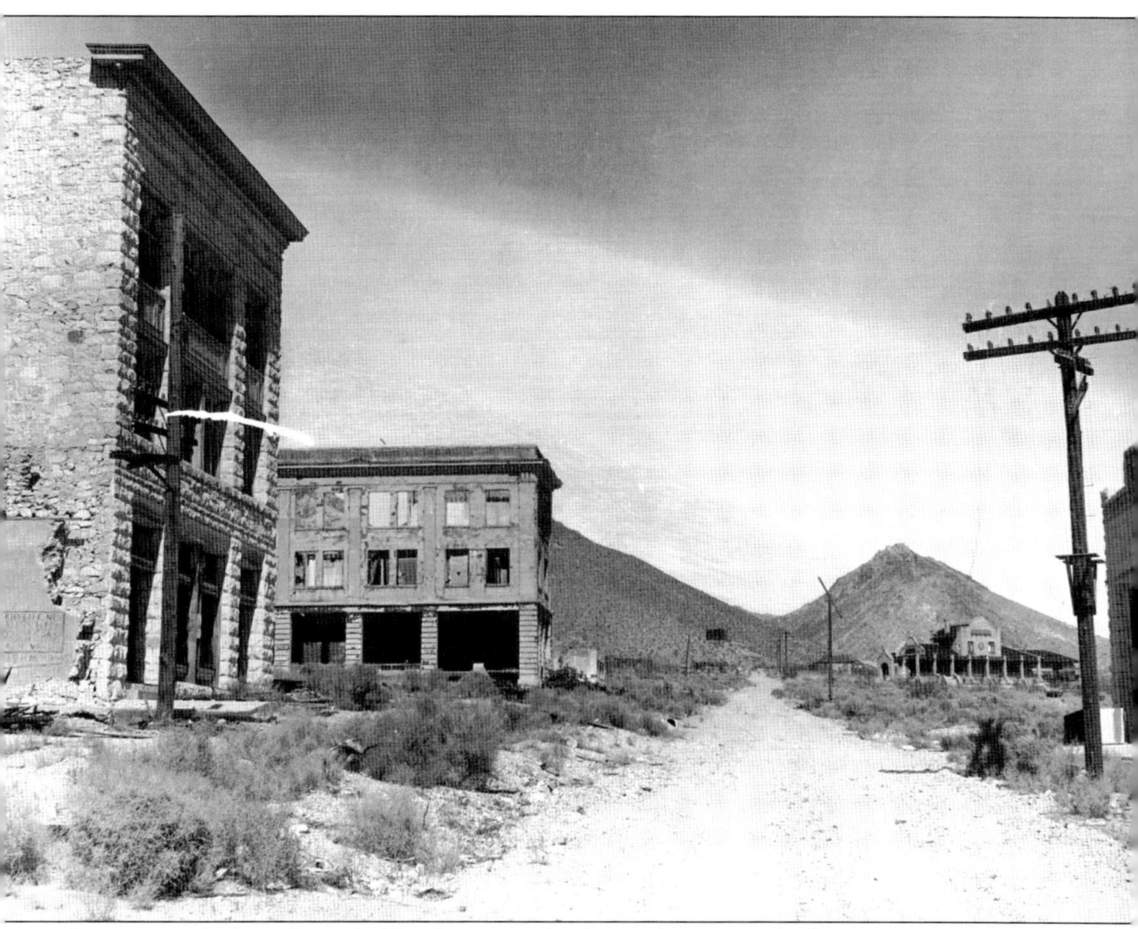

This is a view looking down Golden Street in Rhyolite in the 1960s. The boom-and-bust mining town, located west of Beatty, had been abandoned by 1920. On the left side of Golden Street stands the Overbury building in the foreground and the Cook Bank building in the background. On the right is the Porter building in the foreground and the Las Vegas & Tonopah Railroad depot in the background. Painted on the side of the Overbury building is the following graffiti: "RHYLITE [sic], NEV / PEERLESS 6 FROM / COAST TO COAST / THROUGH ENTIRE / DEATH VALLEY / CHAS. H NEWHAUS / DRIVER." On April 1, 1927, a newspaper article from the *Democrat & Chronicle* explained, "Newhaus of Philadelphia, spent a week in the dread spot with his Peerless six. Mr. Newhaus made the exploration as the climax to his fourteenth cross country trip."

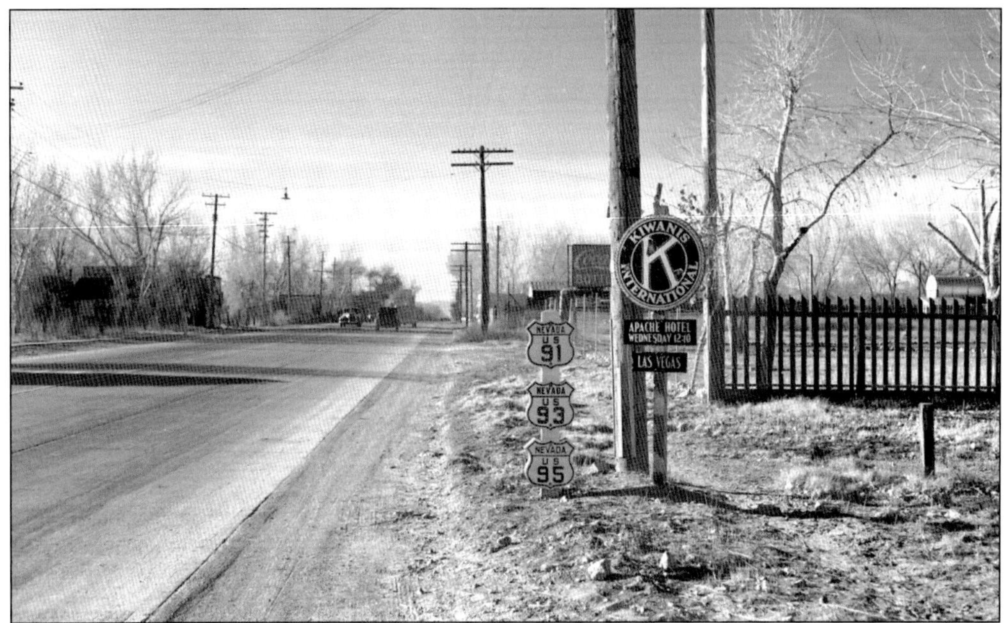

The juncture of US 91, US 93, and US 95 in Las Vegas was the forerunner of today's "Spaghetti Bowl." In the 1930s, the residents of Las Vegas, with a population of 5,165 people, could not fathom the tangle of concrete overpasses and underpasses that would occupy this site in the decades to come. By 1950, the population of the little desert town had swelled to 24,624, showing no sign of slowing down.

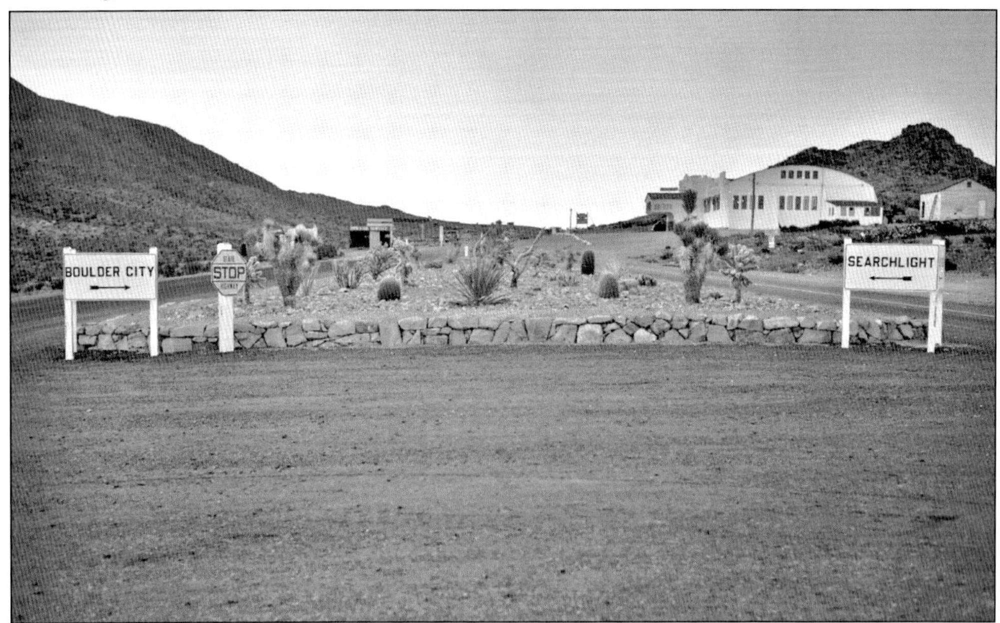

The Railroad Pass junction in Clark County features some of the highway department's new aesthetic landscaping with local barrel cactus, yucca, and Joshua trees. The Railroad Pass Casino, seen in the background, has been in operation since 1931. The same year, the Nevada legislature legalized gambling and lenient divorce laws in a creative effort to stimulate the struggling economy. Their strategy would change the future of Nevada.

Four

A Call to Duty
The Highway Department's Response to the Great World Wars

The Nevada Highway Department was a driving force in shaping Nevada's history, but the department itself was influenced by national and global events, sometimes with unanticipated results. America's belated entry into the Great War was an unexpected boon to the highway department. A stockpile of military trucks, surveying equipment, and field supplies that never saw action in the European Theatre were distributed to the state and beaten into "plowshares" that built roads. The incipient highway department had not been idling while waiting for funding, diverted because of World War I. They had been planning new routes, assessing the condition of the (barely) existing roads, and getting ready for the day when their preparation would pay off.

The period of optimism after the Great War was all too short-lived as the country soon faced another tragedy—the stock market crash of 1929. But the Great Depression, a time of sacrifice and suffering of so many people, was also a time of prolific road improvement. Government relief programs funneled money into road construction as a way to provide jobs and feed hungry families. The collaboration of the Civilian Conservation Corps (CCC), the Works Progress Administration (WPA), and the Nevada Highway Department was an incredible benefit to Nevada's people and roads.

The nation's economic revival started with the onset of World War II, but the war also put the brakes on highway work. The wartime slogan "Use it up—wear it out—make it do" applied to highways as well as darned socks and patched pants. Resources were once again diverted to the war effort, and that meant oil, asphalt, chemicals for paint, metal, machinery, and men were in short supply. Jolting along deteriorated roads during World War II was an act of home-front patriotism.

The "home front" reverted to "home" in the years after World War II, but it was a home that could never be the same as before the war. Atom bombs, baby boomers, and suburbs changed the culture of America. And the new interstate system changed the way Americans traveled, communicated, and lived. The highway department was an integral component in reshaping the physical and cultural landscape of Nevada.

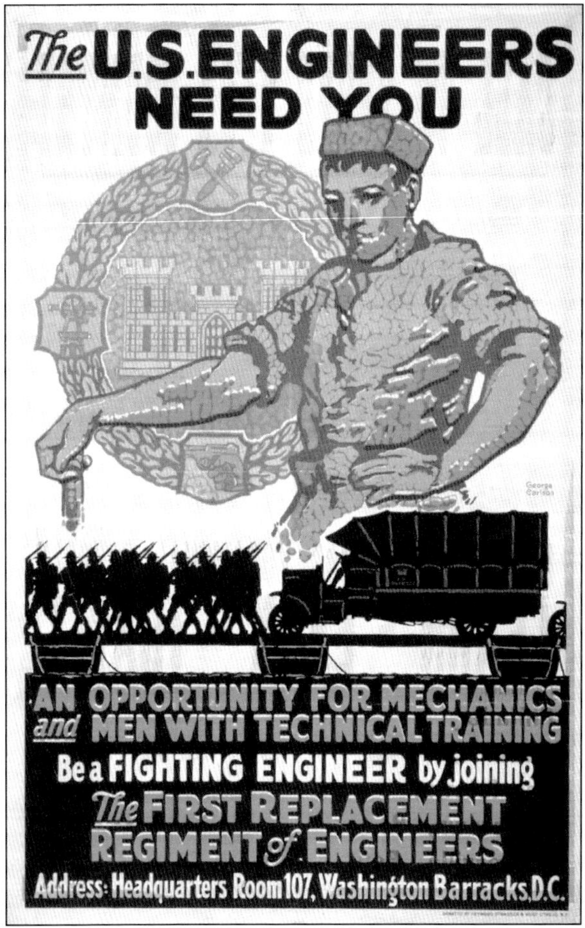

The very first highway department biennial report listed 18 employees who had left the department to enlist in the military. Of those 18 men, six were serving with the US Army Corps of Engineers, including the highest-ranking highway department employee, state highway engineer Robert K. West. (Courtesy of the Library of Congress.)

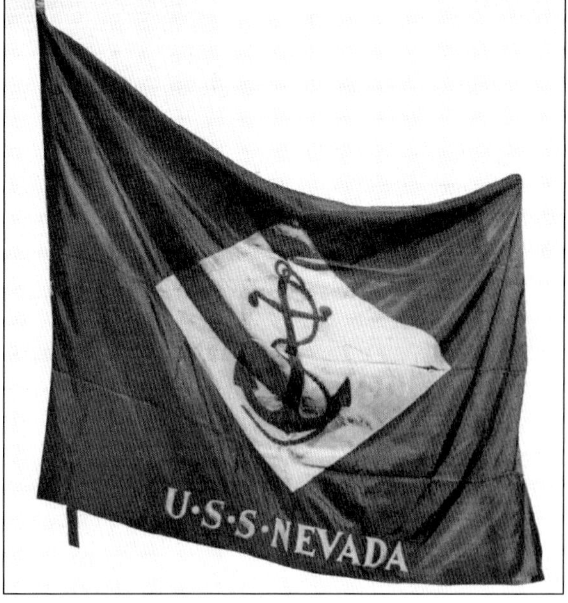

Before Dwight Eisenhower was a war hero and president, he was a 29-year-old major assigned to the 1919 Transcontinental Army Motor Transport Corps Convoy. The purpose of the convoy was to test the military's ability to mobilize across America. For two jarring months, 81 military vehicles drove from Washington, DC, to San Francisco. Their travel across Nevada's rough roads set the convoy a full day behind schedule.

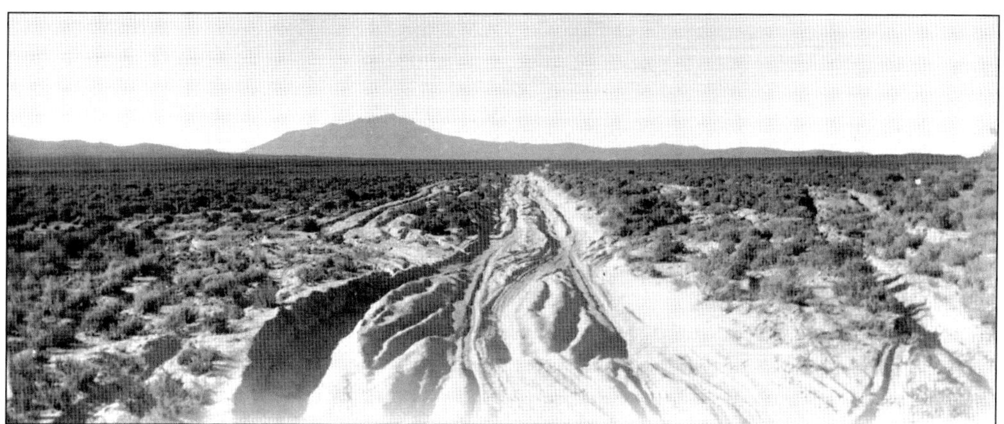

Eisenhower's experience crossing the country on rutted, washed-out stretches of road, like the one in Nevada pictured here around 1923, influenced his decision to support the National Interstate and Defense Highways Act, signed into law in 1956. The law funded the interstate highway system and transformed the American landscape.

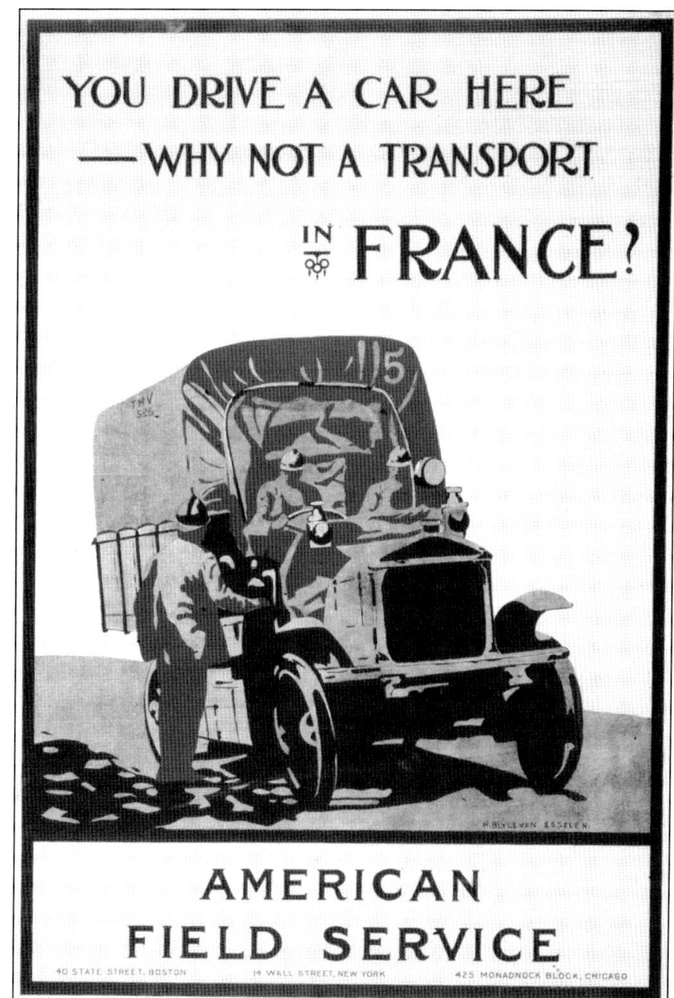

Uncle Sam wants drivers! Many Nevadans put their skills driving on rustic roads to good use for the war effort. After World War I, the military distributed surplus transport trucks, like the one pictured in this 1917 poster by artist H. Blyleven Esselen, to state highway departments. (Courtesy of the Library of Congress.)

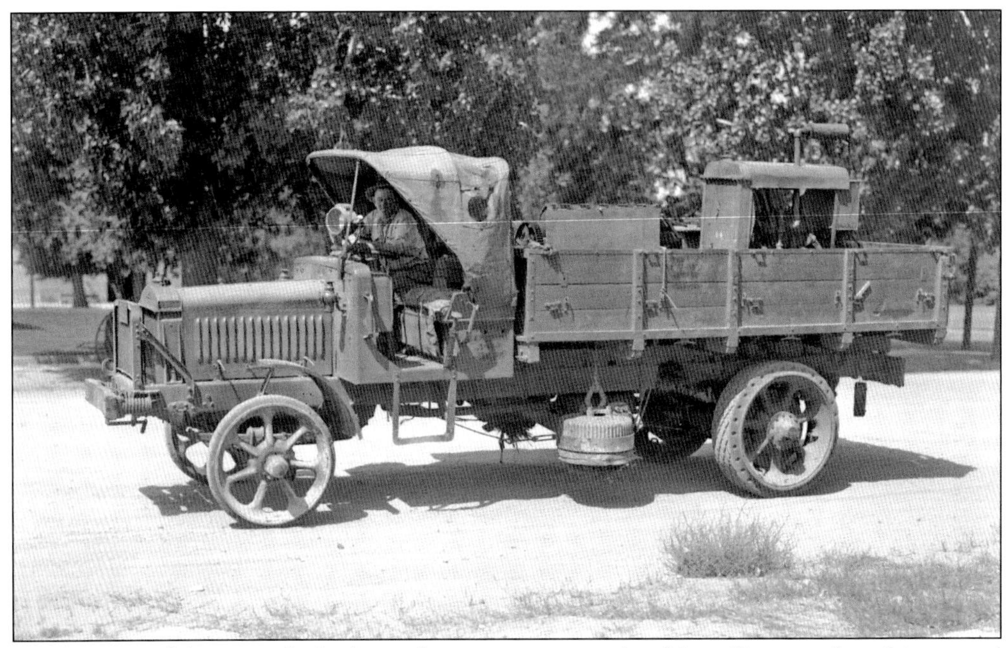

For the price of shipping, the highway department accumulated literally tons of machinery and equipment declared as surplus war material. Equipment was shipped from as far away as Long Island, New York, and included anything from small tools like axes and monkey wrenches to trucks, ambulances, and even entire hangar buildings. This surplus World War I truck was adapted to highway work with a large magnet for picking up metal debris on roads.

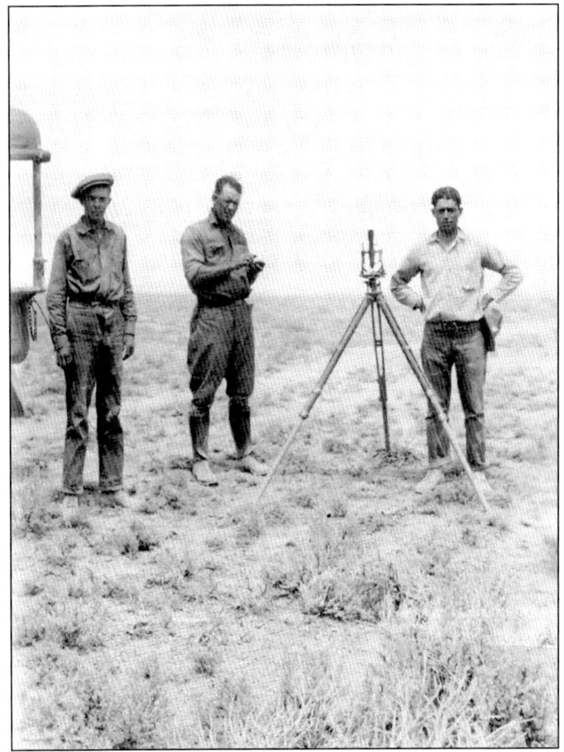

A survey crew is shown at work in the early 1920s. Road construction during World War I stopped before it had even gotten under way. The highway department focused on mapping potential routes instead. The 1938–1940 biennial report summarized the challenge faced by Nevada's early surveyors: "Probably in no State in the West were there more apparently fraudulent and erroneous surveys than in Nevada . . . In some areas these distortions were of such magnitude as to make an intelligent picturization impossible."

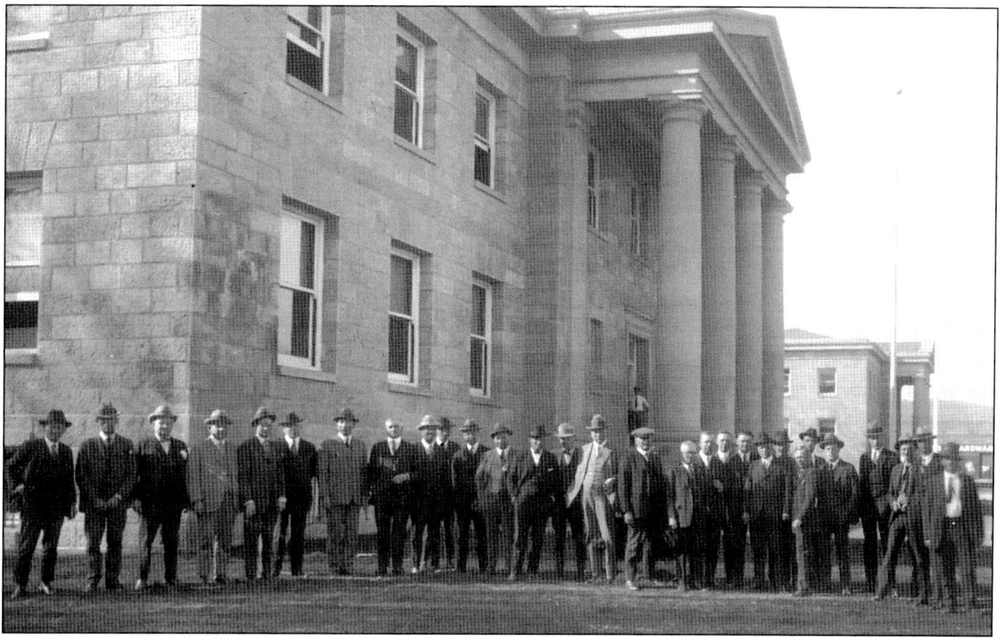

State highway department engineers pose in front of the Heroes Memorial Building in Carson City in the 1920s. Nevada's first and only state architect, Frederic Delongchamps, designed the building, which was dedicated to Nevada soldiers who had died in World War I. Offices for the highway department were housed there until a new headquarters building was finished in 1951.

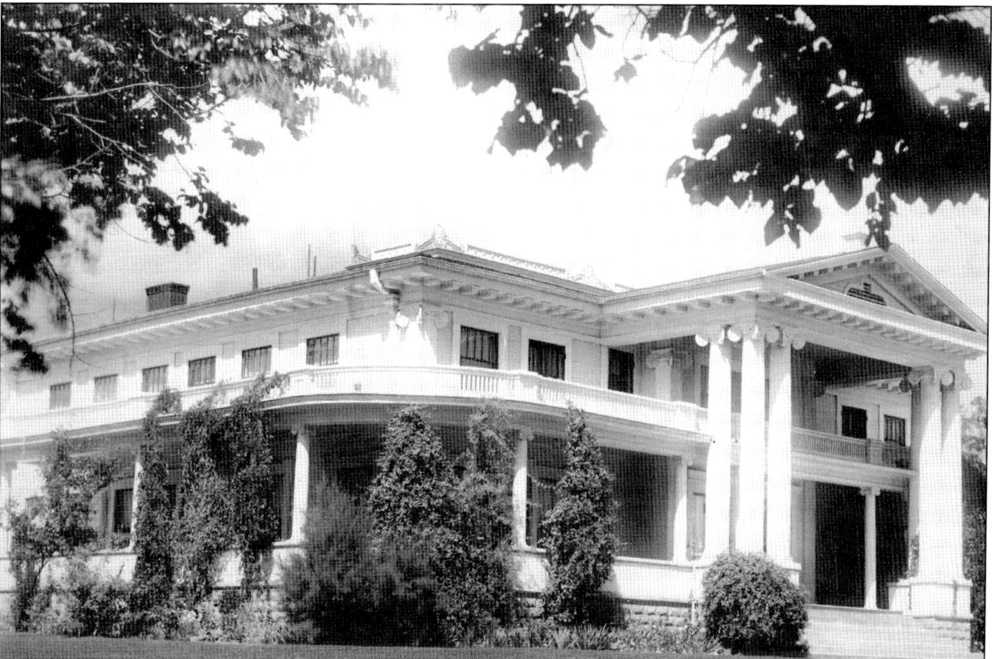

New Deal "alphabet soup" programs kept the highway department going during the Great Depression. In 1937, the WPA contributed $1,000 to grading and paving the street in front of the governor's mansion in Carson City. The cost to the state was only about $30. The WPA also made extensive repairs to the mansion itself, as it was falling into disrepair.

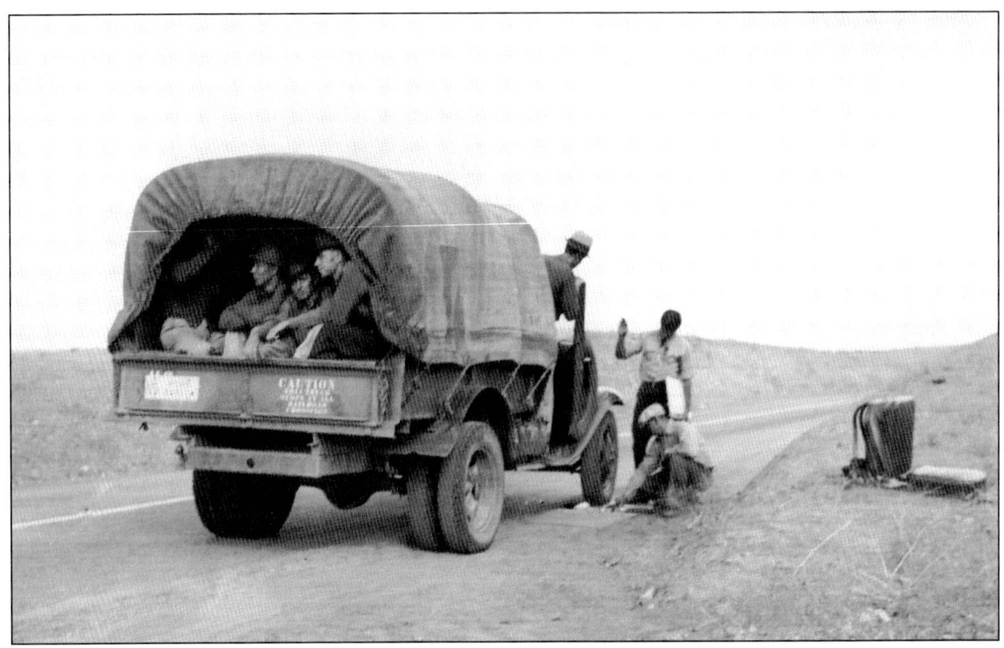

How much does a truckload of CCC workers weigh? Highway department workers are about to find out with the help of a Loadometer in 1936. The CCC and the highway department had a mutually beneficial relationship. The highway department provided training and equipment, and the CCC provided the manpower for many projects in Nevada.

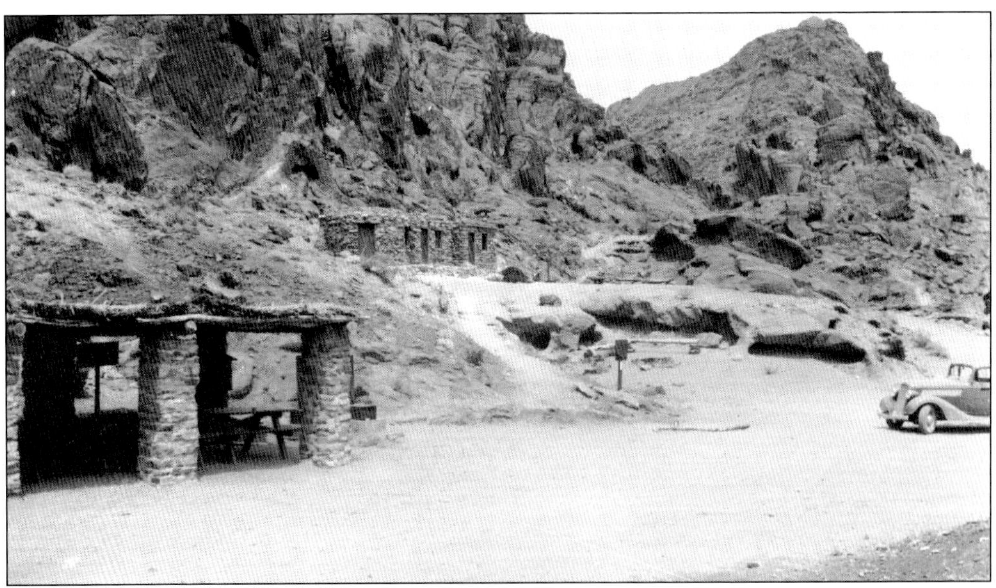

The CCC built the stone tourist cabin and picnic shelter in Nevada's first state park, Valley of Fire, in Clark County. Their handiwork is seen here in 1936, shortly after its construction. The new demographic of "auto-tourist" sought destinations, or at least a wayside stop, where they could be awed by nature. The red-and-orange sandstone formations in Valley of Fire State Park provided a million-dollar backdrop for budget-friendly camping vacations.

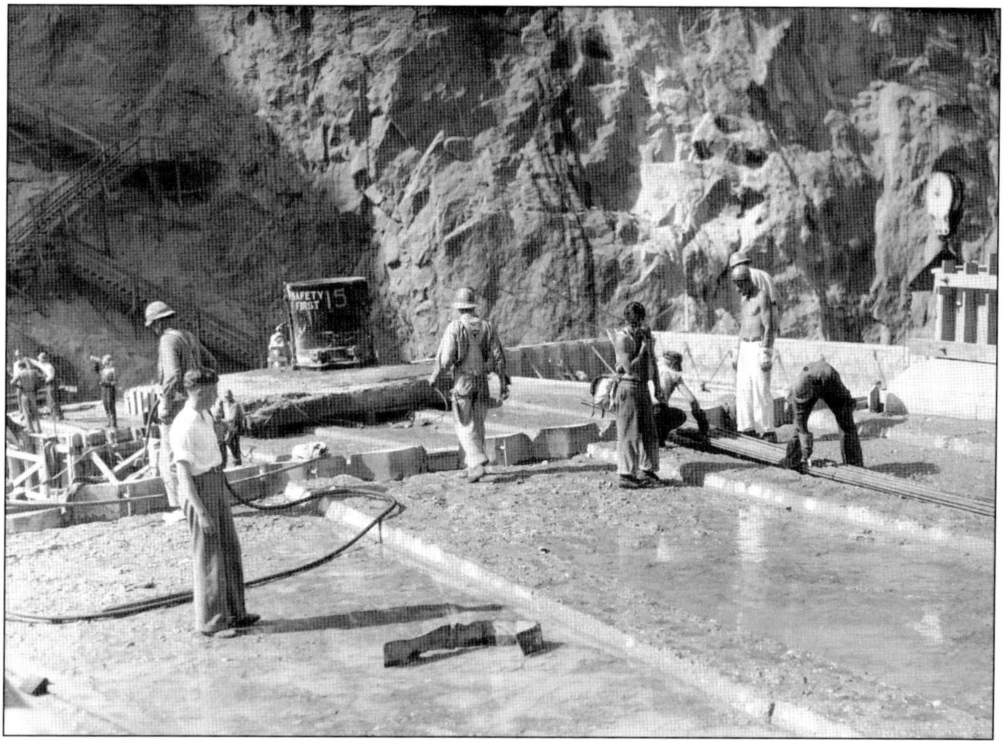

The influence of the Boulder Dam project on southern Nevada's development cannot be understated. When the country's largest federal construction project started in 1931, thousands of men trekked to the dam site hoping for employment. The population of the nearby former railroad town of Las Vegas exploded for the four years it took to build the colossal dam. After completion in 1935, it was tourists who trekked to experience the dam and Lake Mead. About 350,000 visited that first year.

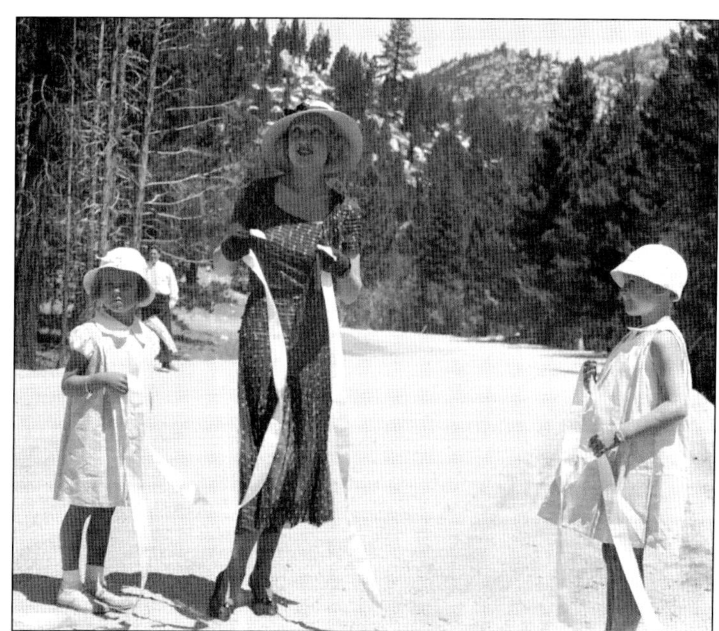

Silver screen star Carole Lombard adds style to the 1933 ribbon-cutting ceremony celebrating the opening of the Rim-of-the-Lake Highway in Tahoe, today known as Route 28. Her young assistants are six-year-old Hatherly Bliss, representing Miss Nevada, and eight-year-old Barbara Blake, representing Miss California. Lombard was living in Nevada at the time to gain residency for her divorce from actor William Powell.

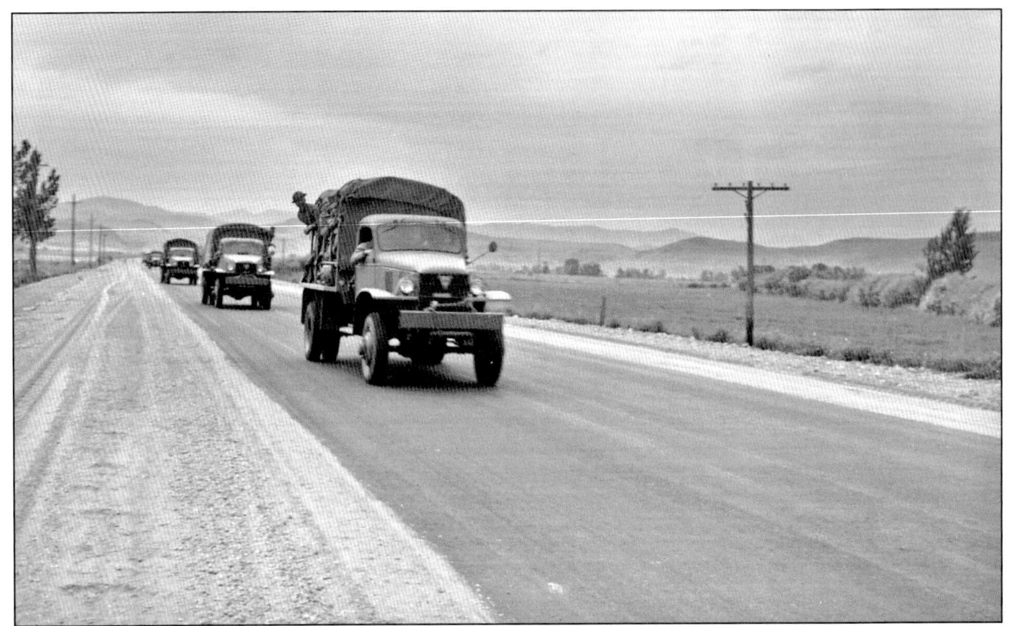

A World War II antiaircraft convoy travels through Nevada along asphalt roads—a significant improvement over the roads encountered during the 1919 Transcontinental Motor Convoy. The 1943–1944 highway department biennial was dedicated "to those very fine young men who have left this Department to go into the service of our Country, and with the sincere hope that they will all return to resume their duties with the Department as soon as the world is safe for decent-living people."

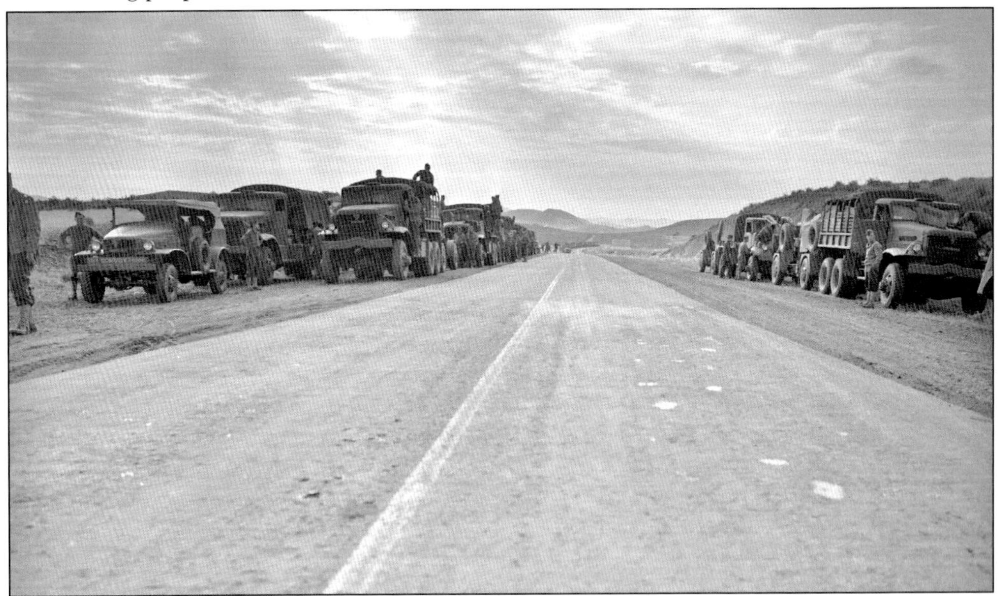

An antiaircraft convoy takes a break on newly widened shoulders in rural Nevada. The highway department widened shoulders specifically to accommodate military convoys. In 1941, the War Department designated 1,445.5 miles of rural roads and 26 miles of in-town roads as part of a system of military highways in Nevada. While other roads deteriorated, the military highways enjoyed maintenance and improvements funded by the federal government.

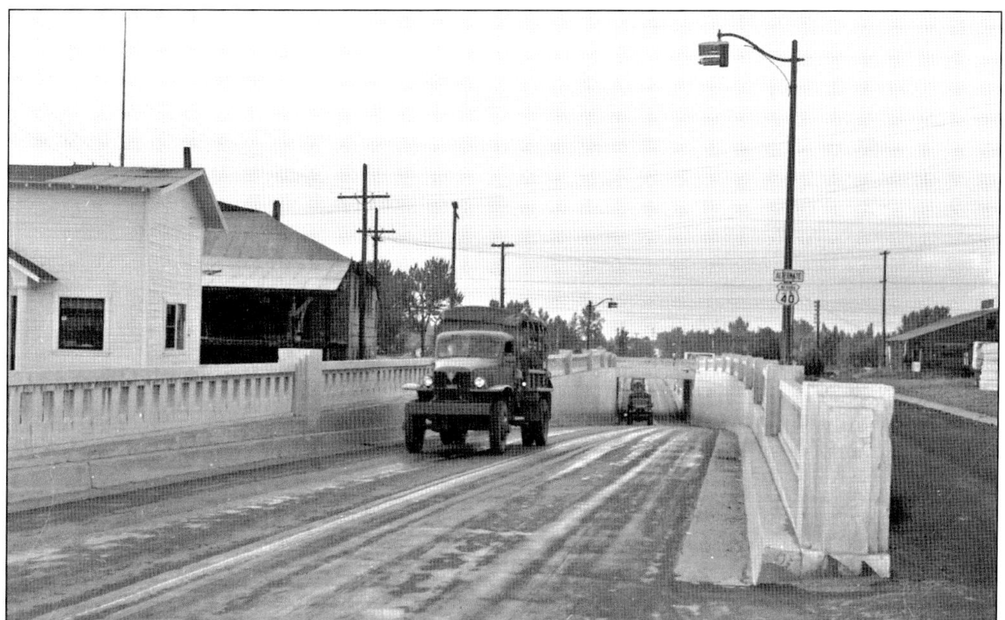

A military convoy passes through the Clark Avenue Underpass in Las Vegas in the 1940s. The underpass, the first of its kind in southern Nevada, eliminated a dangerous at-grade Union Pacific Railroad crossing. Several thousand people attended its opening ceremony in 1937. A particular matter of pride was the topic of the sodium-vapor streetlights that provided a "striking night view," according to the November 1937 edition of *Nevada Highways and Parks.*

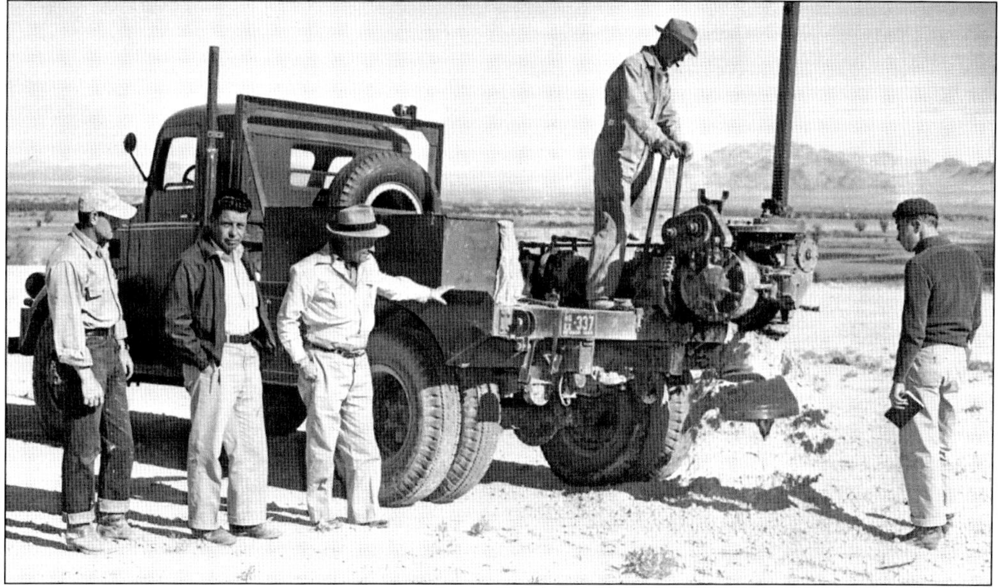

Engineers dig a test hole in February 1949. The highway department struggled to find and keep employees during and shortly after World War II. Skilled labor was drawn away to higher-paying work in federal agencies, defense plants, and the armed forces. From 1948 to 1950, the highway department experienced a phenomenal 75 percent turnover rate. Gov. Vail Pittman had recently passed the Nevada State Employees Retirement Act in 1947, hoping to provide an incentive for employees to stay with the state.

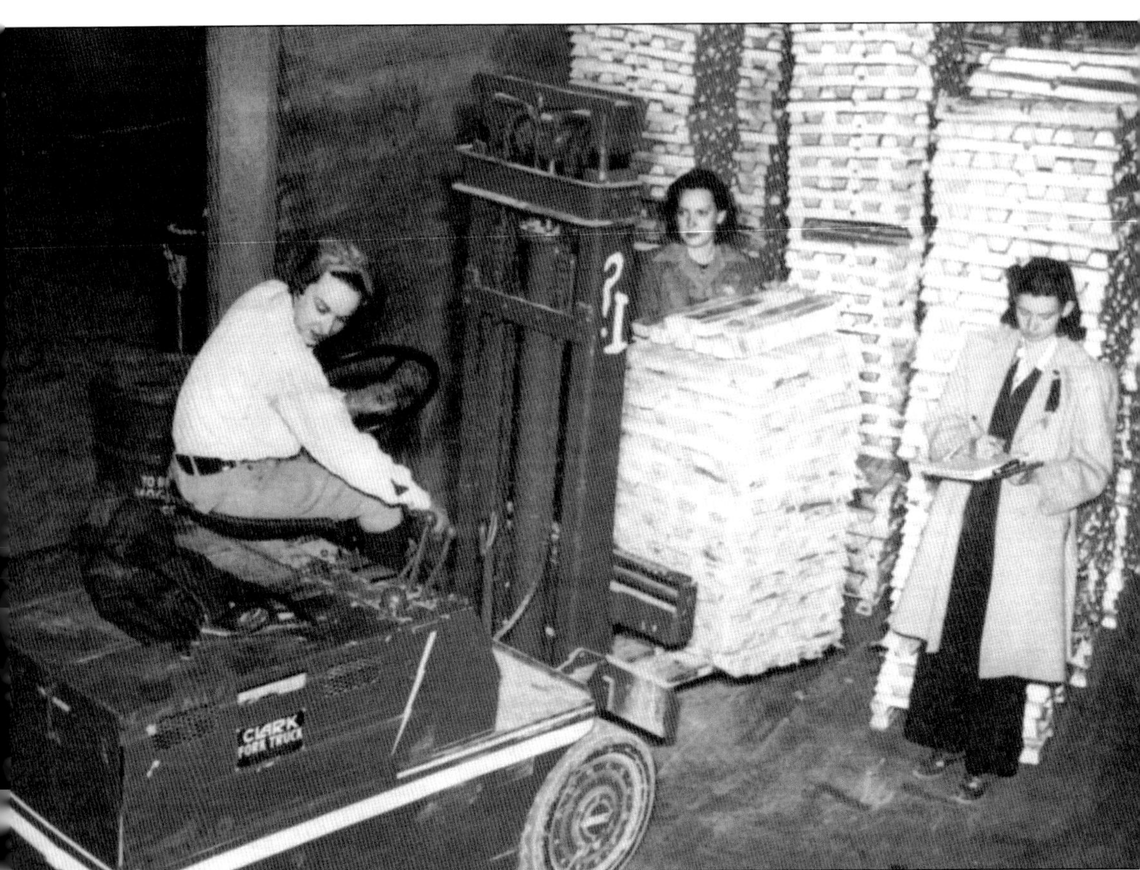

While the disruption in the social norm gave women the opportunity to work at many of what were traditionally male jobs, this was not generally true in the highway department. College education for women typically focused on home economics, secretarial skills, nursing, and teaching. Thus, it was difficult for women to become engineers, draftsmen, or cartographers when they were discouraged, or outright prohibited, from gaining the education needed for these positions. That did not mean, however, that the women of Nevada shirked their duty. To the contrary, while the nation and the world had Rosie the Riveter, Nevada had Magnesium Maggie. Thanks to magnesium-rich deposits near Gabbs, officials built a processing plant called Basic Magnesium Incorporated (BMI) in southern Nevada. When America entered the Second World War, magnesium was a highly sought-after commodity known as "the wonder metal." The BMI plant processed a huge volume of magnesium during the war and many women, such as those pictured here, worked in the plant, operating heavy equipment and keeping the plant functional.

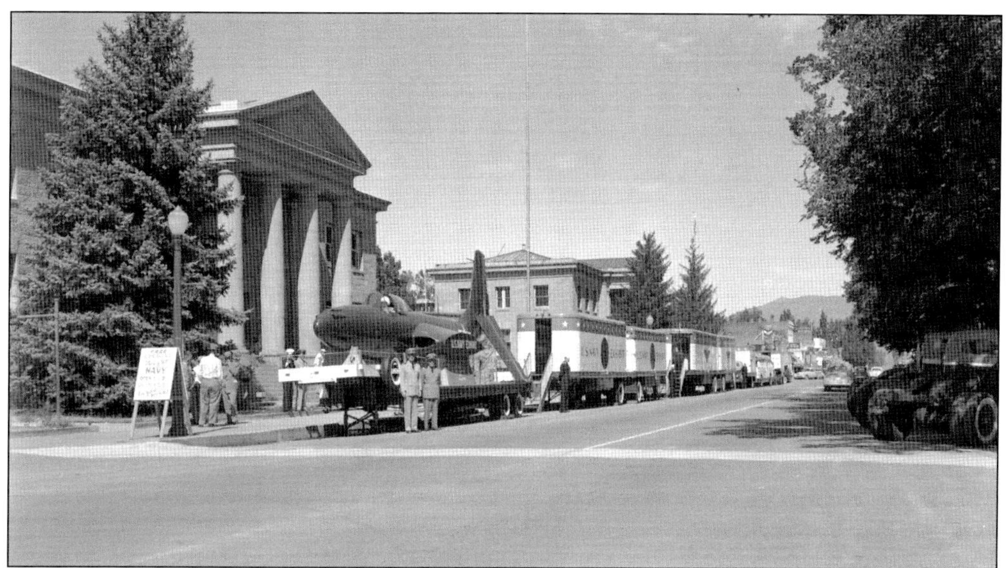

Here, the US Navy puts on a free exhibit along Carson Street in Carson City in September 1951. The Heroes Memorial Building at left housed the highway department offices. In 1944, of the 169 highway department employees serving with the active forces, two were women—Alice Nelson and Elvera Wollitz. As the first woman to work as a right-of-way attorney at the highway department, Wollitz served her country during World War II with the Navy's Judge Advocate General (JAG) Corps.

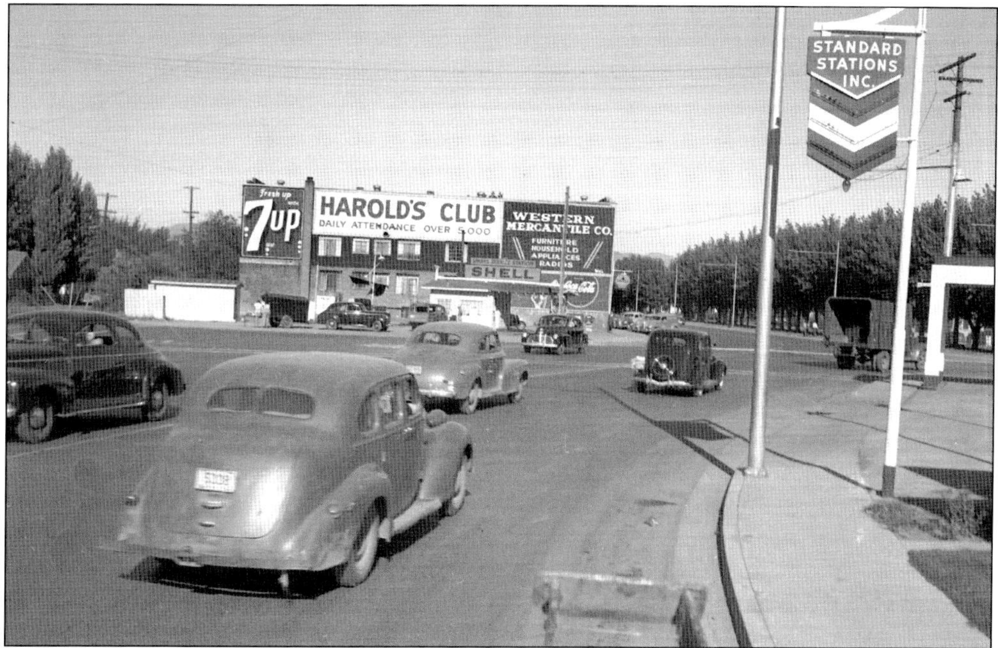

Reno traffic buzzes past a gas station in the 1940s. Strict rations of gasoline and rubber curbed driving for fun. Propaganda posters warned reckless citizens that "pleasure trips" were unpatriotic and that driving alone instead of with a car-sharing club was equal to giving Hitler a lift. Tire rations limited people to four tires per passenger car, plus a spare. Any additional stockpiled tires had to be sold to the government.

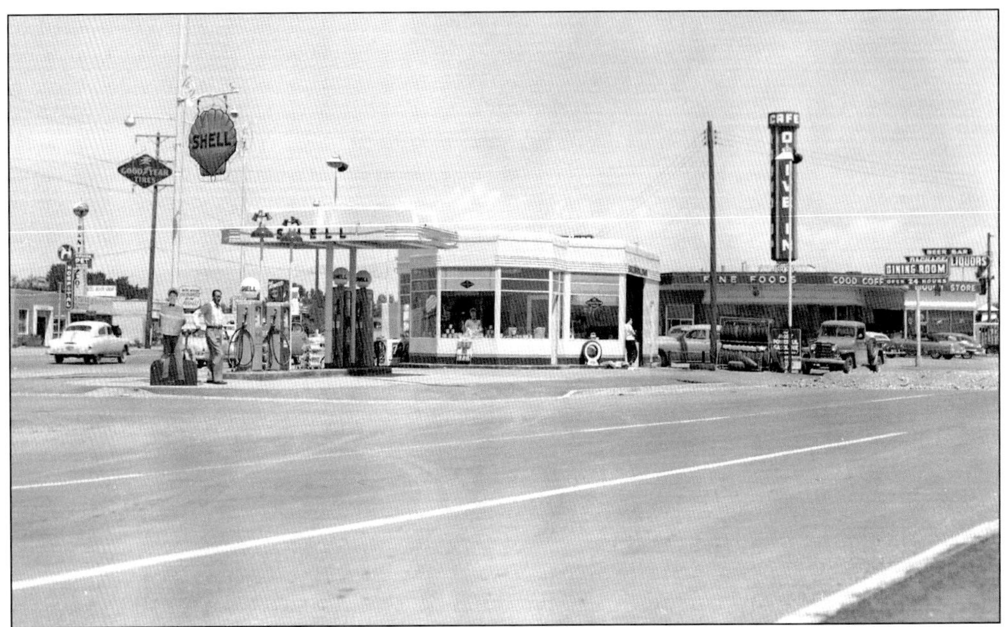

This photograph shows a Shell gas station in Las Vegas. The October 20, 1942, edition of the *Nevada State Journal* warned car owners, "If you or any member of your household, related to you by blood, marriage, or adoption, has more than five tires per passenger car after Nov. 22, you will be denied the privilege of using gasoline in any passenger car you own." The local rationing board enforced the rule by confiscating ration books of violators who failed to file a tire record form.

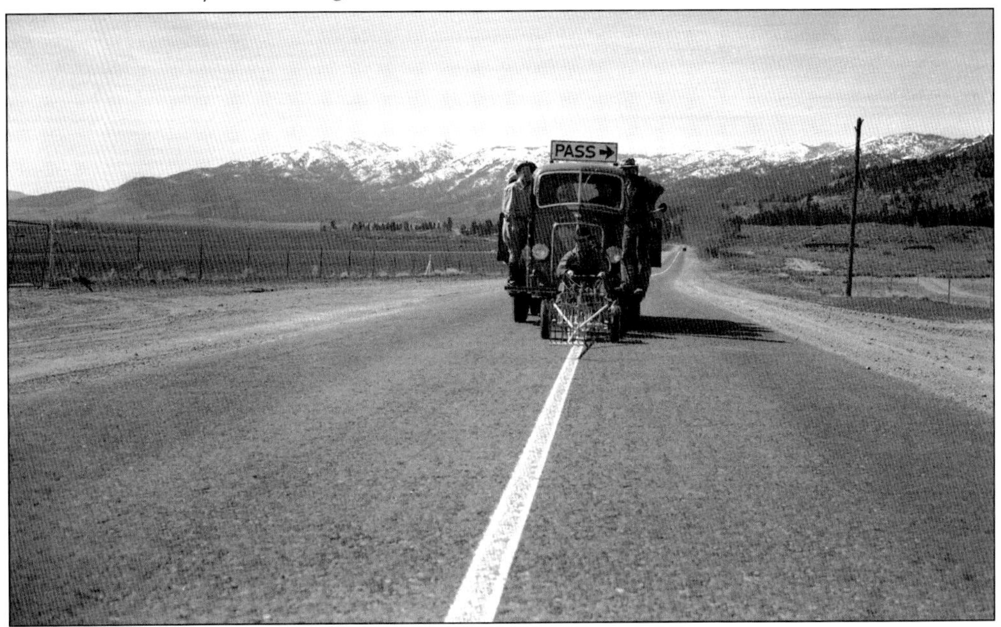

Here is a striping crew at work in 1941. World War II shortages of the chemicals and minerals needed to make paint soon led to the familiar dashed line that runs down highways today. Prior to the 1940s, centerlines were solid and used over twice the amount of paint. The dashed line was an ingenious solution to save paint during wartime rationing. Dashed lines had the added advantage of helping drivers judge their speed.

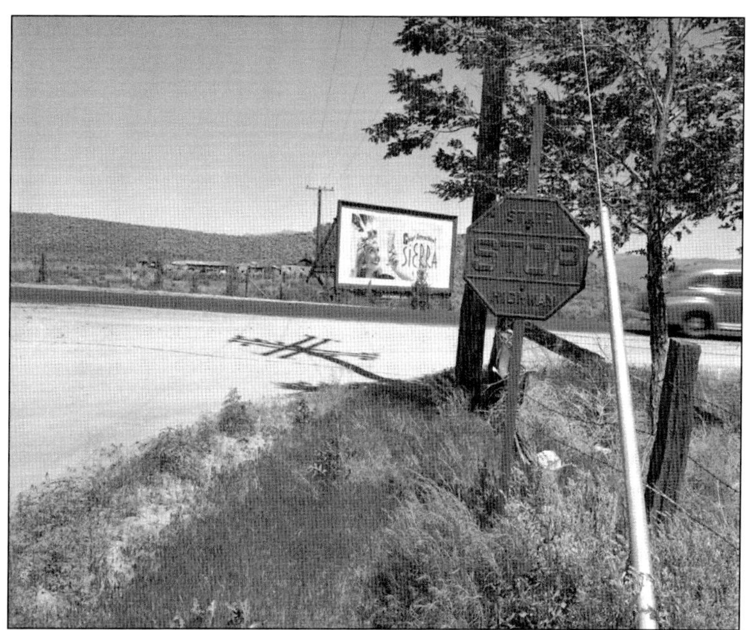

This worn-out stop sign was photographed in Lyon County in 1949. If wartime shortages of paint and metal for new signs had not been a factor, this sign would have been painted yellow with black lettering. Nevada did not adopt the iconic red color for stop signs until 1954. The highway department estimated it would take about five years before all the yellow stop signs could be replaced.

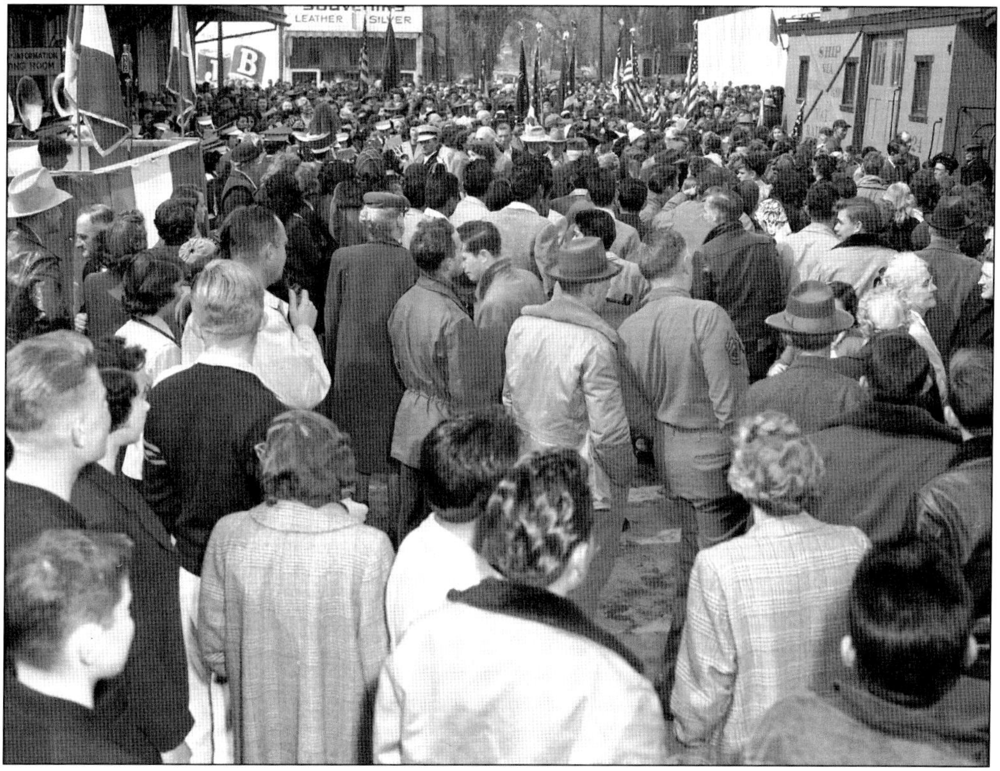

Crowds gather to see the French Merci Train arrive in Carson City on February 23, 1949. After the war, the American people conducted a nationwide food drive to gather grain, canned food, and supplies to distribute to famished European families. The goods were collected by the Friendship Train that traveled from Los Angeles to New York, where the cars were then shipped to Europe. Nevada's only stop on the Friendship Train's route was in Reno.

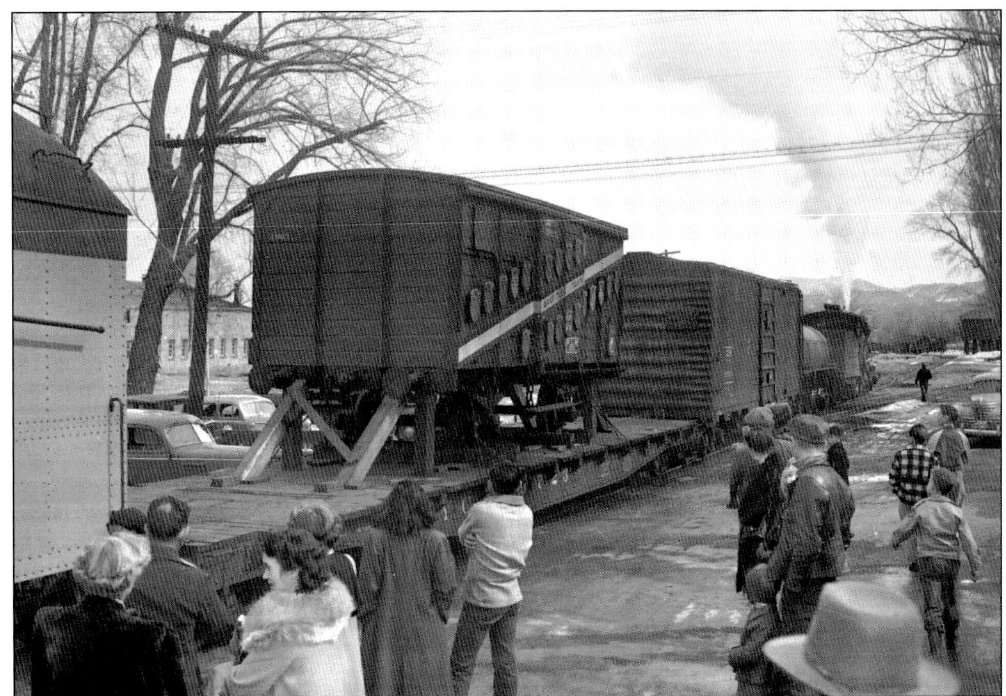

The highway department volunteered its staff and trucks to collect food donations from all over the state and deliver them to Reno for loading onto the American Friendship Train bound for shipment to Europe. In 1949, France showed its appreciation by sending each state a boxcar packed with gifts from individual citizens. Nevada's boxcar arrived by train at the Virginia & Truckee Railroad depot in Carson City.

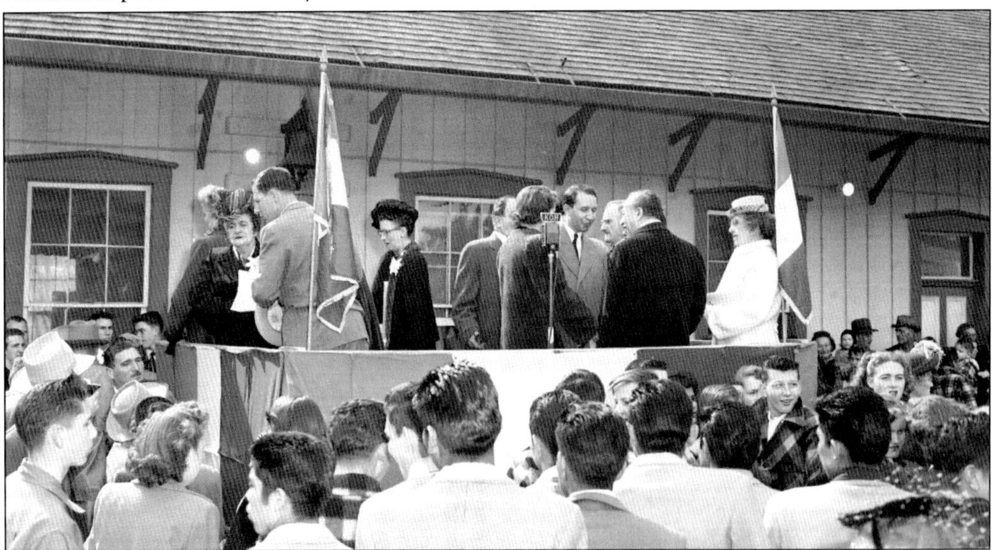

Bands from the Stewart Indian School and the Carson High School and enthusiastic crowds greeted the arrival of the Merci boxcar from France. Nevada's boxcar contained toys, handmade crafts, photographs, art, antiques, military medals, thank-you notes, and hundreds of other tokens of deep gratitude to the American people. The Merci boxcar has been restored and is now on display at the Nevada State Railroad Museum in Carson City.

Schoolchildren were integral to the success of the American Friendship Train. Classes organized food drives and went door-to-door collecting canned goods. Thanks to their efforts and highway department trucks for transport, Nevadans were able to donate two boxcars packed with much needed supplies for European families. Gov. Vail Pittman (back row, second from right) honored the important role that Nevada's children played during this ceremony held in his Carson City office on May 10, 1949.

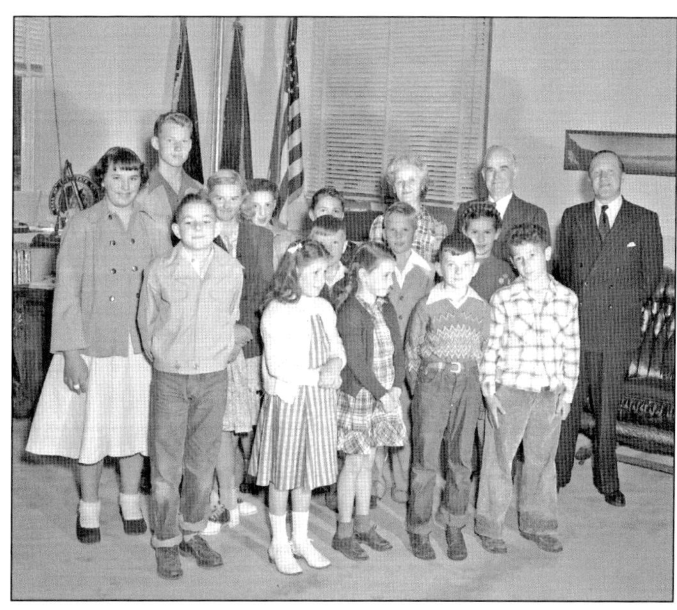

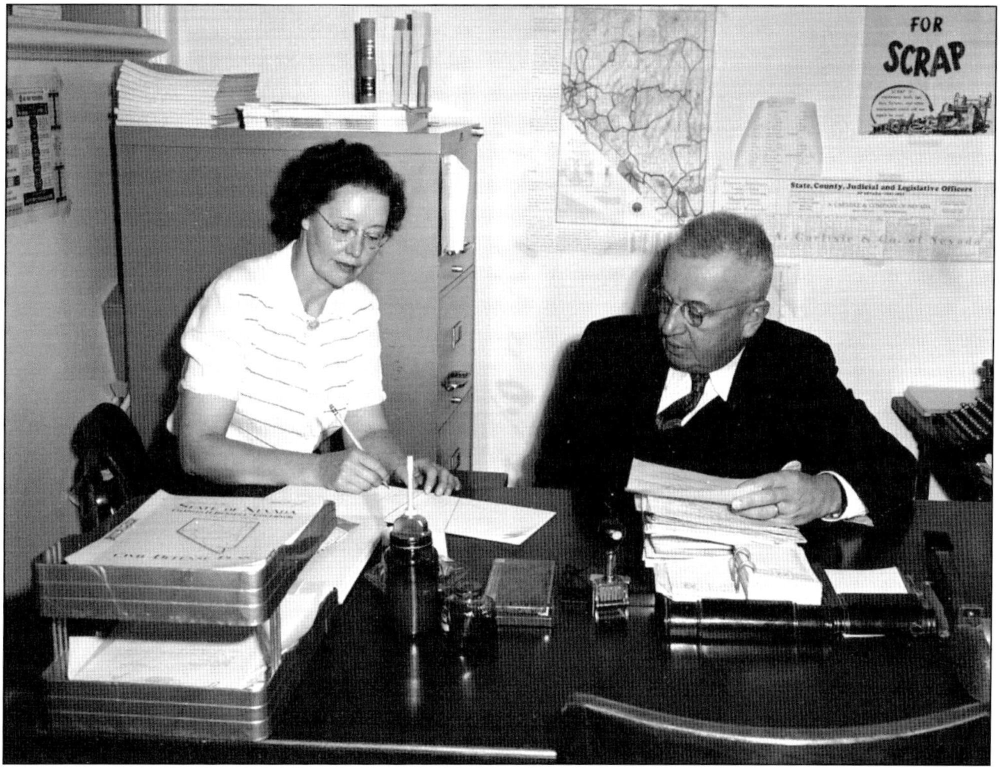

A "Look for Scrap" poster and air raid instructions decorate the office of Nevada's civil defense director, C.A. Carlson Jr. The war was over when the highway department staff photographer snapped this picture in 1951, but definitely not forgotten. The Office of Civil Defense was responsible for preparing civilians for military attacks and natural disasters. One of its more memorable contributions was duck-and-cover drills in which schoolchildren practiced shielding themselves from an atomic blast by hiding under their desks.

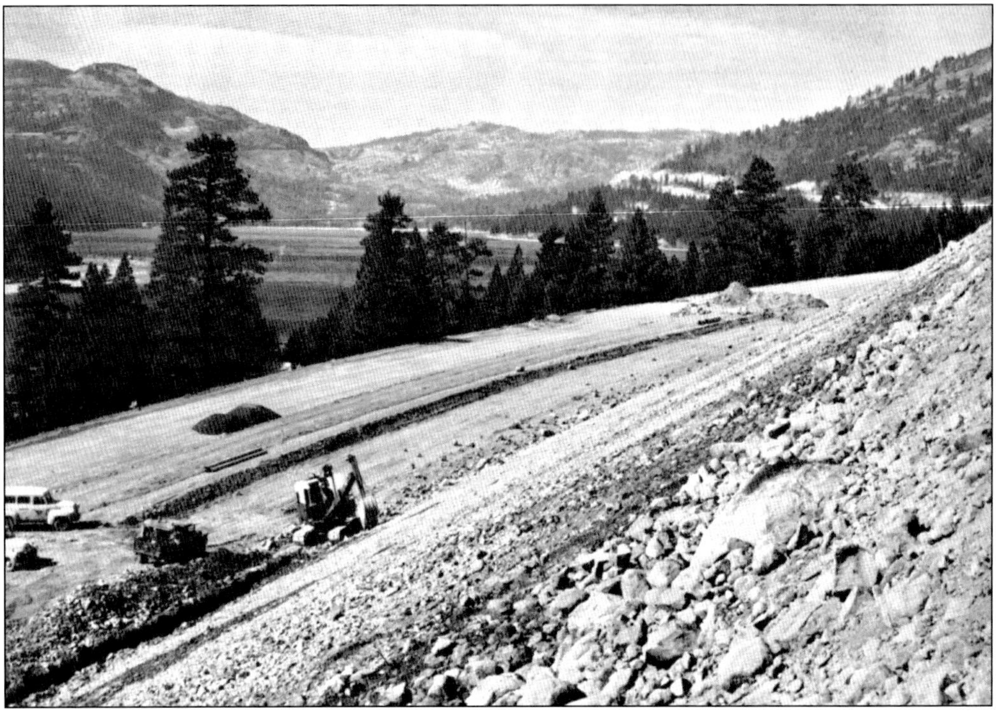

The National Defense Highway System was not just for defense. It was a boon to businesses and improved the daily lives of citizens. But defense was never far from the minds of its advocates. At his 1955 State of the State address, Nevada governor Charles Russell declared, "It is imperative that segments of this [interstate] system joining Nevada with California be completed as rapidly as possible. This is necessary to provide facilities for evacuation of our neighbors from heavily populated coastal areas in event of disasters."

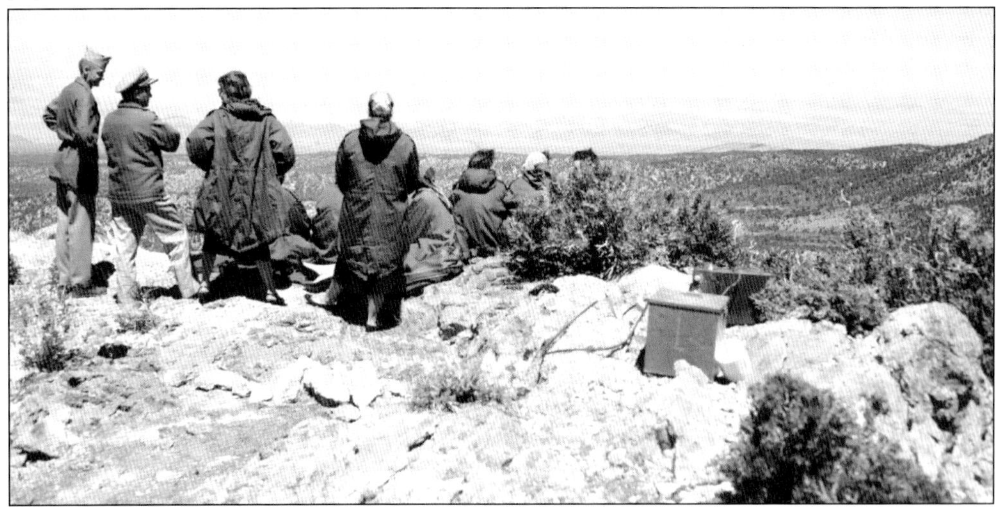

On March 17, 1953, in Yucca Flats, Nevada, the Atomic Energy Commission staged the first public demonstration of an atomic blast. The event was dubbed "Observation Shot," and about 600 observers were invited to witness the explosion. Observers included military personnel, governors, representatives from the civilian defense programs for every state, and highway department photographer Adrian Atwater, along with radio, television, and print media.

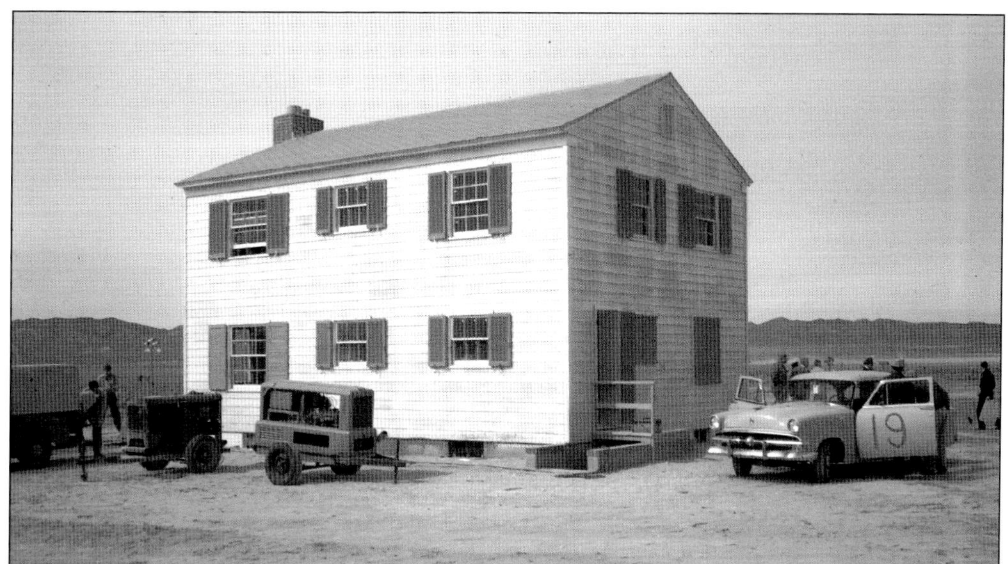

A bus caravan from Las Vegas brought the observers to inspect the "Doom Town" houses before the blast. Two houses had been built. One was located 3,500 feet from the tower that would drop the atomic bomb, and the second house (pictured here) was located 7,500 feet away from ground zero. House No. 2 was fully furnished and inhabited by a family of ill-fated mannequins. The lucky mannequins were placed in the basement fallout shelter.

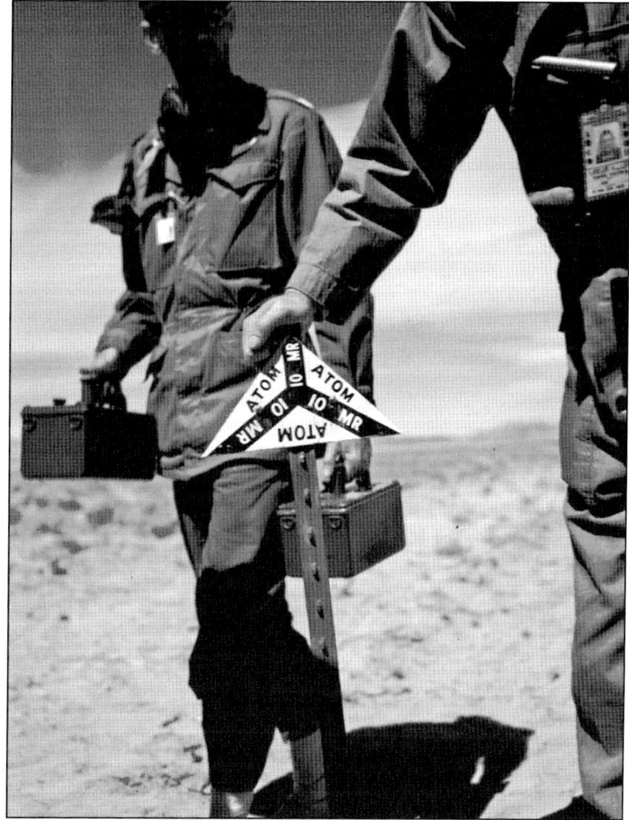

At dawn, four hours after the detonation, Atomic Energy Commission personnel monitor radiation levels with Geiger counters. Safety gear consisted of coveralls, a hat, and booties over their boots. The June–December 1953 edition of the *State Highways & Parks* magazine provided road-trippers with the following reassurance: "There is no danger to travel over Nevada highways from radioactive 'fall out particles.' "

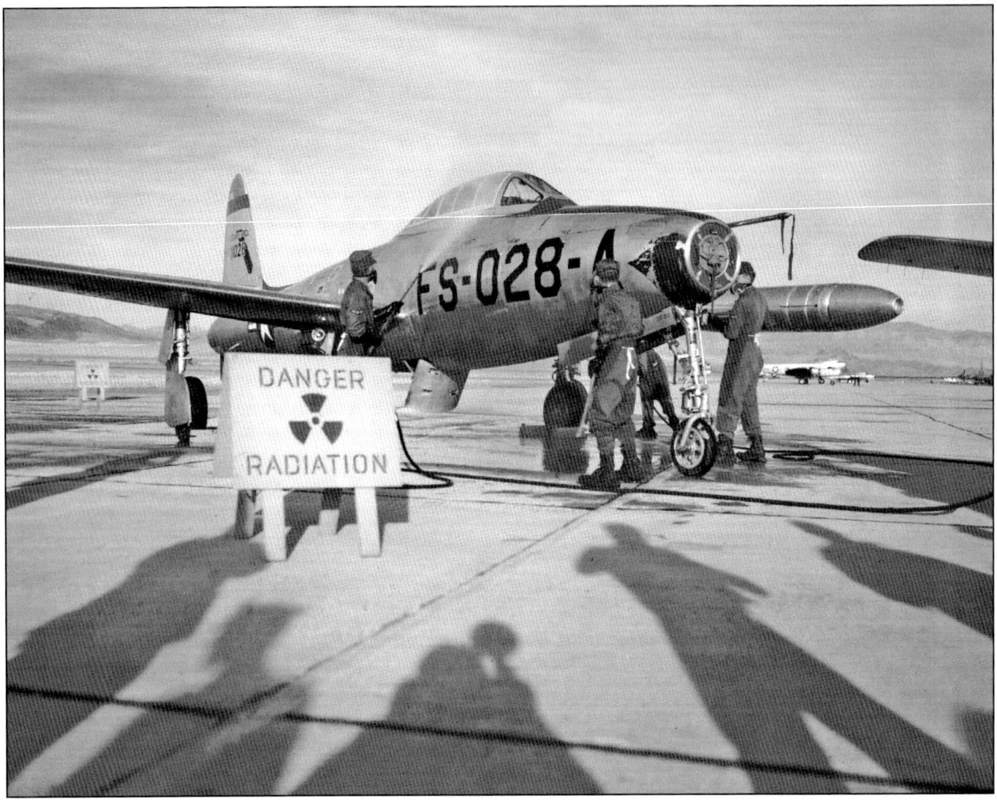

Indian Springs airfield personnel scrub down a radioactive plane after an atomic test. Planes were stationed at Indian Springs, about 20 miles away from Yucca Flats, and protected from fallout by a mountain range. Some A-bombs were detonated by dropping them from a tower, as in the Observation Shot test, while other tests dropped a bomb from a plane. Once, a missile was shot from an atomic canon.

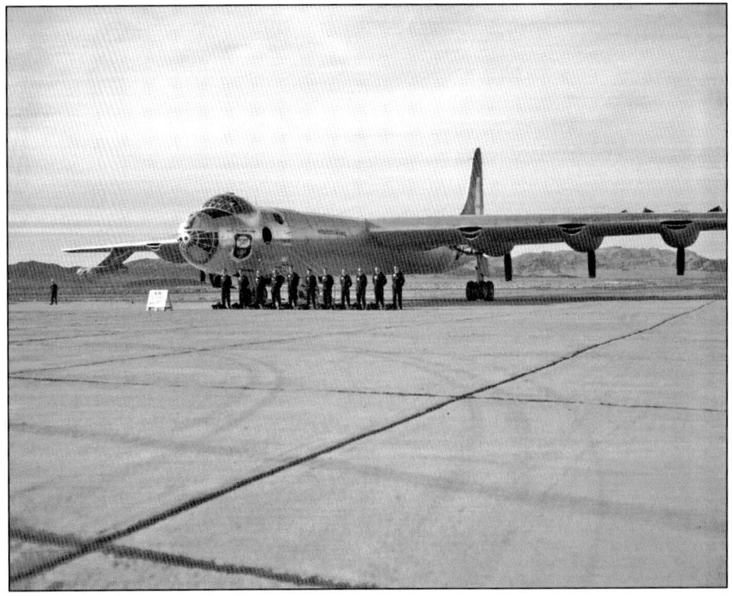

A B-36 is on display at Indian Springs airfield in the early 1950s. The company town of Mercury, about 20 miles north of Indian Springs via US 95, was the gateway to the Nevada Test Site through which all workers had to pass. Most workers preferred to commute from Las Vegas rather than live in Mercury; thus, the highway department expanded US 95 to four lanes between Mercury and Las Vegas.

Five

Nevada's Department
Community Involvement and Seminal Works

With the mission of "providing a better transportation system for Nevada through unified and dedicated efforts," the highway department has often worked toward the public good in ways more subtle than simply building a road. Historically, the department has been involved with assuring motorist comfort, assisting with public works programs, protecting community history, and assisting communities threatened by natural disasters. The department has also been tasked with creating the best travel routes through the Silver State and has had to engineer and construct some truly remarkable structures. Despite its utilitarian nature, road infrastructure has become part of our popular culture and community identity. The authors would like to close this book by highlighting the Nevada Highway Department/NDOT's nearly 100-year commitment to and involvement with the community, some of its impressive engineering feats, and those iconic roadworks that define the Nevada transportation landscape.

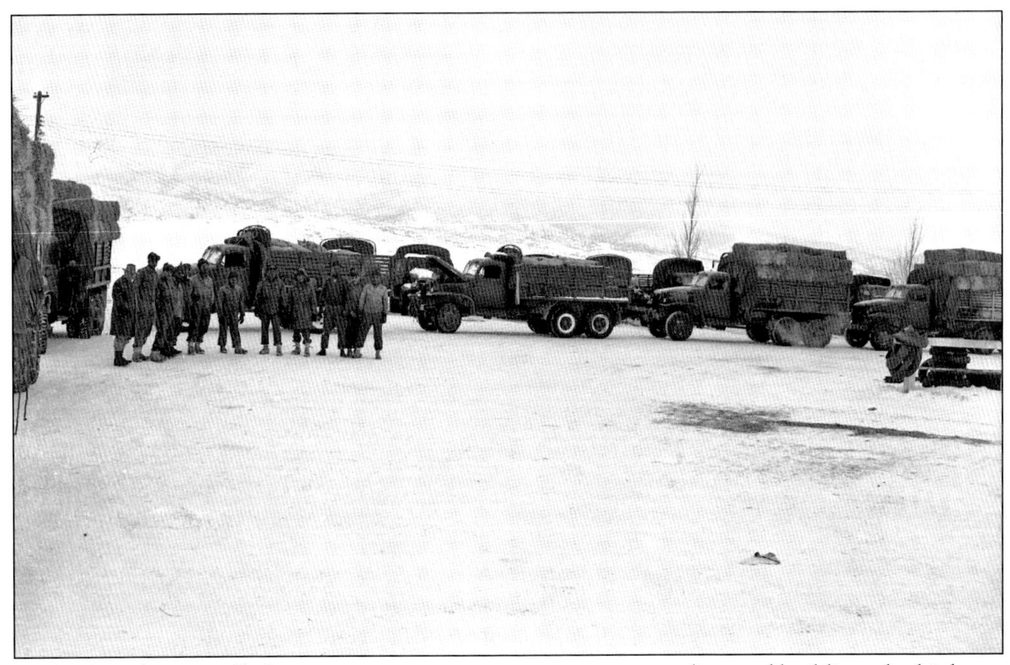

With a long history of helping its community in ways unconnected to road building, the highway department joined forces with the Nevada and California National Guards and the US Air Force in an effort to save stranded, starving livestock in 1949. The eastern part of the state was in crisis due to massive snowstorms that left roads impassible, with no way to get supplies to the animals.

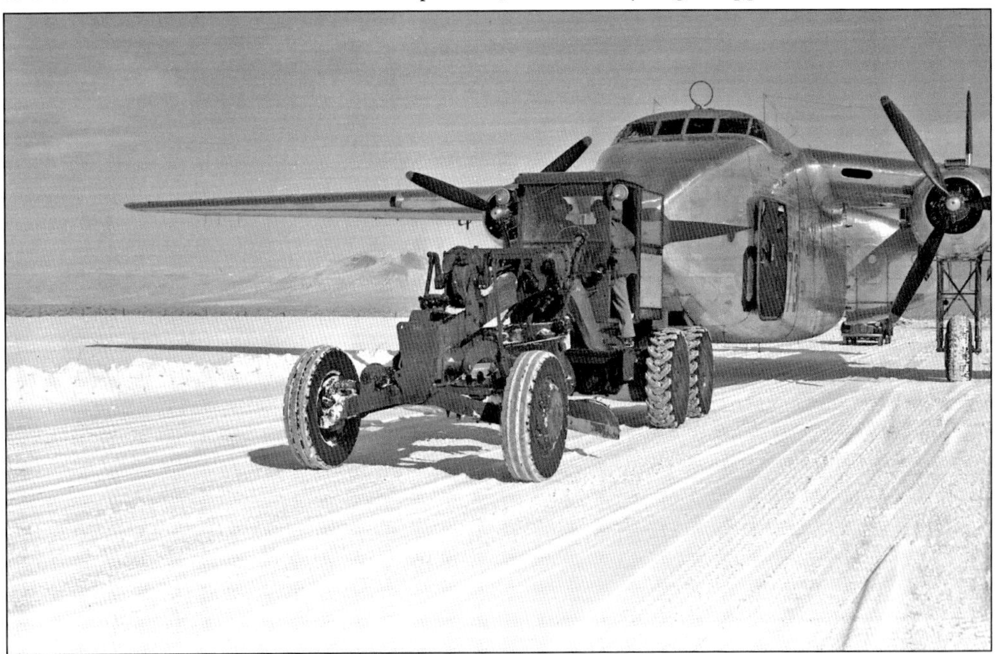

Inspired by airdrops in Berlin, officials devised Operation Haylift in which "flying boxcars" (actually C-82 airplanes) were brought to Fallon and Minden and loaded with hay grown in western Nevada. The hay was flown to areas in eastern Nevada, particularly Ely, and air-dropped to the starving livestock. Within one week, 500 tons of hay were dropped to the animals.

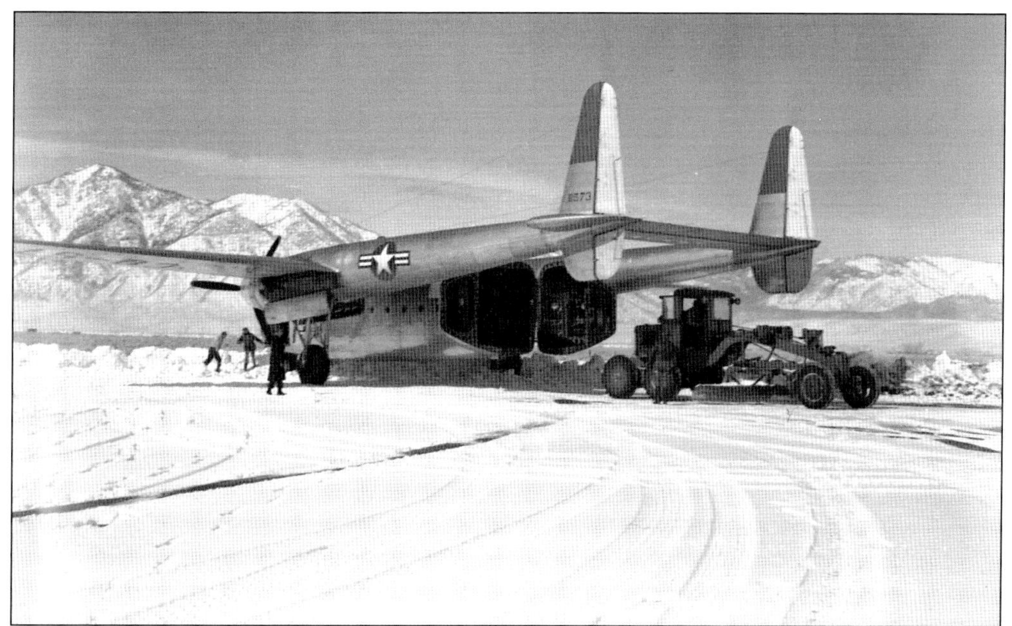

The highway department provided general support to the Operation Haylift efforts by providing personnel, snowplows, and heavy trucks, and by keeping airport roads drivable. In January 1949, an Associated Press photographer described the hay drop: "It's breathtaking to see how they do it, dropping those bales from I judge was a height of from 50 to 100 feet above the frozen, drift-locked wastes of eastern Nevada."

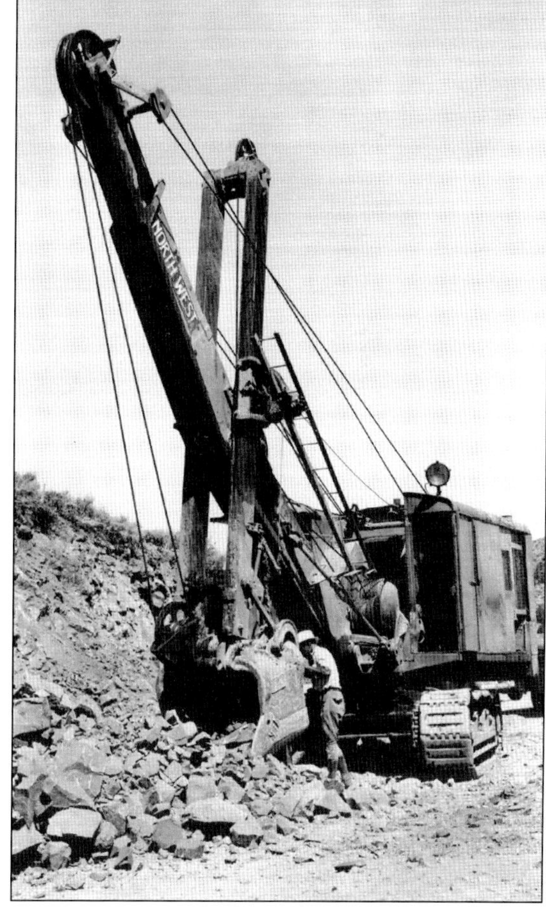

In 1936, the biggest engineering achievement of the highway department was the reconstruction of Geiger Grade, the original 1860s toll road from Washoe Valley to Virginia City. Assisted by the New Deal WPA, the road was widened, and steep grades were decreased. This photograph of the Northwest shovel was taken on a new stretch of Geiger Grade north of Virginia City on August 18, 1937.

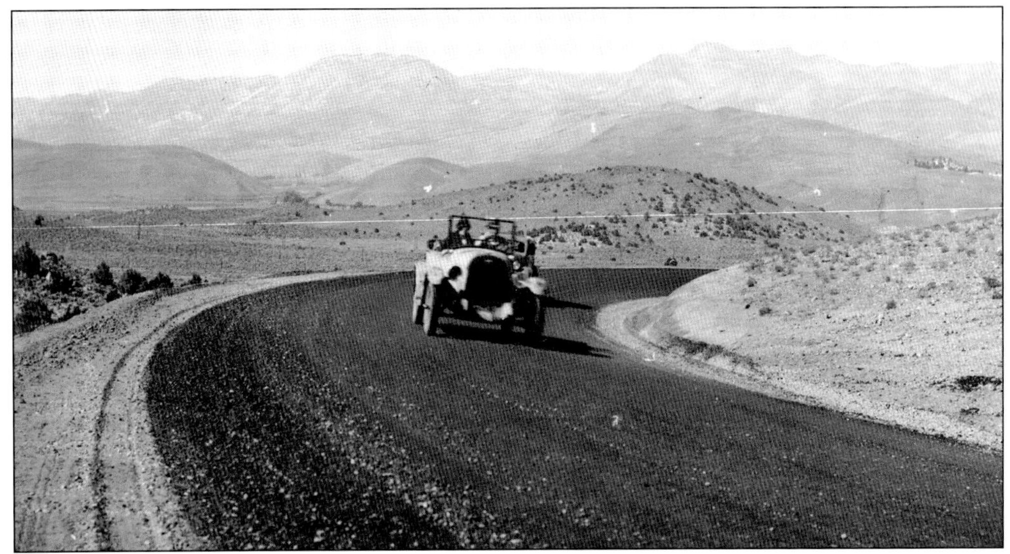

On August 10, 1940, the *Nevada State Journal* stated, "Geiger Grade is scenic and safe if driven carefully. All drivers have to do is to stay on their own side of the road and use sensible speed to make the mountain highway as reliable as their own home driveway." Unfortunately, many drivers did not follow the *Journal*'s advice, and the twisting road was the site of many accidents.

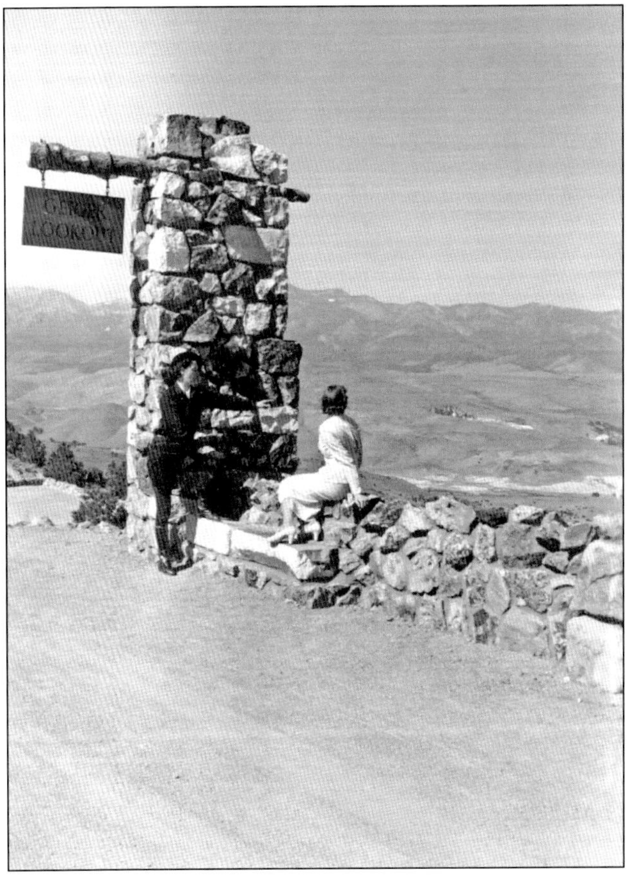

By the 1930s, federal regulations had established that at least 1 percent of federal aid money had to be spent on roadside improvements. Types of improvements included "providing parking space at points of exceptional scenic beauty," like Geiger Lookout Wayside Park, pictured here in 1938. Here, visitors could gaze across the Truckee Meadows and the growing city of Reno, with Mount Rose in the background.

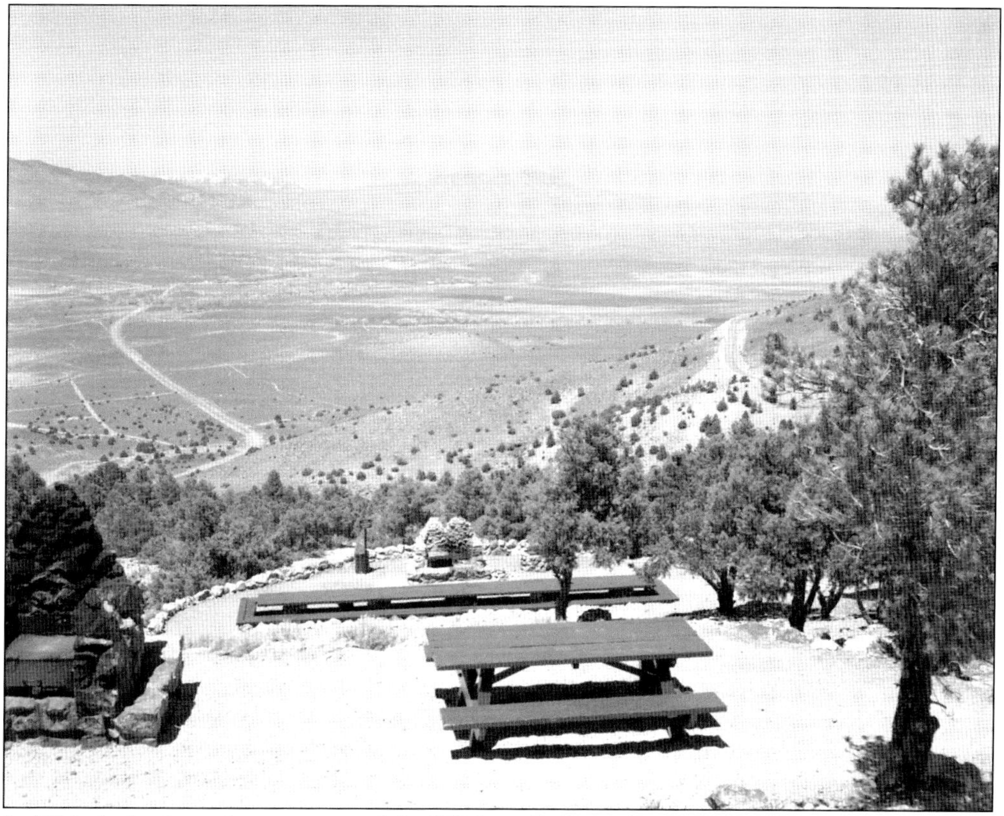

In 1938, the highway department and the WPA worked together to construct a park along Geiger Grade (Route 341), that snaking section of roadway that was the historic lifeline between supplies in Washoe Valley and Comstock bullion. "WPA boys" and highway department day laborers used local stone to build barbecues, wells, restrooms, and a "love seat" at the summit, overlooking the valley below.

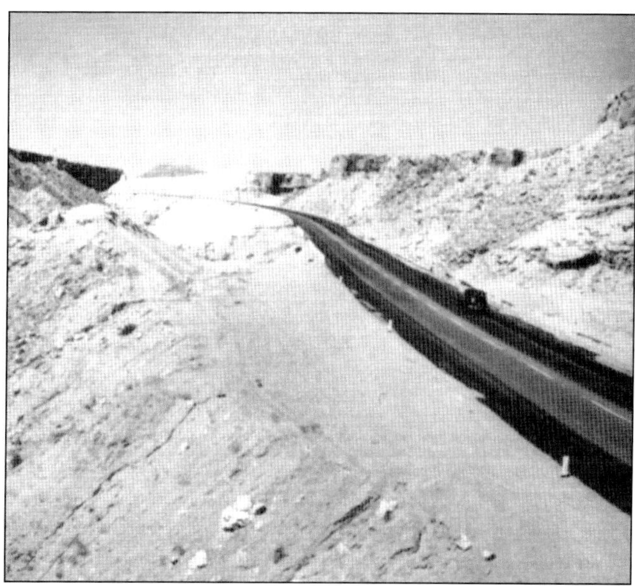

Influenced by the nationwide City Beautiful movement, the highway department worked to make roadways not only functional but also aesthetically pleasing. However, Nevada's desert climate and rural lifestyle provided challenges when it came to planting roadside vegetation. Water conscious even in the 1930s, the department created a policy that no vegetation would be planted in areas where the water table was below 10 feet.

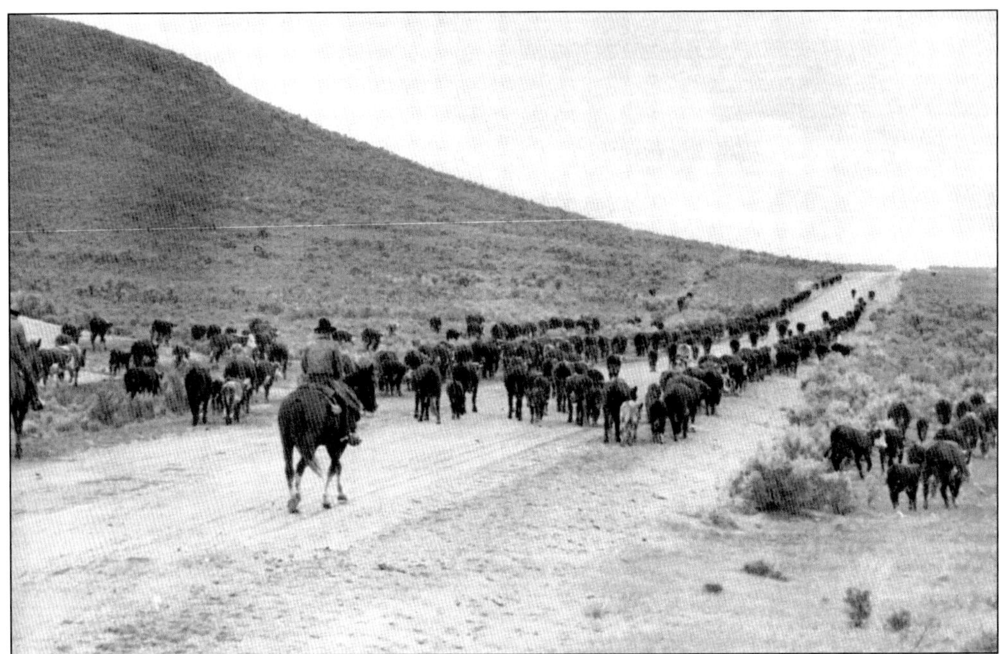

In addition to a lack of water, the practice of driving livestock herds across the highways was another factor that limited roadside landscaping. Herds of cattle and sheep were destructive to the natural vegetation and planned landscapes. The highway department had to balance the needs of the ranchers with that of the motorists; thus, a rather barren roadside occasionally resulted.

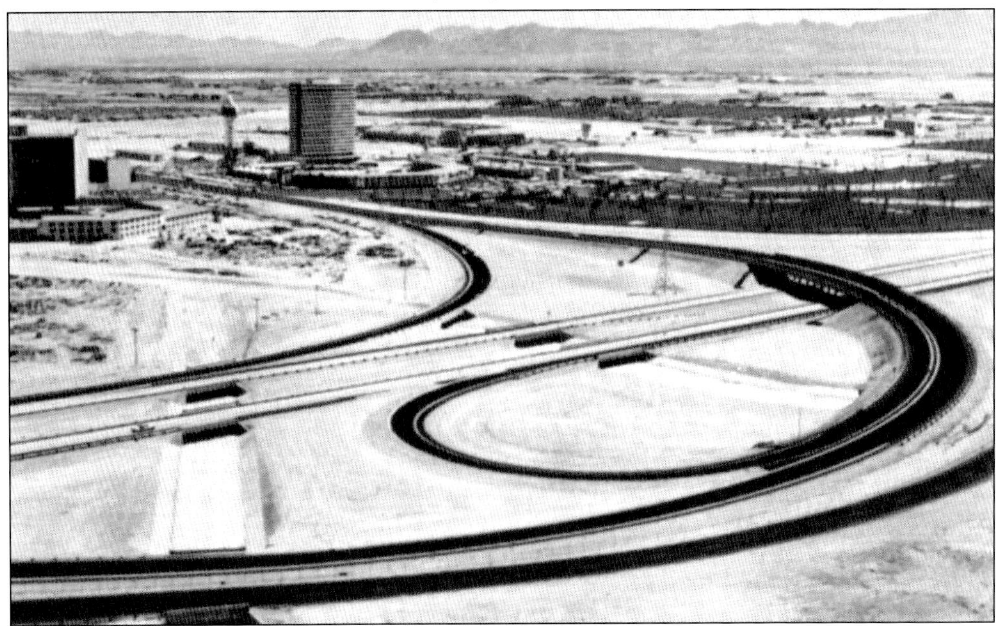

In 1968, the highway department articulated its philosophy of an integrated landscape in its aesthetics manual: "Highways are aesthetic entities involving all the senses, much as a piece of architecture or sculpture does. A road is not just a linear element composed of interlocking forms; it has depth and height, and should be considered as a three dimensional form in all stages of design and construction."

The aesthetics manual further stated, "It is important that design and construction of roads fit the country or city where they are sited. This is the only way in which the problem of reconciling human perception with machine speed can be solved. When a highway is safe to drive on and satisfying to use and observe, the problem of perception has been resolved and the road has both external and internal harmony."

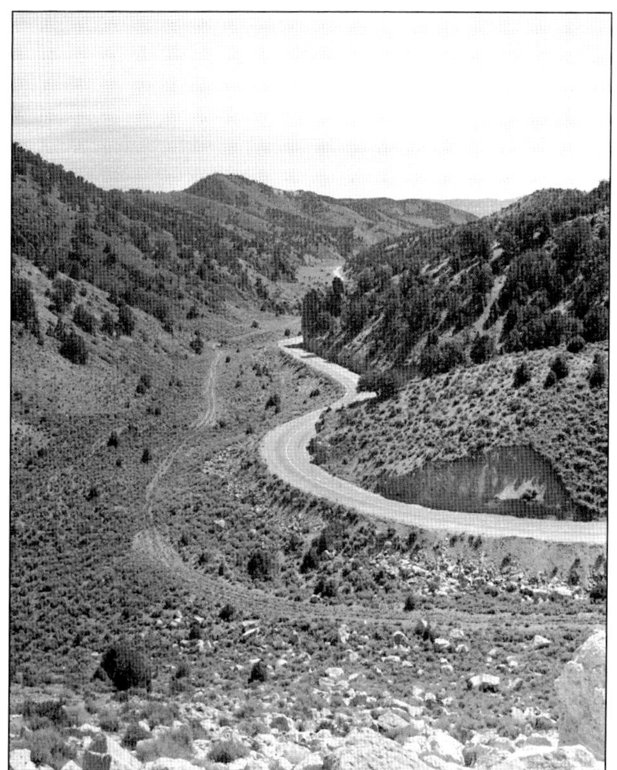

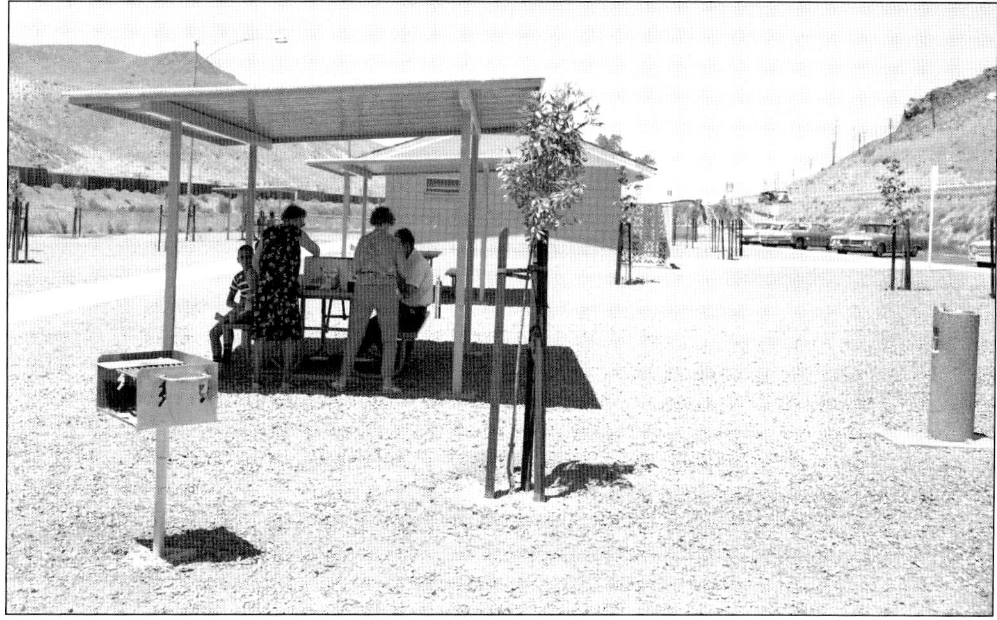

In addition to aesthetics, the highway department also focused on motorist comfort through safety rest areas, which the department defined as, "Places designed for the comfort and safety of travelers, where motorists may stop for short periods of time to rest and relax. They should be functional, visually pleasing, economical to build, easy to maintain, and safe. Rest areas can serve as gateways to the State and to communities, and often incorporate roadside markers."

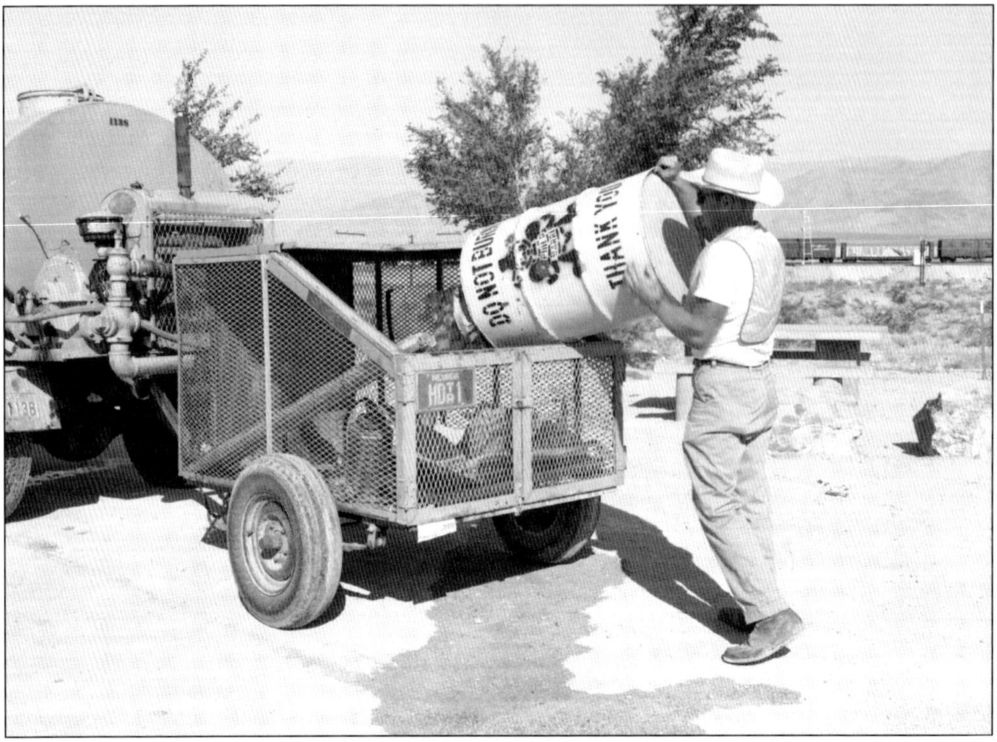

Another effort to keep Nevada beautiful hinged on an anti-littering campaign. The highway department installed hundreds of trash barrels throughout the state, mostly at rest stops, and ensured the trash was emptied regularly. In addition to instructing people not to burn their trash, the barrels featured the whimsical, top hat–wearing litterbug character named Phil D. Barrel.

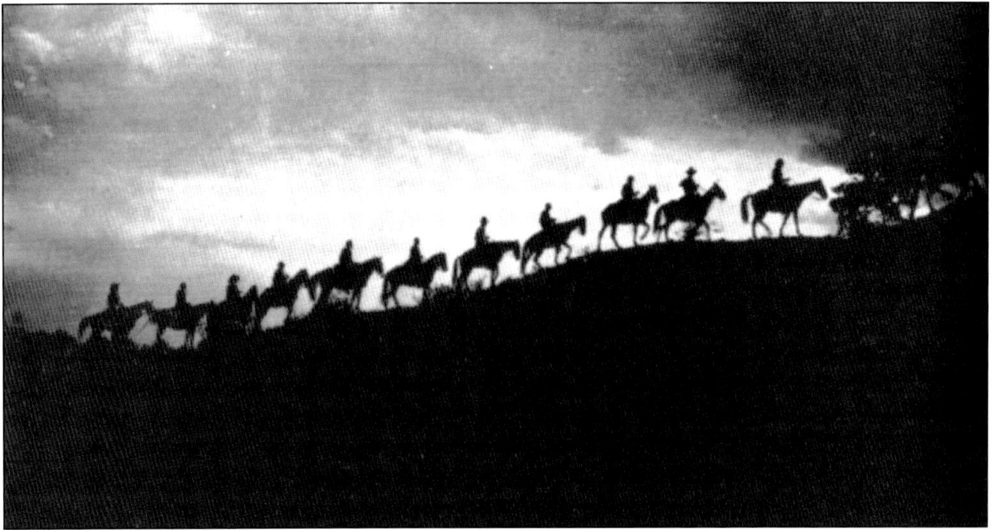

From its inception, the highway department has been on a mission to improve the state. As early as 1925, the department recognized that despite strong patriotism to communities, there was no real sense of being a Nevadan. The department felt that well-maintained and thoughtfully planned highways would help create a "Nevada Spirit" that the state desperately needed to flourish economically and socially within the United States as a whole.

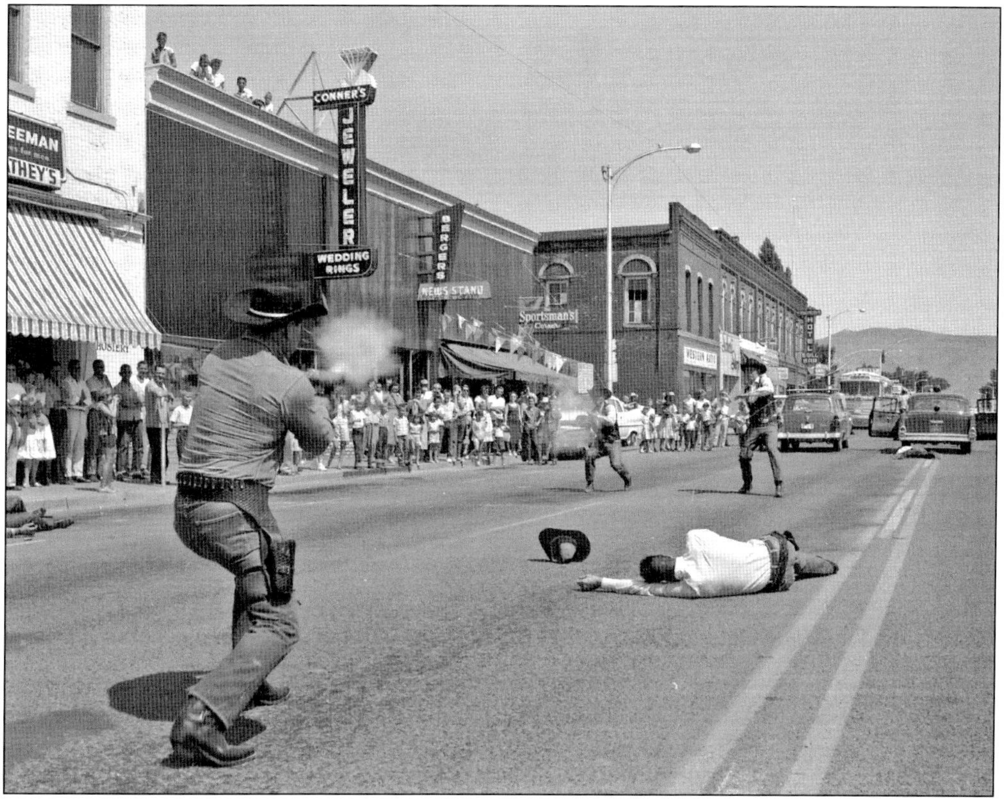

To facilitate the Nevada Spirit and to capture tourist dollars, the department invested in scenic highways, stating, "Nevada is without peer from a scenic standpoint . . . and the romance of the old West has lingered longer in Nevada than elsewhere. All these things can be . . . taken as the means of bringing people to the State," as seen in this gunslinger reenactment on scenic US 50 around 1960.

Scenic highways and the system in general, when feasible, were either built to highlight Nevada's rugged beauty and fascinating history or were often routed to avoid destroying historic structures. For example, these ruins are Pony Express stations located adjacent to US 50, a highway that largely follows the old Pony Express route through Nevada. Presently, the department has a full-time architectural historian on staff, tasked with ensuring that new construction does not radically change historically built environments.

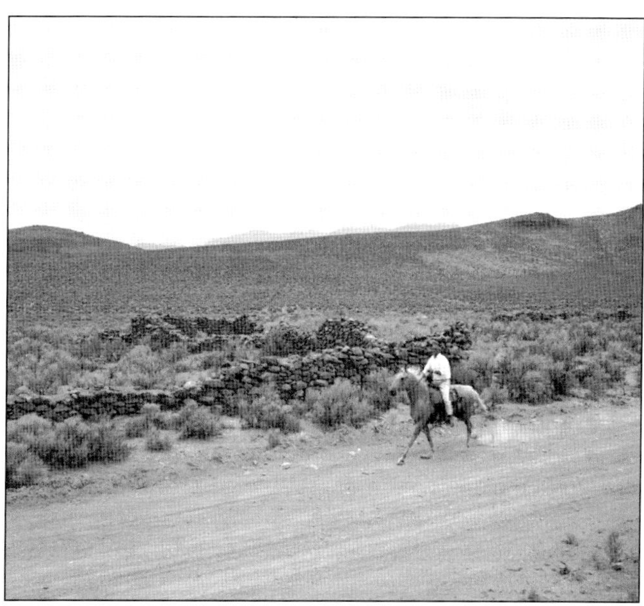

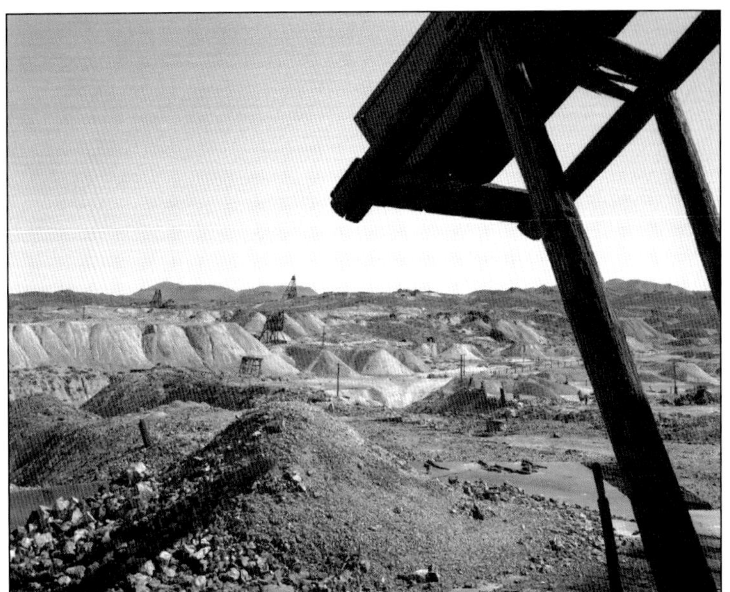

Before a new road is built or an older one repaired, things like "view shed" must be taken into account. For example, the photograph at left shows an old mining operation. A new road could be built through the complex without destroying any of the historic features, but the overall historic feel of the mine would be destroyed because of the out-of-place road and the traffic it would generate.

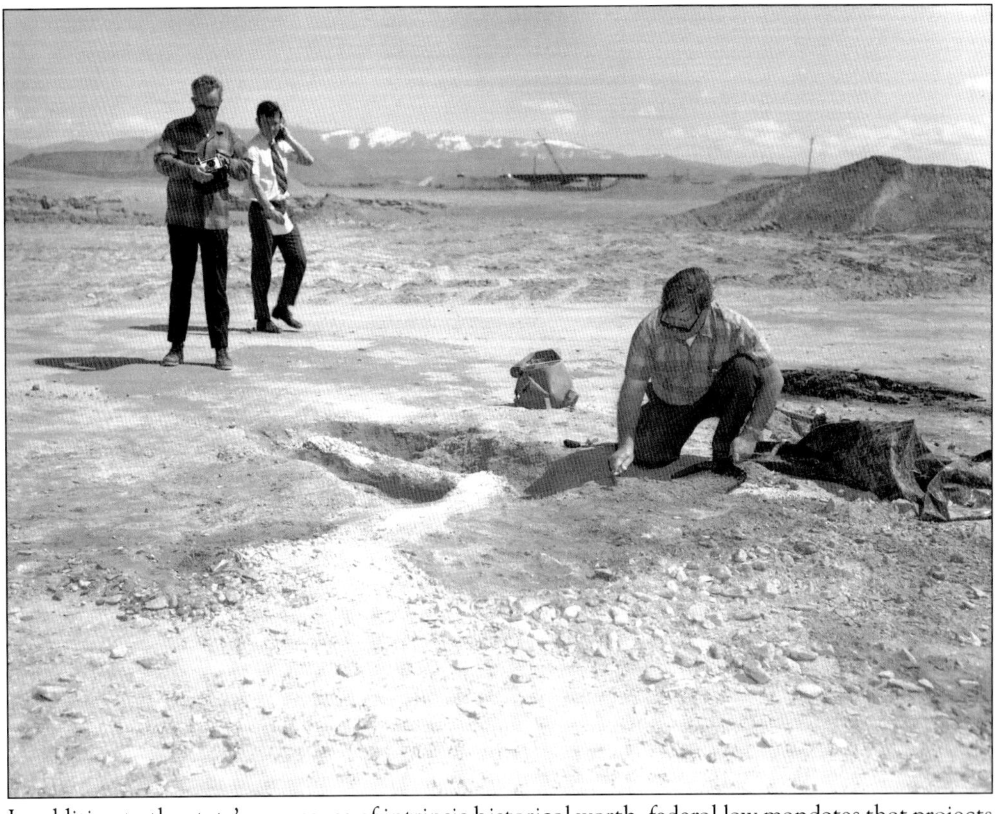

In addition to the state's own sense of intrinsic historical worth, federal law mandates that projects making use of federal money or federal land must take archaeological and historic architectural resources into account. For over 30 years, the highway department has maintained a group of archaeologists to ensure road-building activities do not destroy irreplaceable knowledge of the area's historic and prehistoric past.

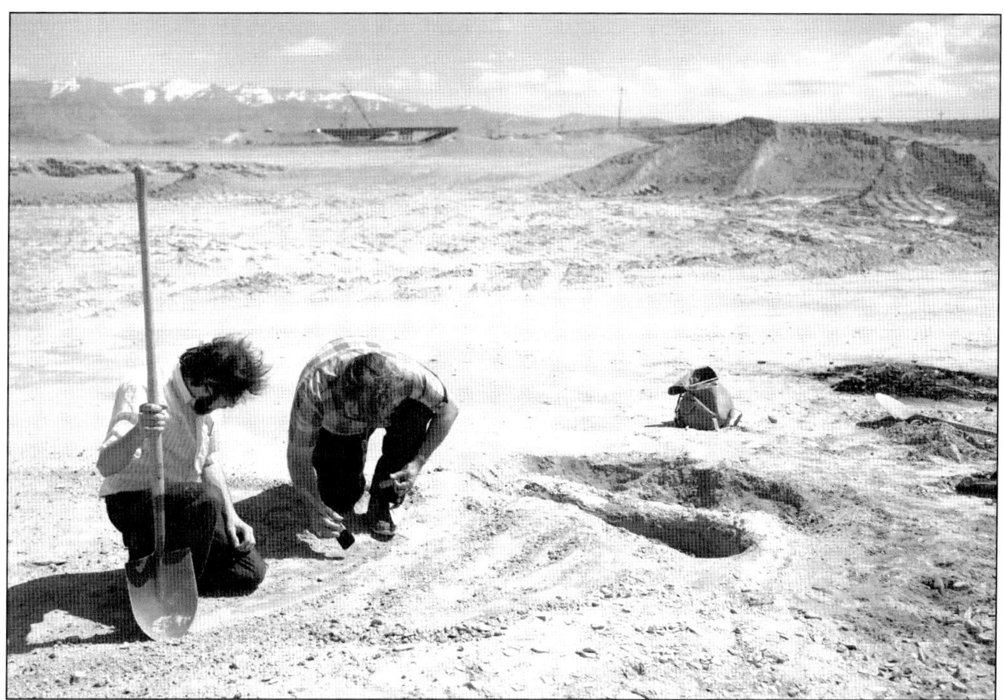

Interesting finds can be anywhere, as exemplified in this picture. Workers found the remains of a mammoth in a highway department material site. While not quite the purview of archaeologists, a team of researchers was nonetheless called in to excavate the beast from the pit and preserve the scientific information embedded in the find.

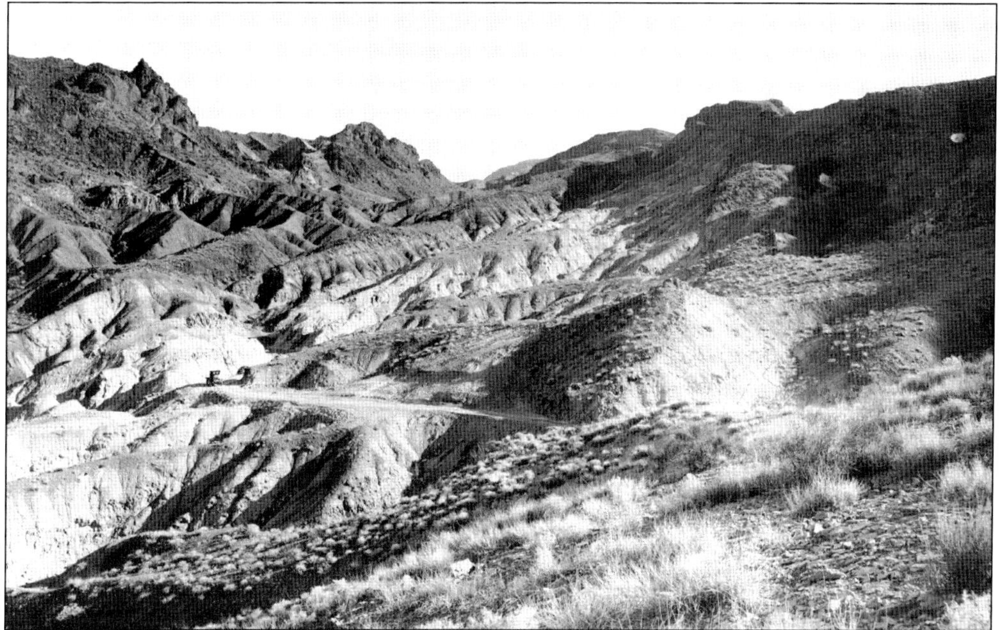

Given the age of Nevada's roadway system, some of the older routes now qualify as archaeology. Finding remnants of routes traveled by the earliest automobiles and seeing views like this showcase the fearless quality of early automobile enthusiasts and the dedication of early highway builders.

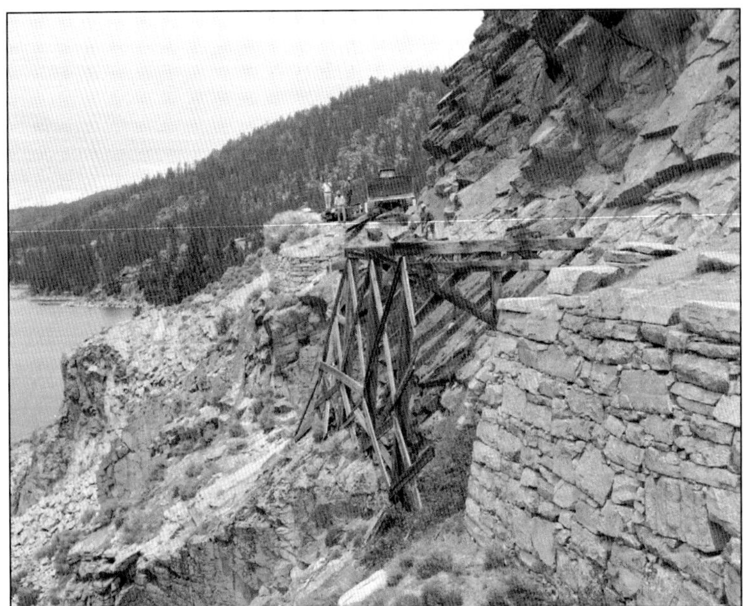

Another example of daring builders and drivers is shown here. Before a tunnel was built through Cave Rock in 1931, a one-lane road dating to the 1860s clung precariously to the side of Cave Rock. The old roadbed was supported by a timber trestle and retaining walls made of dry-stack stone with smaller stone chinking.

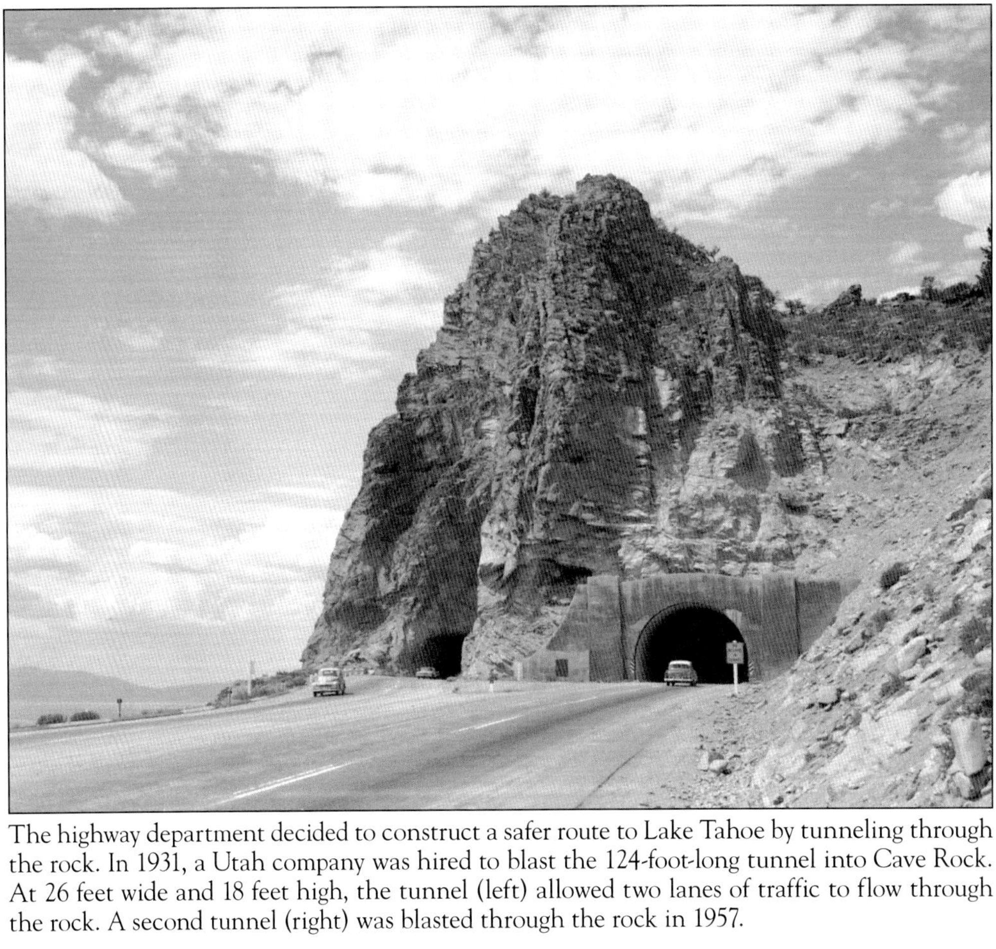

The highway department decided to construct a safer route to Lake Tahoe by tunneling through the rock. In 1931, a Utah company was hired to blast the 124-foot-long tunnel into Cave Rock. At 26 feet wide and 18 feet high, the tunnel (left) allowed two lanes of traffic to flow through the rock. A second tunnel (right) was blasted through the rock in 1957.

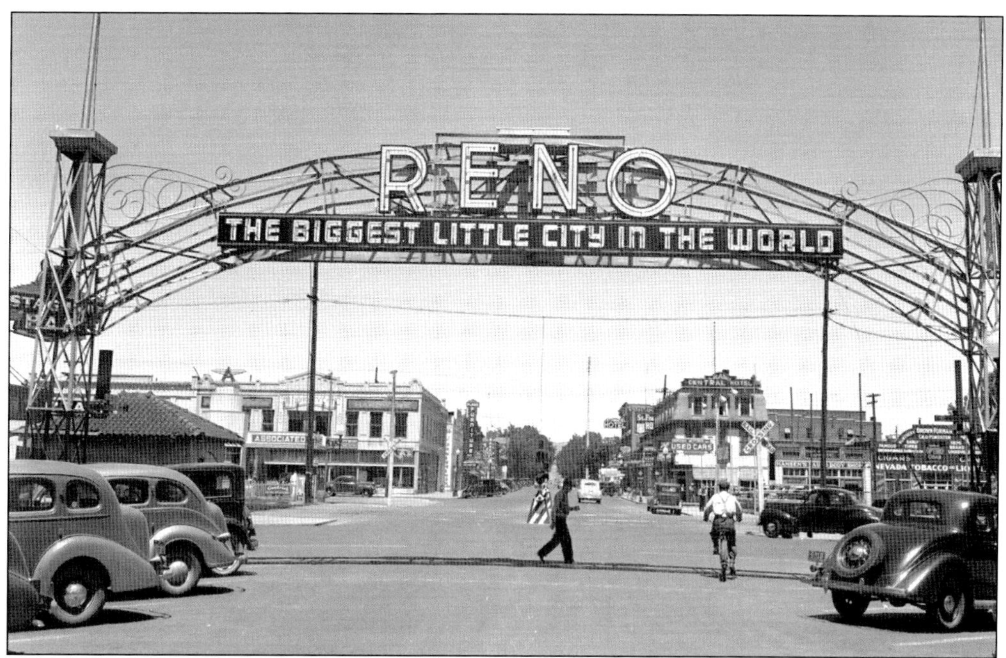

Spanning bustling Virginia Street, the iconic Reno Arch was originally erected in 1926 to advertise Nevada's three-month-long Transcontinental Highways Exposition, a sort of automobile-themed world's fair celebrating completion of the Lincoln Highway (US 50) and the Victory Highway (US 40). The exposition was held at Idlewild Park, built especially for the event.

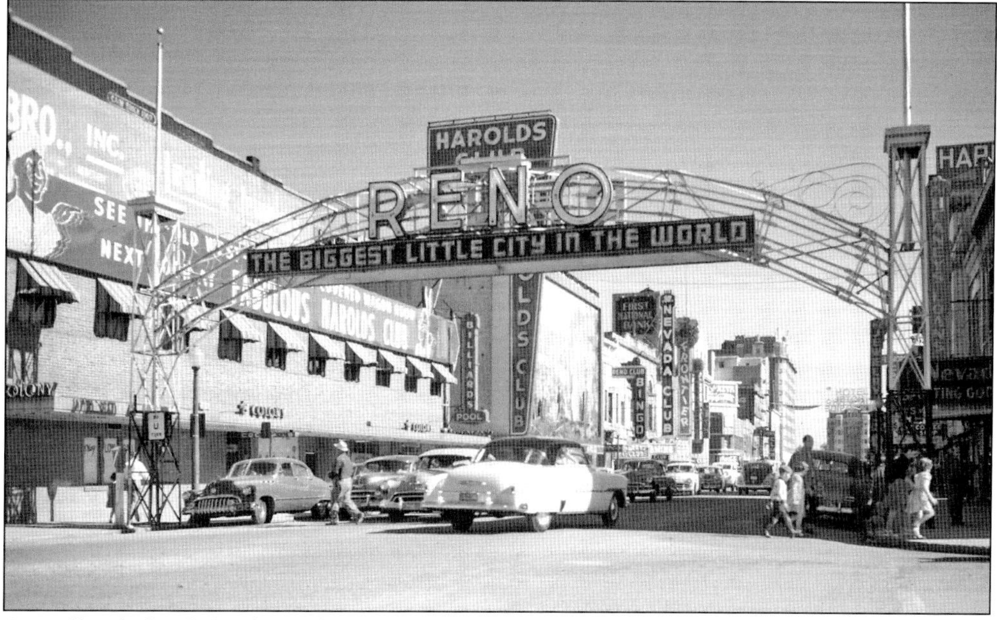

City officials decided to leave the arch standing after the Transcontinental Highways Exposition ended but wanted it emblazoned with a new city slogan. After a contest, G.A. Burns of Sacramento pocketed $100 for the winning selection: "Reno, the Biggest Little City in the World." Burns is often credited with inventing the slogan, but it was actually a nickname promoted by the Reno business community since 1910.

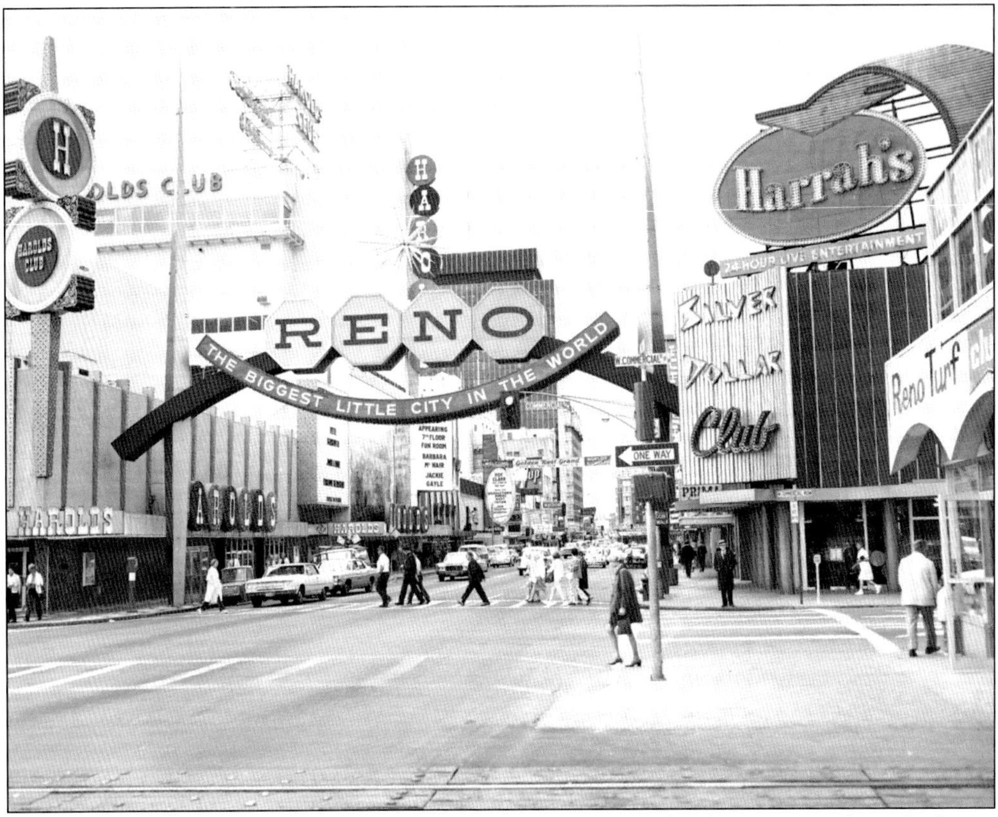

In 1963, the first Reno Arch structure was replaced with this lively Googie-style arch that is plastic paneled and internally illuminated. The first arch migrated to several different locations in the city, finally settling on Lake Street, near the National Automobile Museum, just a few blocks away from its original location.

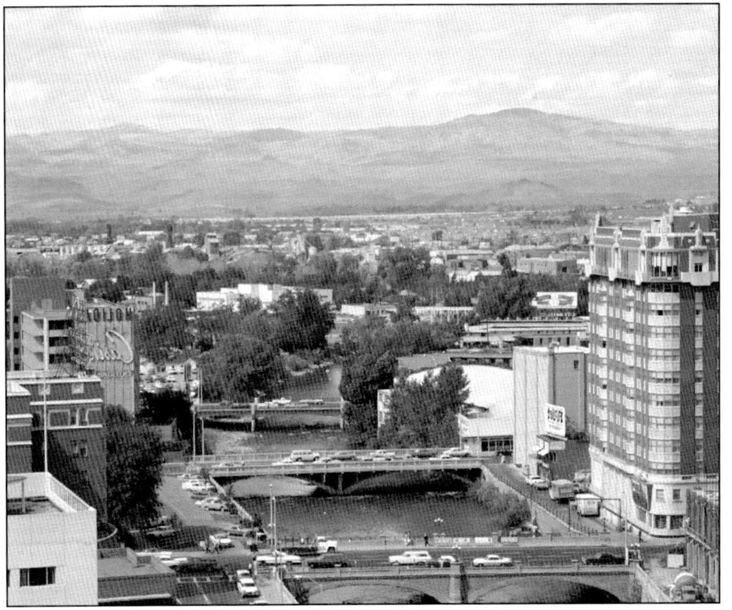

Predating the highway department, the 1905 Virginia Street Bridge in downtown Reno was one of the oldest bridges in Nevada. It was also Nevada's first bridge built of reinforced concrete. This crossing over the Truckee River marks the origins of "the Biggest Little City in the World." In 1861, Myron Lake built a log toll bridge over the Truckee River at this site and started the settlement now known as Reno.

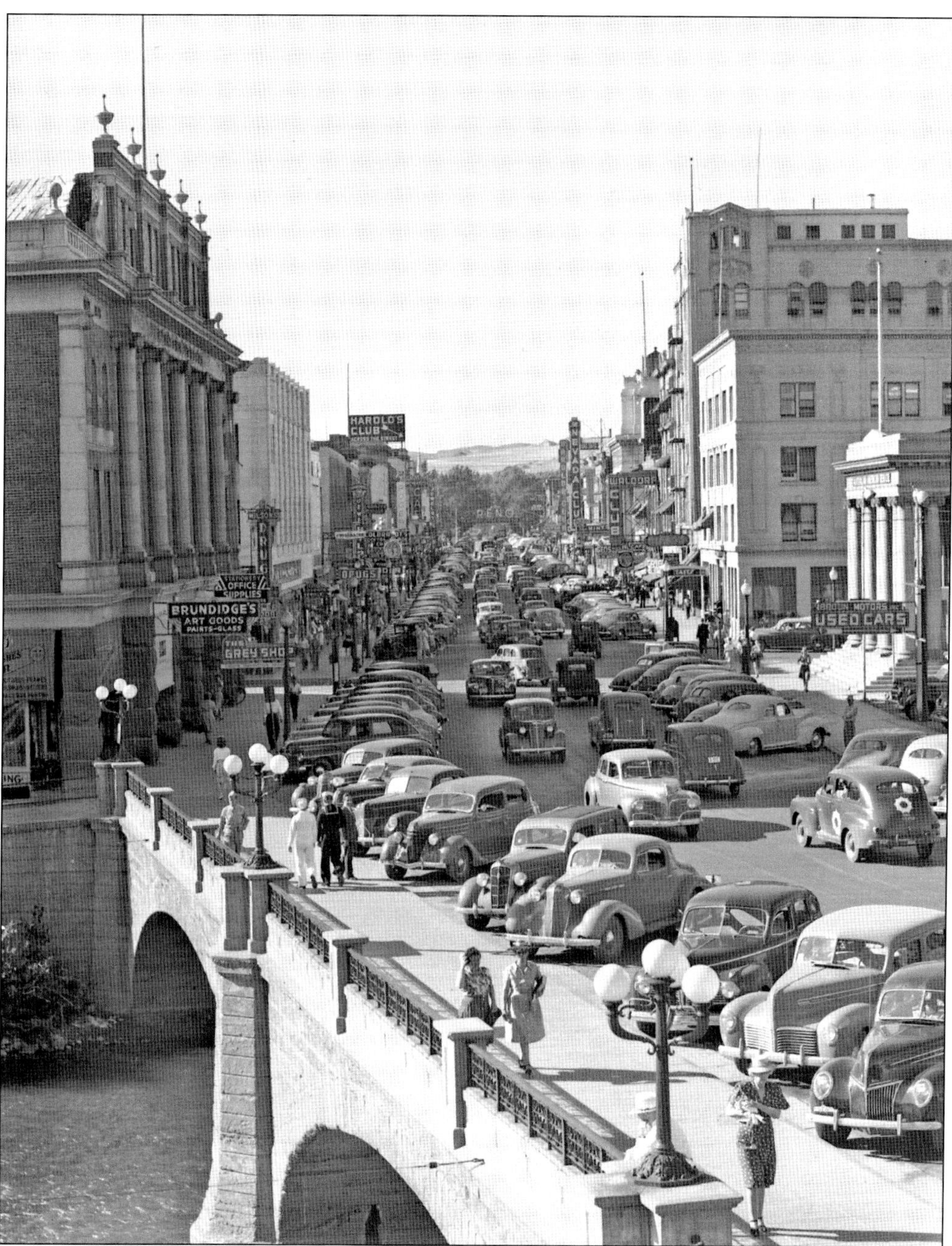

This piece of transportation infrastructure became part of popular culture thanks to Nevada's lenient residency-for-divorce requirement. Unhappy spouses could finalize their divorce at the Washoe County Court House (seen at far right in this 1940 photograph), then proceed to the Virginia Street bridge and fling their wedding rings into the Truckee River. More sensible divorcées likely hocked their wedding rings in one of Reno's numerous pawnshops. After over 100 years of service, this symbol of Reno was demolished in 2015. Flood control plans called for replacement of the bridge with a new clear-spanning bridge.

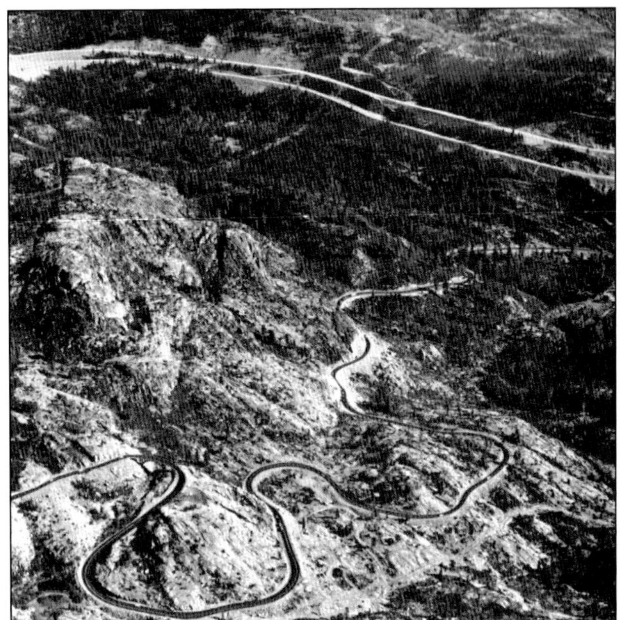

Another major infrastructure project that made travel through the Silver State easier was the completion of Interstate 80, which was challenging because it was the first all-weather route through the perilous Sierra Nevada. Passing close to the last stand of the doomed Donner party, the interstate replaced US 40 in 1964. Pictured are the winding, less safe US 40 in the foreground and the straight, divided interstate in the background.

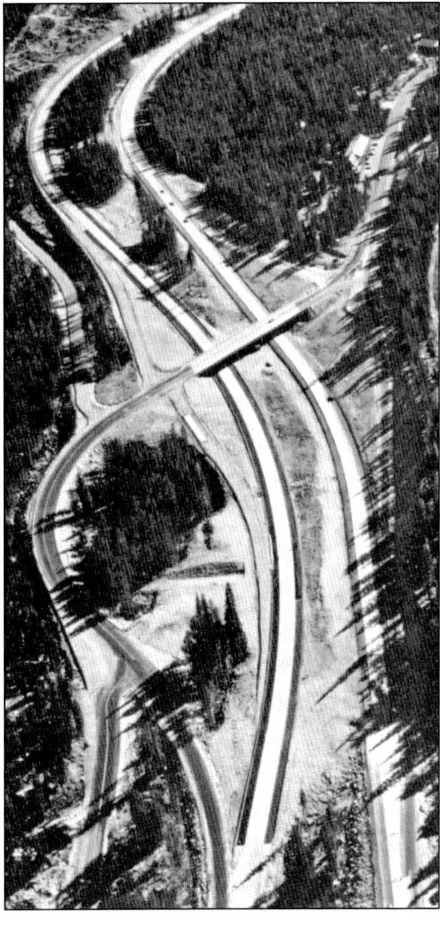

In response to the new interstate, one contemporary writer happily proclaimed, "Gone is the winding . . . two-lane U.S. 40 with its tortuous hairline turns, agonizing traffic jams and hazardous winter surfaces. Replacing it is an engineer's dream of a freeway that rises in a series of gentle curves along a slope above the canyon-bound route, approaching the summit so gradually that motorists may not realize at what point they've crossed it."

In 1964, the highway department celebrated 100 years of Nevada statehood by installing a centennial marker in every county. The Elko County marker, pictured here shortly after installation, commemorated a shortcut on the California Trail. The historical marker featured local "wonderstone," a type of rhyolite, on the base. For Nevada's sesquicentennial celebration, the NDOT and the Nevada State Historic Preservation Office collaborated to restore the now "historic" historical markers.

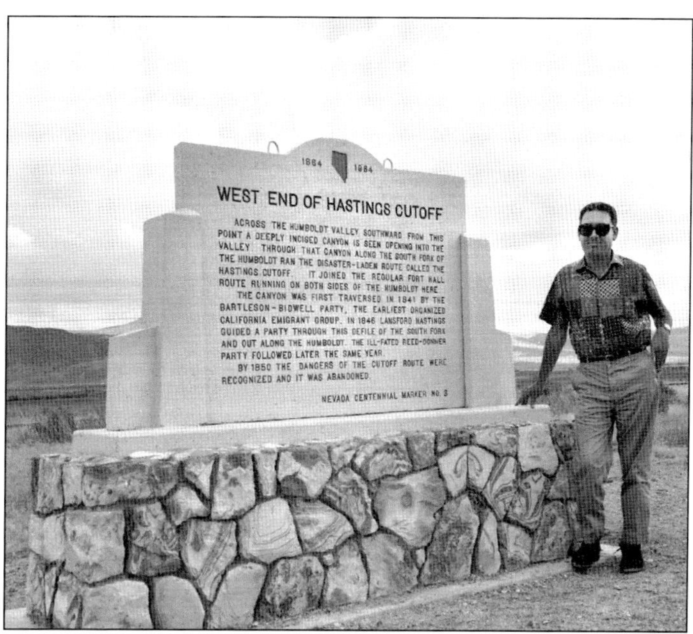

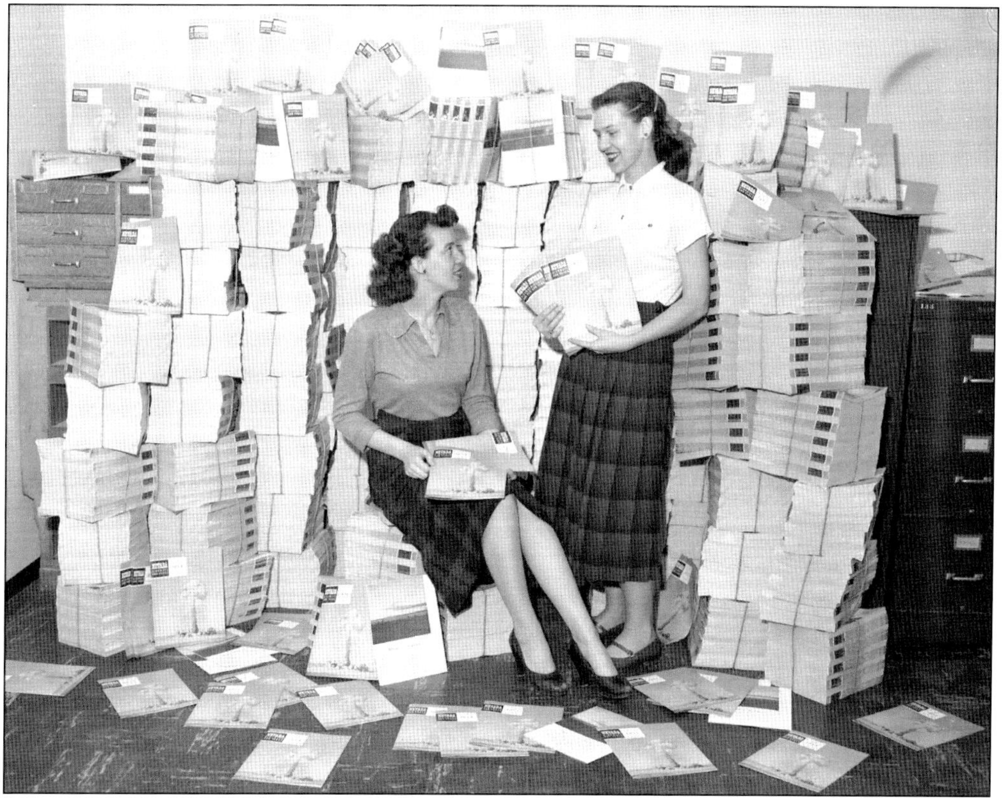

In 1936, the highway department introduced the *Nevada Highways and Parks* magazine, still being published today under the name *Nevada Magazine*. In 1953, these cheerful ladies posed in front of stacks of *Nevada Highways and Parks* magazines ready to be distributed to the public for free. The publication highlighted Nevada's history and promoted scenic road trips through the state.

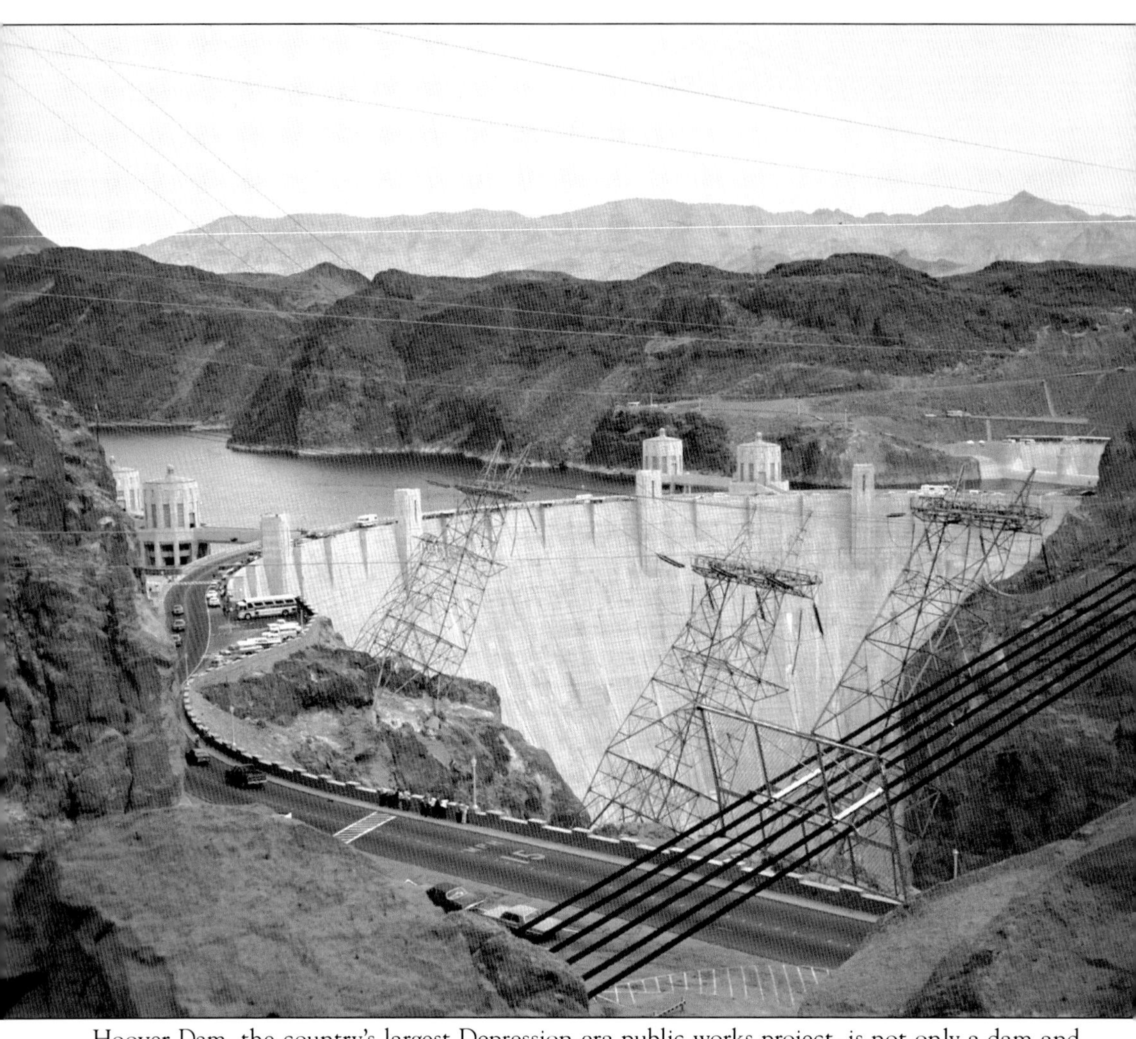

Hoover Dam, the country's largest Depression-era public works project, is not only a dam and hydroelectric power generator, but it is also a road. Crossing the top of the dam, US Highway 95 was the primary route linking southern Nevada with Arizona. Seen here in the 1960s, the two-lane road threaded traffic across the top of the dam at a leisurely 15 miles per hour.

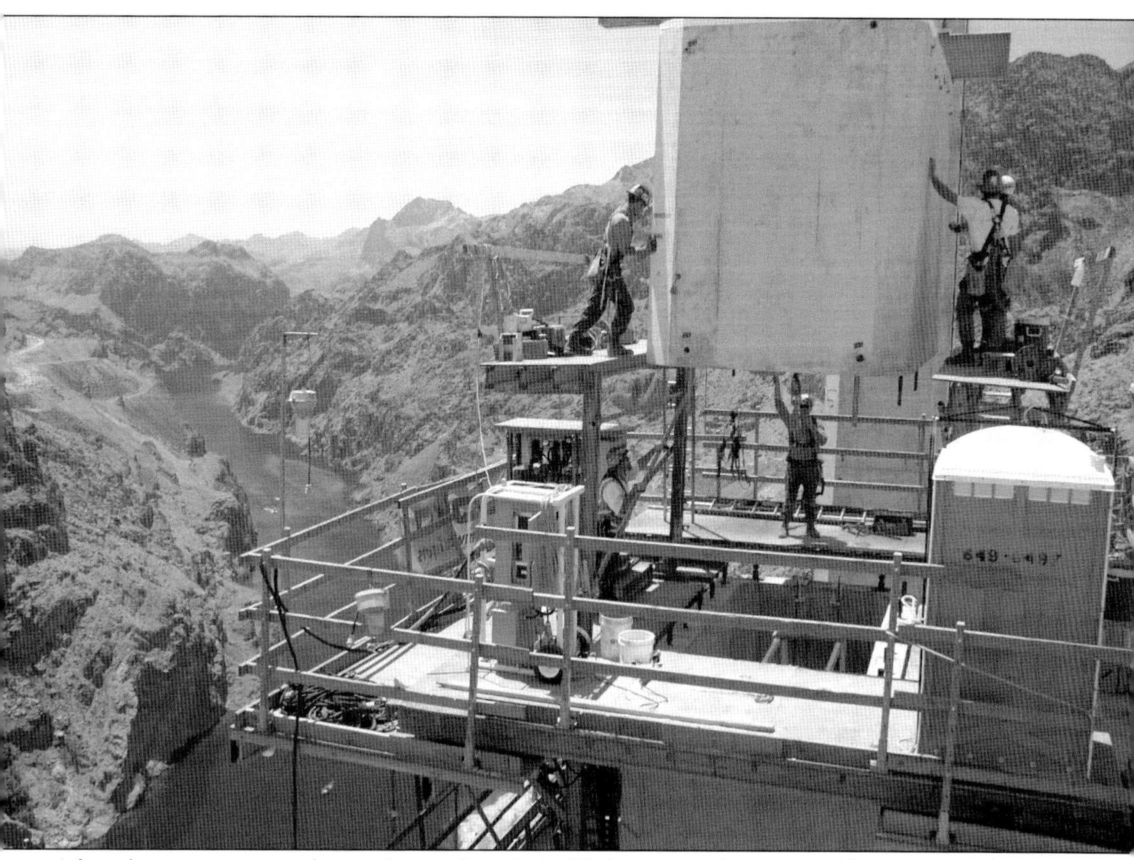

After the terrorist attacks on September 11, 2001, having only one road between southern Nevada and Arizona, and having that road on top of the generator providing power to about 350,000 households a year, was recognized as a national security threat. Shortly after the terrorist attacks, work began in earnest on a bypass that routed US 95 around the dam. (Photograph by Rich Johnston.)

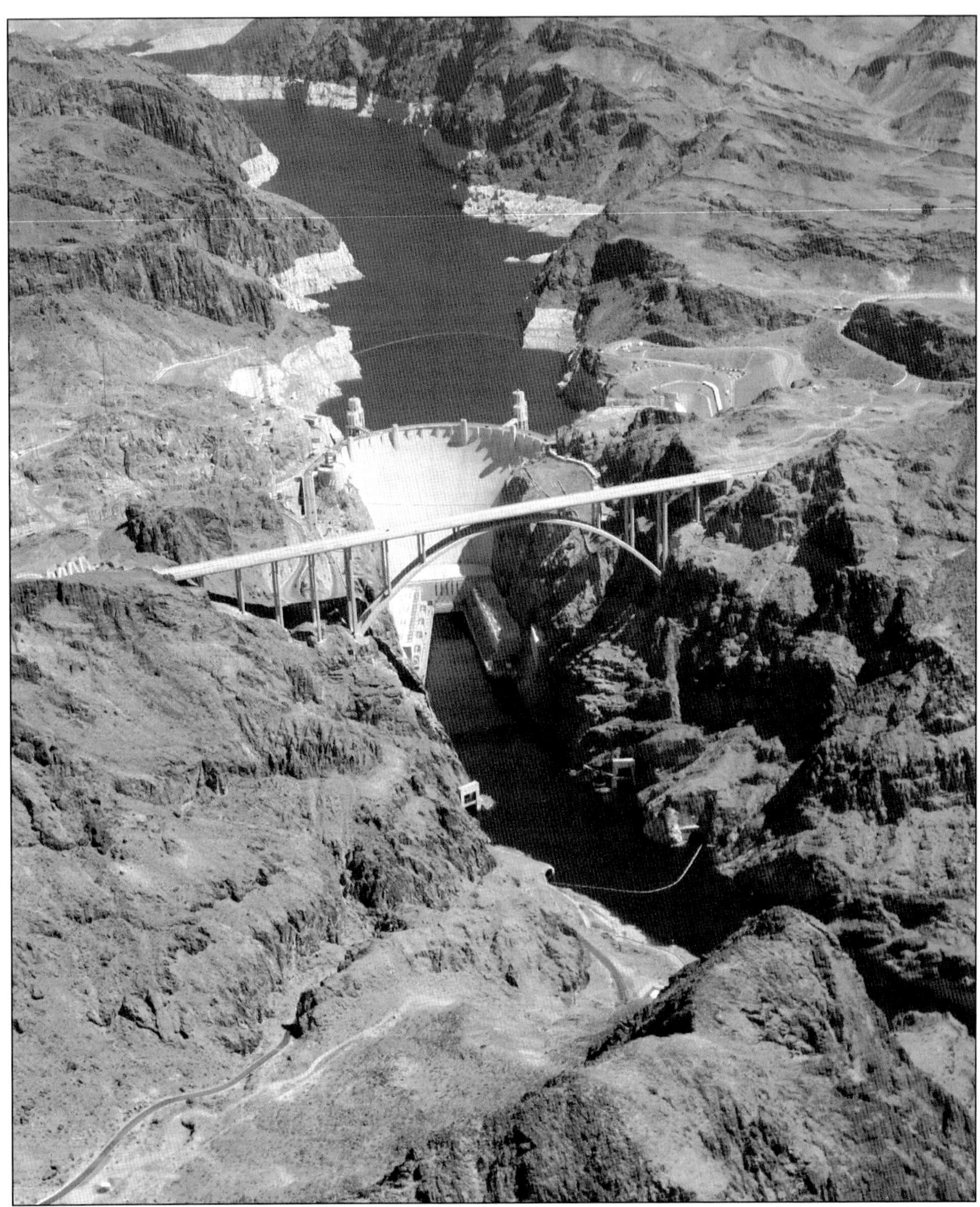

The biggest challenge of the Hoover Dam Bypass Project was crossing the nearly 2,000-foot-wide chasm over the Colorado River. The feat required construction of the widest concrete arch bridge in the western hemisphere. The $114 million cost of the bridge was divided among Arizona, Nevada, and several federal agencies. In 2010, after five years of construction, a collapsed crane, and one death, the Mike O'Callaghan–Pat Tillman Memorial Bridge was opened for traffic. The structure is named after two American heroes: Mike O'Callaghan, who served as Nevada's governor from 1971 to 1979 and as a Silver and Bronze Star veteran of the Korean War, and Pat Tillman, who was a professional football player. After the September 11 terrorist attacks, Tillman enlisted in the US Army and was tragically killed by friendly fire in 2004. The bridge is a symbol of cooperation, sacrifice, and engineering genius worthy of overlooking the monumental Hoover Dam below. (Photograph by Sholeh Moll.)

Bibliography

"Dedicate Bridge with Celebration." *Reno Evening Gazette*. Reno, NV: April 11, 1921.

"France Sends Picture Book to Nevadans." *Nevada State Journal*. Reno, NV: May 11, 1949.

Franzwa, Gregory M. *The Lincoln Highway: Nevada*. Tucson, AZ: Patrice Press, 2004.

Green, Victor. *The Negro Motorist Green Book: An International Travel Guide*. New York, NY: Victor H. Green & Co., 1949.

Hall, Shawn. *Old Heart of Nevada: Ghost Towns and Mining Camps of Elko County*. Reno, NV: University of Nevada Press, 1998.

———. *Romancing Nevada's Past: Ghost Towns and Historic Sites of Eureka, Lander, and White Pine Counties*. Reno, NV: University of Nevada Press, 1993.

———. *Preserving the Glory Days: Ghost Towns and Mining Camps of Nye County, Nevada*. Reno, NV: University of Nevada Press, 1998.

Kolvet, Renée Corona, and Victoria Ford. *The Civilian Conservation Corps in Nevada: From Boys to Men*. Reno, NV: University of Nevada Press, 2006.

"Here's Information on 5-Tire Limit." *Nevada State Journal*. Reno, NV: October 20, 1942.

"Highway Agency Tests Materials Used in Roads." *Nevada State Journal*. Reno, NV: November 14, 1936.

"Highway Department Has Heavy Program for 1923." *Reno Evening Gazette*. Reno, NV: June 2, 1923.

"Highway Jobs Being Pushed." *Reno Evening Gazette*. Reno, NV: March 21, 1924.

Joint Board on Interstate Highways. Report. 1925.

Lewis, Tom. *Divided Highways: Building the Interstate Highways, Transforming American Life*. Penguin Books, 1999.

"Lincoln Highway Gives Nevada More Funds." *Reno Evening Gazette*. Reno, NV: January 29, 1921.

Marriott, Paul Daniel, and National Trust for Historic Preservation. *Saving Historic Roads: Design & Policy Guidelines*. New York, NY: John Wiley & Sons, Preservation Press, 1998.

Nevada Department of Transportation. "Historical State Highway Maps." www.nevadadot.com/Traveler_Info/Maps/HistoricalMaps.aspx.

Nevada Highways and Parks. *Carson City: Nevada Highway Department, 1936–1954*.

Ramsey, Alice Huyler, and Gregory M. Franzwa. *Alice's Drive: Republishing Veil, Duster & Tire Iron*. Tucson, AZ: The Patrice Press, 2005.

State of Nevada. Biennial Report of the Nevada Department of Highways. Carson City, NV: State Printing Office, 1919–1965.

"Tire Ration Violators Warned." *Reno Evening Gazette*. Reno, NV: October 6, 1942.

"Use Tax Number Necessary to Secure Gas Ration Card." *Reno Evening Gazette*. Reno, NV: November 14, 1942.

Weingroff, Richard F. "From Names to Numbers: The Origins of the US Numbered Highway System." Federal Highway Administration. www.fhwa.dot.gov/infrastructure/numbers.cfm.